HEALTH CARE

JOB EXPLOSION!

HIGH GROWTH HEALTH CARE CAREERS AND JOB LOCATOR

Fourth Edition, Completely Revised

Dennis V. Damp

Bookhaven Press LLC
Mc Kees Rocks, PA

Health Care Job Explosion!
High Growth Health Care Careers and Job Locator

by Dennis V. Damp
Copyright © 2006 by Dennis V. Damp

1st Printing 1996   4th Printing 2004
2nd Printing 1998 (Revised)   5th Printing 2006 (Revised)
3rd Printing 2001 (Revised)

For quantity discounts and permissions, contact the publisher:
Bookhaven Press LLC, P.O. Box 1243, Moon Township, PA 15108
http://healthcarejobs.org, E-mail: Bookhaven@aol.com

Distributed to bookstores by:
Midpoint Trade Books, 27 West 20th St., NY, NY 10011
212-727-0190, E-Mail midpointny@aol.com

Disclaimer of All Warranties and Liabilities

Library of Congress Cataloging-in-Publication Data

Damp, Dennis V.
    Health care job explosion! : high growth health care careers and job locator / Dennis V. Damp.-- 4th ed.
        p. cm.
    ISBN-13: 978-0-943641-25-6 (pbk. : alk. paper)
    ISBN-10: 0-943641-25-X (pbk. : alk. paper)
    1. Medicine--Vocational guidance. 2. Allied health personnel--Vocational guidance. 3. Health facilities--Employees--Supply and demand--Directories. 4. Medical personnel--Employment--Directories. 5. Job hunting--Information services--Directories. 6. Employment forecasting. I. Title.

    R690.D36 2006
    610.69--dc22   2006004717

Table of Contents

"The return from your work must be the satisfaction which that work brings you and the world's need of that work. With this, life is heaven, or as near heaven as you can get."

— W. E. B. Du Bois (1868–1963, major African-American scholar)

Acknowledgments

This extensive revision of the fourth edition would have been impossible without the input of the many health care professionals who willingly shared their insights with us for this major update. Especially gracious were those providing the interviews that lead off chapters 4-10: Debra Burton, Stacey Langston, Tamara Theodore, Desiree Griffith, Sabrina Damp, Doctor Paul Zubritzky, and Lily Chan.

A special thanks must go to Erin McMichael Taylor, Paul J. Krumm, and Michelle Macie. Ms. Taylor, our senior editor and research-er for this project, and Mr. Krumm, associate editor, completed an exhaustive search to update this edition's resources. Ms. Macie, our proof reader, was also very helpful. Thanks to their diligence and fore-sight, they have contributed significantly to this revision. The Bureau of Labor Statistics is quoted throughout this work including the newly released 2006-07 edition of the Occupational Outlook Handbook (OOH). Without their extensive employment statistics this book could not have been written. I must also thank Suzan Hvizdash for contributing the section on medical billing and coding.

Many others contributed to this edition, especially those working in professional health care associations who took time to share infor-mation on careers and job hunting. Literally hundreds of health care associations and certification agencies provided information and advice.

Finally, I must thank the millions of dedicated health care workers who provide competent health care services to all of us. We literally could not survive with out their dedication and commitment to quality medical services.

"A man's happiness is to do a man's true work."
— Marcus Aurelius (AD 121-180, Roman emperor)

Chapter

1

THE HEALTH CARE EXPLOSION!

Growing twice as fast as the average occupation, health care practitioner and technical employment is projected to increase 30.3% between 2004 and 2014. Replacing workers who retire or leave their jobs will further increase the number of job openings. Efforts to reduce health care costs may increase demand for technicians, aides and assistants, as they assume duties formerly performed by more highly paid workers.

Between 2004 and 2014, the U.S. will require millions of additional medical workers, including: 212,000 physicians & surgeons, 72,000 physical therapists, 1,203,000 registered nurses, 57,000 respiratory therapists, 1,038,000 health technicians and technologists, 101,000 pharmacists, 273,000 medical assistants, 189,000 dental assistants and 956,000 nursing, psychiatric and home health aides.[1]

Many of the fastest growing occupations are concentrated in the health services field, which is expected to account for 1 out of every 5 new jobs created by 2014.[2] Washington state had a whopping 14,000 health care job openings in May of 2005 alone![3] Factors contributing to job growth include increased use of innovative medical technology, the increase in obesity-related health problems, and the aging population, which will require more health services.[4] Retirement of older workers is expected to cause worker shortages. In some areas, new-hire bonuses of $5000 are common and a few hospitals even offer help with mortgages or rent.[5] Students in fields with the greatest shortages may find employers offering loan forgiveness programs to help repay college debt.[6] The US Army offers registered nurses bonuses of up to $15,000.[7]

WHERE THE JOBS *REALLY* ARE!

The majority (75% or more) of job vacancies never make it to the classified ads. Therefore, individuals must identify viable employment opportunities through associations, newsletters, Internet sites, directories, job fairs, personal contacts, job hotlines, corporations, and other published listings. Alternative hiring resources offer a wide variety of career possibilities.

Health Care Job Explosion offers a distinct advantage over other books of this type. It is two books in one — a comprehensive CAREER GUIDE plus a dynamic JOB FINDER. First, it provides a detailed description of each of the major health care career fields. Second, comprehensive resources are listed for job announcements (publications with job ads, job hotlines, Internet sites for job seekers, and job fairs), placement services, directories, and general information (associations, career-oriented web sites, and job related books).

This dual format permits comparisons between specialties and offers insight into qualifications, cross-training potential, and pay. The job descriptions list occupations with similar skill and training requirements.

Later chapters explore the following occupation groups:

- **Health Technologists**
- **Health Technicians**
- **Dietetics, Pharmacy, & Therapy**
- **Nursing**
- **Health and Social Services**
- **Health Diagnosing & Assistants**
- **Home Health Care & Computers**

The job descriptions offer the most up-to-date information available from the Bureau of Labor Statistics' 2006–2007 Occupational Outlook Handbook, interspersed with succinct input provided from many health care professionals and organizations. Each occupational listing covers the nature of the work, working conditions, employment statistics, training, other qualifications, advancement, job outlook, earnings, and related occupations. Following each job description is a carefully selected list of invaluable career and job resources.

VARIETY AND GROWTH CHARACTERIZE THE FIELD

The opportunities aren't limited to traditional health care occupations. Health care institutions will need thousands of additional accountants, auditors, personnel specialists, directors of personnel, attorneys, buyers, computer programmers, researchers, computer support specialists, chemists, engineers, drafters, computer operators, photographers, file clerks, secretaries, purchasing clerks, and food service helpers. Furthermore, employment growth is not limited to the traditional full-time job. Part time employment is on the increase as well.

4.7 MILLION NEW JOBS

The increased demand for health care services, fed by the growing proportion of elderly in the population, is expected to continue for a full 50 years![8] According to the Administration on Aging[9] the number of Americans over age 65 is expected to grow to 40.2 million by 2010 and to 71.5 million by 2030. Older Americans spend more than twice that of all others on medical services. The health care needs of this population will contribute greatly to the creation of new jobs.

Thirteen of the 20 occupations with the fastest projected growth rate are in health care. (See Table 1-1.) The Bureau of Labor Statistics (BLS) predicts that the private hospital industry is expected to employ nearly 5 million people by 2014, which will make it the seventh largest source of employment growth. Employment in doctor's offices and clinics will also increase and the BLS expects a 56% increase in home health aides.[10] Health care manpower shortages are now commonplace and many health care providers take months to locate qualified personnel. An American Hospital Association survey found that the health care workforce is shrinking while demand for hospital care rose in 2004.[11]

It is not just traditional medical jobs that are growing. According to the Bureau of Labor Statistics, of the seven remaining 20 fastest-growing occupations, five are in computers (an industry with increasing importance in medicine) while two are medical related: medical scientists and forensic science technicians.

Table 1-1

Health Care Projected Employment Increases: 2004 – 2014

OCCUPATION	Growth	Growth plus net replacement
Clinical lab technicians & technologists	69,000	150,000
Dental assistants	114,000	189,000
Dental hygienists	68,000	82,000
Diagnostic technicians & technologists	75,000	129,000
EMTs and paramedics	52,000	74,000
Home health aides	350,000	431,000
Medical assistants	202,000	273,000
Medical records technicians	46,000	69,000
Nursing aides, orderlies & attendants	325,000	516,000
Occupational therapists	31,000	43,000
Personal and home care aides	287,000	400,000
Pharmacy technicians	74,000	107,000
Physical therapists	57,000	72,000
Physical therapy assistants and aides	41,000	58,000
Physician assistants	31,000	40,000
Registered nurses	703,000	1,203,000
Respiratory therapists	27,000	57,000
Surgical technologists	25,000	36,000

Source: BLS, Occupational employment projections to 2014, *Monthly Labor Review*, November, 2005

THE IMPACT OF NEW TECHNOLOGY AND COMPUTERS

Biotechnology, which includes gene therapy, medical devices and drugs, will have a profound impact on the health care industry. New technologies are creating employment opportunities in diverse fields such as magnetic resonance imaging, nuclear medicine, laser surgery, ultrasound, orthopedic engineering, pharmaceuticals, clinical research, and diagnostic testing. With 3.27 billion prescriptions filled in 2004 alone, pharmacy schools can't keep up with the demand for pharmacists: hospitals, drugstores and clinics had 8,000 unfilled positions in 2005.[12] However, outsourcing of jobs overseas is a potential problem in research and development, especially in the pharmaceutical industry.

Computer technology is having a huge impact on the U.S. economy as a whole, as companies are expected to invest heavily in productivity-enhancing software, but the increase in jobs may be tempered by out-sourcing routine tasks offshore. Implementation of new technologies, increased computer networking and computer security will be the main catalysts for demand for certain computer professionals.[13] Even em-ployees who are not computer specialists are often required to have good computer skills. Computers are used in almost all aspects of med-ical research, medical records, diagnostic testing, patient scheduling and other office-related tasks.

WAGE SURVEYS

Hourly earnings in 2004 ranged from $8.89 for home health aides performing simple personal care housekeeping tasks, to $12.39 for dental assistants, $18.65 for radiologic technologists and technicians, $25.75 for registered nurses and $41.12 for pharmacists. Median yearly income of a physician assistant is $67,970 while physicians average $169,500.[14] *Health Care Job Explosion* reports the range of earnings with each listed health care career description and updates can be accessed on the Bureau of Labor Statistics web site (http://www.bls.gov/data/home.htm).

Individuals often fail to negotiate a salary that reflects their intrinsic value and qualifications for the job. This holds true in the health care field where employers must be highly competitive to attract applicants. Knowing the normal salary range in your profession and in your location can be important in deciding which job offer to accept.

EDUCATIONAL REQUIREMENTS

The level of education required for health care occupations varies depending on the field entered. The Bureau of Labor Statistics states that 24 percent of workers in hospitals have a high school diploma or less. Some hospitals and nursing facilities provide training or tuition assistance. Each occupational description listed in the following chapters describes the required education and/or on-the-job training. The re-sources at the end of each occupation's section will help you find appro-priate educational institutions or training programs in your location. It may be useful to contact people in your chosen profession in the town where you wish to work to ask which schools are considered the best. Appendix B provides information on sources of scholarships and other financial assistance for education. Table 1-2 presents an over-view of the level of education required per specialty.

TABLE 1-2

EDUCATIONAL REQUIREMENTS

Group 1 - Occupations that generally require high school graduation or less education or on the job training:

Human service worker	Ophthalmic laboratory technicians
Home health aides	Personal and home care aides
EKG technicians	Psychiatric aides
Dental Assistants	Ambulance drivers and attendants

Group 2 - Occupations that generally require some post secondary training or training below a bachelor's degree:

Radiologic technologists	Nuclear medicine technologists
Radiologic technicians	Physical therapy assistants/aides
Respiratory therapists	Medical records technicians
Surgical technicians	Licensed practical nurses
Medical assistants	Medical secretaries
Dental hygienists	EMTs and paramedics

Group 3 - Occupations that generally require a bachelor's degree or more education:

Physical therapists	Occupational therapists
Psychologists	Chiropractors
Dieticians and nutritionists	Speech-language pathologists
Optometrists	Physician assistants

PREPARING FOR SUCCESS

Individual job seekers are also competing with each other. To give yourself the edge, make sure your résumé looks professional and your interview skills are well rehearsed. Chapter Two of this book has numerous recommendations to help you with both. The Career Resources section of Chapter Three lists books and web sites to help polish your résumé and interview skills.

Follow our recommended job hunting process to expose hundreds of job sources for you to explore. It is advisable to investigate as many career alternatives as possible. You don't want just *any* career, you want the *right* career. It's necessary to explore many related fields to uncover a large pool of job options and to identify a career with the greatest potential for satisfaction and most desirable salary range.

EASING THE CHALLENGE OF FINDING A JOB

The *Health Care Job Explosion's* resources can help you find hundreds of jobs that are not advertised in your local newspaper. Resources include professional associations, Internet sites, employment advertising, directories, and job-related books. Job opening resources are comprised of publications with job ads, web sites where you can post your résumé, job hotlines, placement services, and job fairs. Associations offer career information and advice on education. Some web sites feature employment ads and directories of health care providers as well as career information. Your search through the chapters' resource sections will be guided by the icons defined at the start of each resource section.

CORPORATE LISTINGS

Corporate contacts offer additional opportunities for the health care worker. Thousands of companies manufacture products or provide services to the medical profession. The major manufacturers have large research and development budgets and several operate health care facilities. Research facilities must be staffed by medical professionals, technicians, assistants, and scientists. Other positions include sales representatives who demonstrate complex systems and equipment.

Large corporations like Merck, Medtronic, Johnson and Johnson, and Baxter International realize billions in sales yearly. For example, Baxter employs approximately 48,000 people worldwide in developing, manufacturing and selling medical devices, pharmaceuticals and biotechnology. Baxter's web site allows you to upload your résumé and cover letter into their careers site (**http://www.baxter.com**).

Appendix A provides information on directories, both on-line and print, listing major health care corporations. It's advisable to read the *Value Line Survey* sheet or *Standard & Poor's Index* for detailed information including product lines, gross sales, number of employees, names of the company officers, and other helpful data. These references are available at many libraries or copies may be obtained from full service stock brokers or on the Internet. Companies often have web sites with detailed information for prospective employees and many job search web sites have company profiles.

ADDITIONAL INFORMATION

Uncle Sam employs over 200,000 health care workers at 600 Veterans Administration medical facilities (hospitals, outpatient clinics, and nursing homes) located throughout the United States. Visit their web site at (**http://www.vacareers.va.gov**). Their annual medical care budget exceeds $20 billion. To explore health care jobs with the federal government visit **http://federaljobs.net** or obtain a copy of the author's *Book of U.S. Government Jobs* - 9th edition, available at book stores.

If you are uncertain about which career to enter or even if health care is right for you, *Health Care Job Explosion* is a good place to start. Books such as *1000 Best Job Hunting Secrets*, *What Color is Your Parachute?* and *Tips for Finding the Right Job* – a free Department of Labor pamphlet[15] – can be used in conjunction with *Health Care Job Explosion* to determine your job skills, develop comprehensive résumés, and to help you prepare for job interviews.

REFERENCES

[1] Daniel E. Hecker, "Occupational employment projections to 2014," *Monthly Labor Review*, Bureau of Labor Statistics, November 2005.

[2] Jay M. Berman, "Industry output and employment projections to 2014," *Monthly Labor Review*, Bureau of Labor Statistics, November 2005.

[3] Shirleen Holt, "Rebounding state adds 12,800 jobs; help wanted," *Seattle Times*, Aug. 17, 2005.

[4] Lucy Ament, "AHA survey finds demand for hospital care continues to rise", AHA News Now, November 14, 2005.

[5] Perks: More Than Money, http://www.medhunters.com/articles/perksMoreThan Money.html, downloaded Oct. 16, 2005.

[6] *Ibid.*

[7] Active Duty Nurse Corp Benefits, US Army Nurse Corp, http://www.goarmy.com/ amedd/nurse/corps_benefits.jsp, downloaded Oct. 16, 2005.

[8] Mary N. Haan, et.al., Journal of the American Geriatrics Society, Vol. 45, pages 776-674, 1997.

[9] *A Profile of Older Americans: 2004*, Administration on Aging, U.S. Department of Health and Human Services, 2004, page 13.

[10] Berman, "Industry output and employment projections to 2014."

[11] Ament, "AHA survey finds demand for hospital care continues to rise."

[12] Susan Q. Stranahan, "Want a Red-Hot Job?", *AARP Bulletin*, September 2005.

[13] Berman, "Industry output and employment projections to 2014."

[14] *Occupational Employment Statistics*, Bureau of Labor Statistics, U.S. Department of Labor, November, 2004. http://www.bls.gov/data/home.htm.

[15] *Tips for Finding the Right Job*, Consumer Information Center of the U.S. General Services Administration, 28 pp, 1996. This book, along with other employment information, is available online at http://www.pueblo.gsa.gov/.

Chapter

2

THE NEXUS
MAKING A CONNECTION

I vividly recall taking a school entrance exam when I was nine years old. The examiner held up pictures and asked me what was wrong with each one. I only remember the one I missed; a frontiersman was standing in a forest and firing his musket at several bandits 10 paces away. Three paces to the frontiersman's left was another attacker with weapon raised.

When I first viewed the picture, I couldn't find anything wrong with it. The examiner asked me to look a second time. I asked if all three bandits were the enemy and he nodded yes. I still found nothing wrong with the picture. We spent 25 minutes discussing this singular event.

My perception of the event did not meet with his expectations. He wanted me to say that the frontiersman should be taking care of urgent business — the attacker three paces away. What he didn't realize was that I felt this person was out of the frontiersman's field of view and that he wasn't aware of the imminent danger approaching from his left.

> **Excellent job opportunities are often just three paces away, hidden from our field of view.**

This reminds me of one of my favorite stories as told by Earl Nightingale in his taped Insight series. Earl tells of an African farmer who dreamed about finding a diamond mine. Bound and determined to do what ever was necessary to realize his dream, he sold his farm, and headed for the coast. After many years of fruitless searching he returned to his home to discover that one of the most valuable diamond mines in Africa's history was discovered on the property he had abandoned.

THE JOB NEXT DOOR

Like the African farmer, job hunters are often unaware of valuable employment options within their reach. Most are programmed to respond to local classifieds or to rely on employment agencies. A small percentage of all jobs, less than 25%, are actually advertised in classifieds. To locate the remaining 75%, start knocking on doors.

Networking is the process of opening doors — employment opportunities — through the development of relationships that are mutually beneficial to both parties. The end result is to provide you with contacts that will assist you with your employment and career goals. Networking provides mutual benefits for both parties and offers direct access to people who often know in advance when jobs will become available.

Most health care occupations described in this book have their own association. Contact them for membership information and seriously consider joining the one that will best represent you. These resources often provide job source listings and networking contacts. Directories, discussed in Chapter Three, provide additional contact sources.

NETWORKING PRINCIPLES

Many would have you believe that networking requires complex planning strategies and toastmaster capabilities. Most, including myself, prefer the informal approach. Remember, networking is natural — it's something you do all the time. How? Every time you meet people in your profession, either on the job or in a social situation, and start talking about work, you are networking.

The essential components of a viable networking plan are personal commitment, the ability to identify resources (such as *Health Care Job Explosion*) and above all else, following through with action.

Personal contact is the key!

Motivated job seekers should make every effort to meet face-to-face with key officials long before they submit their résumés. The ability of an interviewer to match a face or telephone conversation to an application prior to the actual job interview can be invaluable. Informational interviews are one of the best ways to set up these meetings.

The importance of professional associations in networking cannot be over-emphasized. If one of the organizations for your profession has a local chapter, attend the meetings and keep in touch with the members by phone or e-mail.

Networking books are available at your public library. These valuable books offer proven networking techniques, introduction letter samples, and formats that you can use to expand your personal network.

Don't forget to search the Internet for networking opportunities and advice. Many sites have articles on networking and/or information on e-mail discussion groups, chat rooms and message boards for professionals. These are especially useful if you are relocating.

IMPROVING YOUR CHANCES

Too often job seekers pin all of their hopes on one effort. Health career jobs are plentiful but they are still highly competitive. The more contacts you make, the better your chances are to find the job you want.

It is important when networking to retain your initial contacts and explore career advancement opportunities with them after you get hired. This can go both ways and you may have the opportunity to reciprocate.

Note your contact's name (correct spelling is important), address, phone number, and a brief summary of the discussion in a journal or binder. It's perplexing when you forget who you talked with and what you talked about. It is also appropriate to send a short thank you note. These contacts will appreciate it and remember your name down the road when it counts.

Begin by using the resources this book offers and build on each contact. Look through your local telephone directory for additional contacts. Do something every day to expand your network. It's very important to define your employment goals, then develop a basic action plan to achieve what you set out to do.

I've been on many selection panels. Interviewers naturally have an opinion of who the best candidate is from reviewing résumés and employment applications. They are also highly influenced by anyone who has had personal contact with any of the job applicants. I can't stress enough just how important a face-to-face informational interview is and how dramatically it can influence a selection panel!

Those most technically or professionally qualified may not be hired. Officials look at a wide range of criteria; special skills, education, motivation, personality, ability to present one's views orally and in writing, organizational knowledge, and the ability to get along with others. Through networking, job seekers impart a positive image to the organization long before the interview. Supervisors want motivated employees who can work independently, have the basic skills and training and, most importantly, can get along with co-workers and patients. As long as you have the basics, don't be over concerned about others having more experience or training. If you demonstrate that you are really eager to learn, you may have the advantage over someone who gives the impression that they are a "know-it-all." With the constant technological advances in health care, many supervisors know that employees who enjoy learning new skills will be long-term assets.

Selections are often based more on personality, positive attitude, and motivational characteristics than you can imagine. Organizations prefer to spend funds to educate someone technically marginal than to hire a "problem child" who may disrupt the work environment. I've personally counseled many applicants who weren't selected because of these intrinsic characteristics. These individuals knew they were highly qualified and couldn't understand why they weren't selected.

It is a true statement that supervisors deserve the employees they have. Once a supervisor observes unacceptable behavior or performance, it's his or her responsibility to counsel the employee immediately to correct the deficiency. The primary goal of the supervisor is to improve the employees' performance or behavior. It's unfortunate that many supervisors go to great lengths to avoid constructive confrontation and often ignore behavior and/or performance problems until they get out of control. This is a disservice to the employee and to the organization.

TURN DISAPPOINTMENT INTO A POSITIVE EXPERIENCE

Many selecting officials will counsel candidates who were not selected. Ask if you can spend 15 minutes discussing what you could do to improve your chances. This is very important information. Even if the company doesn't plan to hire in the near future, the information you obtain from this counseling session will help you with future interviews and résumés. And it may be a big boost to your self-esteem! Maybe the interviewer thought you were wonderful, and the only reason you weren't hired is that there were several other equally good candidates.

Find out how to improve your chances for future positions. Do you need to improve your proficiency, complete additional training, or improve interpersonal skills? Ask the selecting official for a candid counseling session and handle it professionally. The job has already been filled, so find out what you need to do to be considered next time. Be courteous and thank the supervisor for his/her time and assistance.

I often hear recent graduates talking about how scarce jobs are. While talking with these individuals, I find many are doing very little to locate job openings. They tend to focus their search on traditional classified ads and placement services. Health care is an excellent field for networking to locate jobs that aren't listed in the classifieds. If you're motivated, willing to write a letter of introduction, and make a few phone calls, jobs are available. Most towns have medical facilities and large cities have thousands of health care providers, including nursing homes, hospitals, rehabilitation centers, veterans hospitals, and private physicians' offices.

The Secret to Success Is That The Harder You Work, The Luckier You Get.

INFORMATIONAL INTERVIEWS

Call or write potential employers and ask to talk with a personnel specialist or a specific specialty supervisor, ie; radiologist, registered nurse, etc.. Briefly explain what you are interested in and ask if he/she would be willing to talk with you in person about career opportunities. If you're uncertain whether or not specific job skills are needed by a local health care organization, ask for the Personnel or Human Resources Department and query them concerning available positions.

For your informational interview have a copy of your résumé and a cover letter describing your desires and qualifications. These job hunting tools are essential. Your résumé and cover letter must have a professional appearance and be customized to fit your job goals. Hire a résumé writing service or follow the advice in a book such as *1000 Best Job Hunting Secrets* by Diane Stafford and Moritza Day. The resources in Chapter Three include résumé advice books and web sites.

The informational interview will help you investigate familiar and diverse employment opportunities. It's best not to limit your informational interviews strictly to supervisors or personnel specialists. Any employee can provide important information. The outcome of these interviews will help you make an objective career decision and hopefully develop a company contact to help you land a job.

Many supervisors and employees are willing to talk about their job even when no vacancies exist. These interviews often provide insight into secondary careers and upcoming openings that can be more attractive than what you were originally pursuing.

When contacting people to request interviews, add that you will only take 15 minutes of their time. Time is a critical resource that most of us must use sparingly. If the supervisor's schedule is tight, you might suggest meeting in the hospital cafeteria during lunch. Some health care workers need this rest period for themselves, but others use it as a social hour and may even introduce you to co-workers who walk by.

Visit **http://healthcarejobs.org** for up dated information and helpful networking links.

It is wise to ask *specific* questions to get the information you need. Write them down and take them with you. Amend the following interview questions to suit your individual needs:

INFORMATIONAL INTERVIEW QUESTIONS

EXPERIENCE AND BACKGROUND

1. What training and skill is needed for this type of work?
2. How did you personally prepare for this career?
3. What experience/training is absolutely essential?
4. What do you find most and least enjoyable with this work?
5. How does my background compare?

CREDENTIALS

Of the items listed below which do you consider most important?

1. Education	4. Personality
2. Special skills	5. Organizational knowledge
3. Former work experience	6. Other

GENERAL QUESTIONS

1. What advice would you give to someone interested in this field?
2. How do I find out more about jobs, and how are they advertised?
3. Does this company hire from this office or do they hire through a centralized personnel office?
4. Is there career advancement potential?
5. Is travel involved?
6. Are you required to work shifts?
7. What type of additional training would be helpful?

REFERRAL

1. Are there others I should talk to?
2. May I use your name when I contact them?

If an interview is not granted ask permission to send a cover letter and résumé for the company's prospective employee file. You can expect numerous rejections while pursuing these methods. Don't get discouraged. A good manager is always on the lookout for needed talent. If you present yourself professionally and have the necessary background, you will make a connection. Persistence pays when networking. Many promising candidates give up prematurely before giving their efforts a chance to work.

INTERVIEW PREPARATION

When going for the interview dress appropriately for the position applied for. Also be on time and don't forget a copy of your résumé.

It isn't uncommon for prospective employers to open up a dialogue with you to discover your suitability for various positions within the company. Be prepared and visit your local library or bookstore to pick up a book on interviewing techniques such as *101 Dynamite Answers to Interview Questions: Sell Your Strength!* , by Caryl & Ronald Krannich, Ph.Ds. If you can't find this book, a librarian can find you another title. Don't overlook publications like *Career Magazine* (www.careermag.com).

Most interviewers will ask you to tell the group about yourself. They purposely leave the question open to your interpretation. Many applicants I interview limit their response to work experience and education. It's important to some degree but remember, they already read your application and résumé and know your background. Give them a brief overview of your education and experience and then expand on your personal life and outside activities. This lets the interviewers see you as a person and not simply a robot that has punched all of the technical buttons to get to where you are. Tell them about your outside interests; make it interesting and personable.

Many organizations are now involved with QWL, Quality of Work-life, and they need people-oriented workers to improve productivity and to use their creative talents for the betterment of the organization and the people in it. "Participative" management is becoming pervasive within many organizations, including government.

Another leading question is: "What did you like and dislike most about your present or past employer?" Remember that no matter how you actually feel, be diplomatic. Interviewers are looking for divisive behavior, attitude problems, overconfidence, and cooperative intent with this question. If you truly hate your current employer or company, soften the answer with tact. Employers are looking for employees who will support their organization, not bring it down. For instance, this answer to "What did you like least about your current job?" was very creative and, I believe, sincere: "I enjoy my work and I voluntarily take a considerable amount of work home. This tends to take time away from the family. I resolved the conflict by devoting one day off each week entirely to family activities. Actually, this has helped me at work also. I'm more energized because of the one day break each week." This creative response indicated that the individual was highly motivated to take work home voluntarily. Secondly, he was able to overcome the negative aspects affecting his family.

I'm surprised by how many people are totally candid with this question. One individual I interviewed bad-mouthed his boss for thirty minutes. His negative attitude over-shadowed the rest of the interview. Needless to say he didn't get the job. It's acceptable to talk about difficulties with a supervisor but it must be done tactfully.

INTERVIEW FOLLOW-UP

After you've had your first interview, sit down for a few minutes to collect your thoughts and add items to your action plan. Take your plan and start penciling in your changes. Remember that a plan is simply a starting point and it evolves as you progress through it.

If the person you interviewed indicated that additional training would be helpful, look at what you need to do to get it. Many positions require computer skills so if you have them, put this on your résumé and consider bringing it up in the interview. Even if the job you are applying for doesn't directly require it, many companies find it helpful.

How about communications skills? If you need to improve your ability to talk to groups, contact a local chapter of Toastmasters International and join one of their clubs. They have an excellent program developed to improve all facets of oral presentations. The cost is minimal and you will expand your network simply by joining a club.

I was a manager participating in a local Toastmasters Club I helped to set up in the late 70's. I became a competent Toastmaster in my group and met a diverse cross section of managers and specialists. One member was anticipating a layoff. She had specific experience that we needed in my organization. I referred her for an interview and she was hired for an engineering position. She has since been promoted several times and now holds an upper management position.

Don't forget to put your activities such as Toastmaster membership, computer users group participation, volunteer work, Little League Management, etc. on your résumé. This proves that you are self-motivated. This is a highly desirable attribute. I always look at extra-curricular activities when I am hiring. Many managers volunteer or join clubs such as Toastmasters. If two people are equally qualified, this can often be the determining factor in selections.

THE NEXT STEP

The remaining chapters provide detailed occupational descriptions with extensive career advice and job source listings. Before going on to specific occupations, read Chapter Three to locate general job or career information sources for most occupational groups.

Good luck with your job search. Remember, it isn't as much a matter of luck as persistence. Follow the guidance in this and other stated references and you can't help but make a connection.

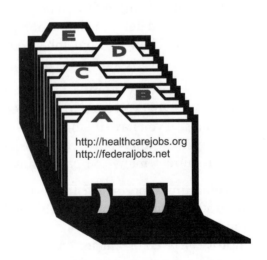

http://healthcarejobs.org
http://federaljobs.net

"Obstacles are those frightful things you see when you take your eyes off the goal." — **Hannah Moore**

Chapter

3

JOB SOURCES FOR EVERYONE

This chapter presents job resources that are useful for many health care occupations. Associations or publications that focus on a narrow range of professions or on a single specialty are placed with the discussion of specific professions in the following chapters. After reviewing these resources refer to the Table of Contents and Index to locate more job sources for your specific vocation.

A number of periodicals and directories in this chapter are available at libraries. Many publishers will send complimentary review copies of their publications upon request. Others, like *USA Today*, are available at most news stands. Many are available on the Internet. Professional journal advertising practices are changing. In order to provide faster service, some are posting job openings on the Internet, rather than in print publications. It would be wise to check current advertising volume before subscribing if jobs are your only interest.

Several excellent books, such as the author's *The Book of U.S. Government Jobs* and *Post Office Jobs*, target federal government employment and are valuable resources for those seeking jobs with Uncle Sam. These titles are available at your local library or bookstore or you can call 1-800-782-7424 to order copies.

HOW THE RESOURCES ARE ORGANIZED

Each occupation's resource section will offer one or more of the following, with icons to help you find exactly the services you want.

📖 JOB-RELATED BOOKS

Recommended books that provide career advice or offer general job search guidance. If your library doesn't have a book you want, ask about interlibrary loans, a free service at many school and public libraries.

📄 JOB ADVERTISING SOURCES

Newspapers - Start with the classified and display ads in your local newspaper. Include national newspapers such as the New York Times and USA Today. Many have employment pages on their web sites.

Special purpose periodicals - These listings provide classifieds for specific careers or occupational segments. Job ads number from a dozen to thousands per issue.

Professional association publications - A number of associations' newsletters (print or electronic), journals, Internet sites and other publications list classified ads and provide networking contacts.

Internet - The Internet has changed the way job seekers access classified advertising. Many professional associations have employment ads on their web sites. Many web sites focus solely on employment ads and advice. Some specialize in health care, such as **http://healthcarejobs.org**. Internet service providers and search engines often have career sections on their home pages.

〽️ JOB HOTLINES and E-MAIL JOB NOTIFICATION

Job Hotlines - A number of health care facilities, businesses, and government organizations offer job hotlines. The charge for this service varies, but many are free. To find job hotlines, call the employment department (human resources) of hospitals or local government agencies.

Alternately, use an Internet search engine by entering the name of your state, county or city and the key words "job hotline."

E-mail job notification - Also called Job Alerts or Job Agents, many of the Internet sites listed in chapter three have services using e-mail to notify you of jobs that fit your specifications. Most are free, but to access some you must be a member of the sponsoring association.

℞ JOB FAIRS

Job Fairs - Organizations occasionally conduct jobs fairs throughout the country. They provide direct contact with potential employers and offer a wide array of career literature and job listings. "Mini-job fairs" are often held at annual professional conventions. Ask your professional association(s) if recruiters will be present at meetings.

✍ RÉSUMÉ MATCHING SERVICES

Résumé Matching Services (Placement Services) - Trade, professional, and government organizations operate placement services, often referred to as résumé matching services. Résumés are matched to vacant positions. Computers are often used to analyze résumés and match them to job vacancies.

State government services are free, while others charge the applicant and employers often pay a fee to use the service. Many states, professional associations and private recruiters have their job placement services on web sites. Many professional associations and web job sites will allow you to post your résumé free.

☤ ASSOCIATIONS

Associations. Health care associations provide a wealth of valuable information, career guidance, and services to members and, often, to students. They may advertise job vacancies in their publications and web sites, sponsor annual job fairs, and offer placement services. Position wanted ads may also be accepted. Services and member benefits can be extensive. The AAPA (American Academy of Physician Assistants) is an excellent example. They offer a directory of accredited programs, career guides, résumé assistance, publications, internet job listings, CME credit logging service, and insurance. They also have 57 local chapters to facilitate networking. Hundreds of organizations provide similar services.

Membership cost varies. Students can join many professional associations at reduced rates. Nonmembers can often purchase subscriptions and publications or receive free career information.

Some publications of associations may be listed in the Resource sections under the publisher's name, if the publisher provides a special service, such as Lippincott's *Nursing Center* on the web.

Write for a sample newsletter and association membership information. Many publications and directories are available at university medical libraries or you may be able to read a copy at your local medical center. Also, your local public library may be able to obtain some materials through inter library loans.

   DIRECTORIES

Directories - Directories provide detailed listings of association members, companies, medical practices, allied health providers, homes for the aging, laboratories, specialists, research facilities, special care facilities, and much more. They offer abundant resources for the job hunter.

It's best to research the companies that interest you. The more information you have concerning a potential employer the better. This information can help you select companies with the best benefits, comprehensive retirement packages, and working conditions. Individual contacts can steer you to personnel directors, under staffed offices, and provide inside information on the working environment. Some of the employment Internet sites provide employer profiles.

Directories are available from thousands of organizations. Prices range from free to several thousand dollars for extensive packages. Many directories are now published on CD ROM in a database format for computer users. Computers offer key word sorting and fast access to any of thousands of retrieval formats. A diligent search of the Internet may turn up the directory you want online at no charge. Libraries have many directories; ask for them at the reference desk.

Searchable directories of thousands of health care facilities and home health agencies are available through several Internet sites listed in the Resource section of this chapter.

⌐ INTERNET SITES

The Internet - Information Capitol of the 21ˢᵗ Century

The Internet is an important source for employment opportunities, career information and networking. If you do not have a computer, many public and college libraries can provide Internet access. Most of the above resources can be found on web sites. Many commercial web sites are devoted entirely to job ads. The larger Internet service providers may provide their members with employment ads or links to employment web sites.

Networking on the web can be accomplished through message boards, chat rooms or e-mail lists. The e-mail list process allows you to send messages to a central server and then it sends out your message to every subscriber on the "list." In that way, members of a specific profession can join with others in discussing topics through a centralized e-mail exchange. Some Internet sites provide message centers or chat rooms where students or professionals can "discuss" their careers.

This edition of *Health Care Job Explosion* provides URLs, (Internet site addresses,) for numerous professional organizations and job ad sites. Listings also include sites with links to medical centers and hospitals that may have employment offices (human resource centers) to contact. E-mail lists can be located by search engines or through professional associations, while message boards may be accessed through your Internet provider's interface menus or association web sites.

The Internet is a rapidly evolving information source, so expect some of the URLs (addresses) to have changed by the time you begin your job search. Visit **http://healthcarejobs.org** for updated book resource listings. Conducting a search of the web on your own is more effective if you follow a few simple guidelines. (If you are unfamiliar with the Internet, ask a librarian to show you how to get started.) First, read the Internet search tips section of your search engine. Second, there are many web search engines available in addition to the one your Internet service lists on its main menu. Some search engines, such as Yahoo, are set up with directories (categories) so they offer easy access to job listings and other information. Also many web sites provide extensive links to job search sites, professional associations, résumé tips and interview advice.

One final word on Internet searches. Expect a search to locate about 40% of the web sites that fit your search criteria. Therefore, if you don't find your target on the first try, refine your technique using the search engine's help section, and then try another search engine. Each engine uses a different method of indexing web sites, which may produce very different results. Why are we emphasizing search engines when we are listing hundreds of web sites for you? *New sites pop up daily and web addresses change, so an hour or so invested in learning how to "surf the net" will pay off by saving many hours—and much frustration—later!*

The Internet is an important source for employment opportunities, career information and networking. The resource section begins with a few sites that teach you how to use the Internet. If you do not have a computer, many public and college libraries can provide Internet access.

Appendix A provides a comprehensive guide to locating health care companies that may also offer job opportunities. Also included are web sites that list medical companies. Contact their employment offices for job possibilities.

One resource that we can't list specifically is your local college or university. Many have career descriptions available at a central information office, in individual departments, or on their web sites. Most do not require you to be a student to access information.

A warning is in order for those who post their résumé online. Criminals search résumés and pose as overseas companies looking for people to work on commission cashing checks. They ask you to deposit checks in your account, wire the money to an overseas bank and keep a fat commission. The checks are stolen and your bank account can be wiped out. Beware of all work-at-home offers and report suspicious offers to the Internet Crime Complaint Center (**http://www.ic3.gov/**). More fraud and safety advice can be found at **http://www.monster.com**.

RESOURCE GUIDE

Resources are listed alphabetically by association or title. <u>The outstanding resources are underlined</u>. The icons below will guide you.

For a full explanation of these resources see the second page of Chapter 3.

SURFING LESSONS:
HOW TO USE THE INTERNET EFFECTIVELY

Google (http://www.google.com) The Help Center can be found by clicking on the word "more..." It is loaded with web search tips.

Search Engine Watch (http://www.searchenginewatch.com) This site keeps you informed on the best search engines. Like everything else on the web, search engines are constantly undergoing changes. Check the "Web Searching Tips" to learn how to fine tune your search skills.

Spider's Apprentice (http://www.monash.com/spidap.html) This site teaches you how to use the web and evaluates the major search engines. Check in Search Engine Listings for Medical Search Engines. Even advanced surfers can benefit from this site's great information.

NETWORKING SUPER SOURCE:
LISTSERVs (MAILING LISTS or E-MAIL GROUPS)

Google (http://www.google.com) Click on the word "more" and search for groups concerned with health care professions, or start one.

Yahoo! Groups (http://groups.yahoo.com) This site makes it easy to find people to chat with or set up your own list and exchange mail with your fellow students or professionals.

Some search engines provide direct access to mailing lists in their directories. You can use the words "newsgroup," "mailing list" or "Listserv" with a topic keyword in any search engine. Not all lists are public. Private groups can be found by contacting your professional association.

SEARCH ENGINES

Many search engines have employment or classified sections; most that are organized by categories are a type of directory that can greatly simplify searching and increase the number of relevant sites you find.

About.com - **(http://careerplanning.about.com)** One of the most extensive career advice and job search sites. Hundreds of informative articles and links to job sites.

Alltheweb - **(http://www.alltheweb.com/)** Spider's Apprentice (above) ranks Alltheweb as runner up for "Biggest, Fastest, Most Comprehensive" and for "Best Advanced Search Refinement."

Altavista - **(http://www.altavista.com/)** Spider's Apprentice (above) rates Altavista as having the "Best Advanced Search Refinement."

AnyWho - **(http://www.anywho.com/)** Provided by AT&T, this site has Yellow Pages, White Pages and a reverse lookup.

Google - **(http://www.google.com/)** Today's leading search engine. To access the directory (which is connected with the Open Directory Project), click the word "more" then "Directory" then "Health."

Open Directory Project - **(http://www.dmoz.org)** Netscape volunteers evaluate all the sites indexed in this directory. Still the best directory on the Internet. Hundreds of annotated links to employment web sites under two categories: Health and Business.

Yahoo! - **(http://www.yahoo.com)** An old standard, this search engine and directory has several helpful features. It has a HotJobs section with career advice. To access employment web sites in the directory, click "Directory" and type in "Health Care Job and Employment Resources."

EDUCATION RESOURCES

Many of the search engines above and resources below include advice or school directories among their other services.

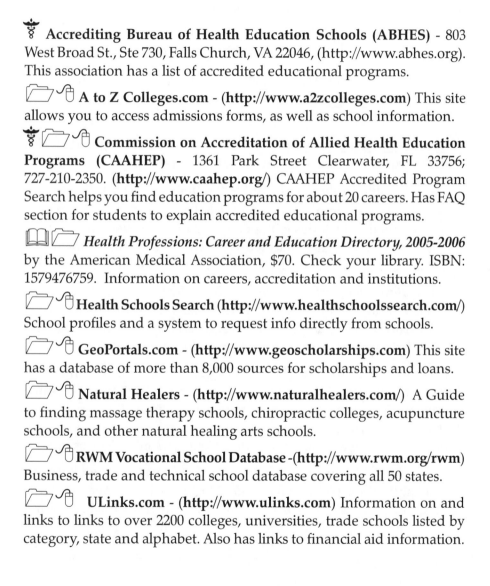 **Accrediting Bureau of Health Education Schools (ABHES)** - 803 West Broad St., Ste 730, Falls Church, VA 22046, (http://www.abhes.org). This association has a list of accredited educational programs.

A to Z Colleges.com - (http://www.a2zcolleges.com) This site allows you to access admissions forms, as well as school information.

Commission on Accreditation of Allied Health Education Programs (CAAHEP) - 1361 Park Street Clearwater, FL 33756; 727-210-2350. (http://www.caahep.org/) CAAHEP Accredited Program Search helps you find education programs for about 20 careers. Has FAQ section for students to explain accredited educational programs.

Health Professions: Career and Education Directory, 2005-2006 by the American Medical Association, $70. Check your library. ISBN: 1579476759. Information on careers, accreditation and institutions.

Health Schools Search (http://www.healthschoolssearch.com/) School profiles and a system to request info directly from schools.

GeoPortals.com - (http://www.geoscholarships.com) This site has a database of more than 8,000 sources for scholarships and loans.

Natural Healers - (http://www.naturalhealers.com/) A Guide to finding massage therapy schools, chiropractic colleges, acupuncture schools, and other natural healing arts schools.

RWM Vocational School Database -(http://www.rwm.org/rwm) Business, trade and technical school database covering all 50 states.

ULinks.com - (http://www.ulinks.com) Information on and links to links to over 2200 colleges, universities, trade schools listed by category, state and alphabet. Also has links to financial aid information.

CAREER RESOURCES

This chapter presents job and career information resources that are useful for many health care occupations. For directories of health care-related corporations, check below and in Appendix A.

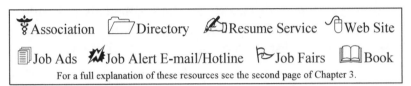

For a full explanation of these resources see the second page of Chapter 3.

Health Care Careers and Jobs (http://healthcarejobs.org) The Health Care Job Explosion Web site. Check here for updates.

Federal Jobs Net (http://federaljobs.net) The U.S. Government is the largest employer in the United States. Explore all occupations. Information includes job openings, pay scales, veterans and the disabled recruitment, and job search techniques and resources, including valuable web site links. Several books to aid your job search are available.

1000 Best Job Hunting Secrets - by Diane Stafford and Moritza Day. Published by Sourcebooks, 2004. ISBN: 1-4022-0218-0. $10.36. Formatted with 1000 numbered paragraphs, this book is both informative and fun to read. Extensive résumé, cover letter and interview advice.

Absolutely Health Care - This award-winning site **(http://www.healthjobsusa.com)** lets you search for full time, part-time or traveling jobs by state and job category. Employers directory links to the facility or recruiter web sites. Post your résumé and receive e-mail job notices. Check the Education Resource Center. Don't miss this one!

American Association of Cardiovascular and Pulmonary Rehabilitation (AACVPR) - 401 North Michigan Avenue, Suite 2200, Chicago, IL 60611; 312/321-5146. Their site at **(http://aacvpr.org**, aacvpr@smithbucklin.com) has Career Links where members can post résumés, view job ads or sign up for job alert emails. Members include, MDs, PhDs, PTs, Eps, RNs, RRTs, RCPs, RDs, EdDs. Extensive directory of certified rehabilitation programs.

American College of Sports Medicine (ACSM) - P.O. Box 1440, Indianapolis, IN 46206-1440; 317/637-9200. **(http://www.acsm.org)**

Offers placement service to members. The Web site has a brochure on careers in sports medicine to download.

American Heart Association CareerMatch - Post your résumé, view company profiles and job ads by location or profession at **http://aha.medcareers.com/seeker/**

American Medical Association (AMA) - 515 N. State St., Chicago, IL 60610; 800/621-8335. (**http://www.ama-assn.org**) Membership consists of physicians and medical societies. Web site has information on careers as a physician and in allied health. The DoctorFinder give you access to 690,000 doctors. Publishes the *Health Professions Career and Education Directory*, a book on careers and educational institutions.

American Public Health Association - 800 I St. N.W., Washington, DC 20001-3710; 202/777-2742. (**http://www.apha.org**, comments@apha.org) Membership includes a diverse cross section of the medical community. Offers a number of services to members including a job placement service, research, training, and networking though Special Interest Groups. Has a student membership available. Web site includes job listings and membership directory (members only).

American School Health Association (ASHA) - 7263 State Rt 43, P.O. Box 708, Kent, Ohio 44240; 330/678-1601. Targets all medical specialties that are utilized in school systems. (**http://www.ashaweb.org**, asha@ashaweb.org) The web site has networking for members via a Listserv. *Journal of School Health*, 10 issues per year, free to members, includes both display and classified advertising.

America's Career InfoNet - (**http://www.acinet.org/**) One of the best career planning sites, ACINET has an excellent assortment of resources to help you find a career that fits your personality, get information on financial aid, check employment trends, find counseling, plan a job search and locate job openings. State profiles have extensive resources: links to educational institutions, city web sites, employment needs for specific careers and links to state job banks. Don't miss it! This site is part of CareerOneStop, an integrated suite of national career web sites at **http://www.careeronestop.org/**.

America's Job Bank - A service of the Public Employment Service, and part of the above, this site at **http://www.ajb.dni.us** allows searching for a job using a menu of occupations, keywords, or various occupational codes. There are over one million jobs–excellent site design.

Contains links to the state public employment services, to employers' web sites and private placement agencies' sites.

Association for Gerontology in Higher Education - For information about a variety of job opportunities working with the elderly try **http://www.aghe.org**. The site links to job ad sites.

ASAE Services, Inc. (http://info.asaenet.org/) This site lists thousands of associations and provides information on careers working for the associations themselves.

BestJobsUSA.com - (**http://www.bestjobsusa.com**) This Web site is both a job bank and recruitment center, with health care career/job search section. Post your résumé for free and search for career fairs. Read articles and interviews with health care professionals.

Billian Publishing - (**http://www.billianhealthdata.com**) Current publications, which may be in your library, include *Assisted Living & Extended Care Facilities Directory, Managed Healthcare Organizations* (HMO, PPO and POS facilities) and *Hospital Blue Book.*

Black Collegiate Services - 140 Carondelet Street, New Orleans, LA 70130;832/615-8871. (**http://www.black-collegian.com**). *The Black Collegian* has two annual career issues. Award winning web site has "Search Jobs" and "Post résumés" sections, with job alert agent. They also have a Military Opportunity Job Bank.

The Book of U.S. Government Jobs - *Where They Are, What's Available, & How to Get One* by Dennis V. Damp, ISBN: 0-943641-23-3, $21.95 plus $5.75 shipping. Available with check or money order direct from Bookhaven Press, P.O. Box 1243, Moon Township, PA 15108, or by credit card at 800/782-7424 or **http://www.federaljobs.net/**

CareerBuilder.com - (**http://www.careerbuilder.com/**) It provides résumé posting, job searching and job alerts to e-mail you the results of your job searches. There is extensive advice on career-related issues. Career fairs section lists events around the country.

TrueCareers - (**http://www.careercity.com**) This web site has articles on careers and job hunting. Search employment ads by state or use the Diversity Center for minority job seekers.

Career Magazine - Published by National Career Search. Good for career information, including videos. Their Internet site is located at **http://www.careermag.com** and has job openings, employer profiles, a résumé listing service, résumé writing tips, a "healthcare & medicine" section and job search alerts. Very well organized.

📖 *Careers in Health Care* - by Barbara Mardinly Swanson, Hardcover, 192 pages, $10.95. Published by McGraw-Hill, 2005. ISBN: 0071438505. Can be downloaded from Amazon.com.

📖 *Careers in Healthcare (Success Without College)* - by Robert F. Wilson, Paperback, 184 pages, $8.95. Published by Barrons Educational Series, 1999. ISBN: 0764108034

📖 *Careers Inside the World of Health Care* - by Beth Wilkinson, Hardcover, $19.35. Published by Globe Fearon, 1999. ISBN: 0130231940

📖 *Careers in Sports Medicine* - by Barbara Moe, Rosen Publishing Group, 2002, $26.25, ISBN: 0823935388. Includes physicians and physical therapists, exercise and fitness specialists, nutritionists and others.

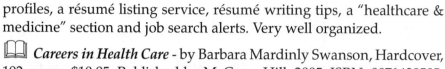 **Caregiver Jobs Clearinghouse** - http://carecareers.net/ This site offers a jobs database, links to employers and the ability to post résumés online for long-term health care workers.

College Grad.com - **http://www.collegegrad.com**. This site has a healthcare/medical category allowing you to search for entry-level job opportunities. There is advice on job search strategies and a section for employer research. free career magazines. Post a résumé.

Consumer Information Center - Pueblo, CO 81009; 888/878-3256. (**http://www.pueblo.gsa.gov**) This service is provided by the U.S. government. Employment section has lots of good links to career info. Many employment information or small business pamphlets can be downloaded free or ordered for a small fee.

Commission on Accreditation of Rehabilitation Facilities (CARF) - 4891 E. Grant Road, Tucson, AZ 85712; 520/325-1044. (**http://www.carf.org/aging**). CCAC site lists accredited continuing care rehabilitation providers across the country, organized by type of care, with links to facility Web sites when available.

DiversityConnection.org - Institute for Diversity in Health Management (**http://www.diversityconnection.org/**) This organization's goal is to expand leadership opportunities for ethnic minorities in health services management. Scholarships are available. Jobs are posted and notices can be e-mailed to you. Post your résumé.

DoctorDirectory.com - (http://doctordirectory.com) This is a very efficient directory of doctors and hospitals by specialty and state.

Doctorline (http://doctorline.com) The web site has addresses and phone numbers of health care professionals in conventional and alternative medicine.

Dorland Healthcare Information - 1500 Walnut Street, Suite 1000,Philadelphia, PA 19102; 800/784-2332. (http://www.dorlandhealth .com). *Case Management Resource Guide* is the largest directory of healthcare services. *Dorland's Medical Directory* has contact information for thousands of physicians. Both may be available at libraries.

eRésumés & Résumé Writing Services - (http://www.erésumés.com) This site is a top-notch guide to preparing e-résumés, résumés that looks good when delivered by e-mail.

explore: HealthCareers.org - Funded by the Josiah Macy Jr. Foundation and the Association of Academic 'Health Centers. (http://explorehealthcareers.org/, contactus@explorehealthcareers.org) A free online health careers resource for students and advisors. Has extensive listing of health careers from the aide level to M. D. level. Has overview of each health career, how to find a career, how to pay for training, and estimate of how long training takes. Also has links to enrichment programs for students who would like to try out what life might be like in particular health professions and a Diversity Matters section.

Federal Research Service FedJobs Career Central - (http://www.fedjobs.com, E-mail: info@fedjobs.com) 800/822-5027 or 703/281-0200. FRS is a private company offering information on federal job vacancies for a monthly fee. This online database of federal jobs is updated every work day. The web site lists job fairs, has career chat and résumé advice. Several books are available. Members receive application kits and daily e-mail notification of jobs.

FedWorld Federal Jobs Search - U.S. Department of Commerce Technology Administration, National Technical Information Service, Springfield, VA 22161; 703/605-6000. (http://www.fedworld.gov/jobs/ jobsearch.html, helpdesk@fedworld.gov). You can search this site by keyword and limit the search to a single state. U.S. government job openings include Army and Air Force Reserve. FedWorld downloads files from the FJOB bulletin board system, see USA Jobs below.

Ferguson Publishing Company - c/o Facts On File, Inc., 132 West 31st Street, 17th Floor, New York, NY 10001; 800/322-8755. (**http://www.fergpubco.com**, CustServ@factsonfile.com). Publishes many books on careers, including: *Career Opportunities in Health Care, Careers in Focus: Medical Technicians*, and *Careers in Focus: Therapists*. Also sells the Career Exploration on the Internet CD-ROM. High school and college guidance counselors and libraries frequently have these guides and many others from Ferguson.

Free $ for College for Dummies by David Rosen, Publisher: For Dummies, 2003, $19.99, ISBN: 0764554670. Financial aid resources.

Government Job Finder by Daniel Lauber. (paperback, $16.95.) Published by Planning Communication. Everything you need to find a job in local, state, and the federal government. ISBN: 1884587321, 4th edition published in 2006.

HealthCareerWeb - (**http://www.healthcareerweb.com**) Search job ads, post your résumé, have openings e-mailed to you, apply online, find job fairs, and get advice on health care and military jobs.

HealthcareRecruitment.com - Lists job openings and provides career resources such as résumé advice, finding schools and career videos online. (**http://www.healthcarerecruitment.com/**) Post your résumé and receive job alerts. Links to 200 free industry magazines. Part of a network of job sites in nursing, radiology, pharmacy, rehabilitation, clinical laboratory technology and many more specialties.

HealthCareSource.com - (**http://www.healthcaresource.com**) This very well-organized site has over 33,000 jobs from clerical workers to physicians. Post your résumé or look through their list of employers organized by state. Access the web sites of hundreds of employers. Can't beat this one for ease of use!

Health Direction - (**http://www.healthdirection.com**) Search jobs by state and/or post your résumé. If you want to experience different areas of the U.S., this web site has a travel nurse section.

HEALTHeCAREERS.com This site, sponsored by many professional associations, provides job search tools by discipline, location, and organization. Post your résumé. Call 888/884.8242 or visit (**http://www.healthecareers.com/**, info@healthecareers.com). Receive e-mail notification of new job postings.

🗁⁀🖰 **Healthfinder (http://www.healthfinder.gov)** This web site, sponsored by the U.S. Department of Health and Human Services, provides access to many types of libraries, online journals, state health departments, hospitals and not-for-profit organizations.

⁀🖰 **Health Profession Network (HPN)** - 1850 Samuel Morse Drive, Reston, Virginia 20190; 703/708-9000. (**http://www.healthpronet.org/**, information@healthpronet.org) They represent health *organizations* not individuals, but the site has detailed career information.

♉🗁⁀🖰 **Health World Online (http://www.healthy.net)**. The web site contains directories of holistic practitioners and schools as well as access to local professional groups for networking and directory of associations.

⁀🖰 **Health Hippo (http://hippo.findlaw.com)** This site is mainly concerned with health legislation, it does provide extensive links to job sites and career information under "Hippjobs." Take a break from your job search and explore "Tragically Hipp."

📄💥✍⁀🖰 **HireHealth.com - (http://www.hirehealth.com)** Over 150 companies post jobs here for pharmaceutical, biotechnology, medical and healthcare professionals. Create a job agent, submit résumés to companies directly from the site and view profiles of some of the companies. Information on Life Science Career Fairs and careers in the pharmaceutical field. Network on Discussion Boards.

🗁⁀🖰 **HospitalWeb** - Massachusetts General Hospital Department of Neurology. (**http://neuro-www.mgh.harvard.edu/hospitalweb.shtml**). This site lists links most of the hospitals on the web, in U.S. and globally. There are also links to medical companies and organizations.

📄💥✍⁀🖰 **HotJobs.com - (http://hotjobs.yahoo.com/)** This well-organized site lets you search for jobs by category and create an agent to e-mail you notices. Career Tools offer résumé tips, interview tips and networking.

📄💥✍⁀🖰 **IMDiversity.com - (http://www.imdiversity.com)** Well-organized site for minorities has employer profiles, job ads and extensive career advice. Post your résumé and create a job notification agent.

Internet Career Connection Visit (http://www.iccweb.com) . This site, provided by Gonyea & Associates, Inc. has extensive online career and employment resources, including Help Wanted-USA, Worldwide Résumé/Talent Bank, Recruiters an Placement agencies, Government Employment and much more. The Government Jobs Central area contains advice written by Dennis V. Damp. Versatile search options are provided.

JobBank USA (**http://www.jobbankusa.com**) Established in 1995, this resource has job ads in all fields, not just health care. Post your résumé, use the Job Search page and/or create a job agent to e-mail job notices to you. This site provides yellow pages, e-mail list networking, career fairs, career advice, corporate directories and more.

JobCentral - (http://www.jobcentral.com) Job searches by state, résumé posting, career advice, networking, employers directory. This site, provided by the Direct Employers Association, was given a top rating for ease-of-use by *PC Magazine*. Try the Advanced Search.

Job Finders Online (http://jobfindersonline.com) Publishes and/or sells 400 helpful books, including topics such as international jobs, career advice, schools and financial aid. Download a catalog.

job-hunt.org (http://www.job-hunt.org) Very well designed site with hundreds of links to Internet job ads, state employment sites, and job hunting information. Advice on creating a "CyberSafe" résumé.

JobHuntersBible - (http://www.jobhuntersbible.com) This site is a supplement to Dick Bolles' book, *What Color Is Your Parachute? A Practical Manual for Job-Hunters and Career-Changers*, published by Ten Speed Press. It has extensive information on job hunting and résumé writing. The "Contacts" section of this site explains how to use Listservs and newsgroups for job hunting and networking. Bookmark it!

jobscience.com - (http://www.jobscience.com) Post your résumé, search job ads by field, company or state, create a search agent to e-mail you about jobs. Well-organized. Lots of career resources.

Kids into Health Careers - Bureau of Health Professions, Parklawn Rm. 8A-09, 5600 Fishers Lane, Rockville, MD 20857. U.S. government-sponsored site at **http://bhpr.hrsa.gov/kidscareers** provides students, parents and educators with information on health careers, education, financial aid, diversity programs and other federal programs.

▤◠ **Lippincott, Williams & Wilkins (http://www.lww.com)** Located at 351 West Camden Street, Baltimore, MD 21201-2436; 800/882-0483. (custserv@wwilkins.com) Williams and Wilkins is a major publisher of medical and scientific journals. All of the employment ads from their journals can be found online at **http://www.lww.com/classifieds**.

▱◠ **Lookups (http://www.melissadata.com/Lookups/)** Look up addresses, postal codes, place names or similar information? This site provides 18 databases, accessible from a single page.

▤✎◠ **MedCAREERS (http://www.medcareers.com/)** Over 20,000 health care job ads can be searched by profession, specialty, region or state. Post your résumé and view company profiles. The web site has a section to government medical careers and Internet job hunt advice.

▤◠ **medhealthjobs (http://www.medhealthjobs.com/)** Provided by Valley Forge Publishing this site has job postings for physicians, nurses, allied health, pharmacists and others.

▤✄✎◠ **Med Hunters (http://www.medhunters.com)** Register (free) with MedHunters to allow employers access to your profile. You can also search specific categories for jobs world wide. Post your résumé and set up an agent to e-mail you job notices. Over 19,000 job ads online.

▤◠ **Medical Ad Mart - (http://www.medical-admart.com)** Compiles classified advertising from medical journals. The focus is on physicians, veterinarians, physician assistants, nurses, and nurse practitioners.

▤✎◠ **Medical Workers.com - (http://www.medicalworkers.com)** Search for jobs and view details about employers, apply for jobs online, post your résumé at . Job ads are for physician jobs, radiology jobs, nursing jobs, pharmacy jobs, medical jobs and other health care workers. Both recruiters and facilities post here.

✎◠ **Med Options USA** - 6542 Hypoluxo Road, Suite 294, Lake Worth, FL 33467; 800-863-8314. info@medoptions.com. These free placement services are located at **(http://www.medoptions.com, http://www.rehaboptions.com and http://www.nurseoptions.com)** will give your profile to prospective employers and the employer can contact you directly. Professions served include: nurse practitioner, physician assistant, PT, PTA, speech language therapist, OT, COTA, midwife, RN, nurse management, pharmacist, respiratory care and more.

▤⚡️✎☞ **MedZilla.com** - **http://www.medzilla.com/** Search ads, post résumés, use their job agent, and view lists of jobs available at specific facilities for jobs in biotechnology, pharmaceuticals, healthcare and science.

▤✎☞ *Monster's healthcare site* - Monster.com was one of *PC Magazine's* 101 Top Websites in 2005, and their healthcare site is loaded with information. Visit their site at (**http://www.medsearch.com** or **http://healthcare.monster.com**). Be sure to read their Safe Job Search advice. Post your résumé, network sign up for free newsletters.

☤▤☞ **National Health Service Corps (NHSC)** - 800/221-9393. (callcenter@hrsa.gov) The NHSC is a federal program whose mission is to increase access to primary care services for people in areas with shortages of health professionals by recruiting health care workers. (**http://nhsc.bhpr.hrsa.gov/**) Among other benefits, they offer student loan repayment and scholarships. America's Health Care Heroes.

📁☞ **National Hospice and Palliative Care Organization (NHPCO)** - 1700 Diagonal Road, Suite 300, Alexandria, VA 22314; 703/837-1500. (**http://www.nhpco.org**, info@nhpco.org) Has a search engine to locate a hospice by state, county, city or hospice name.

▤☞ **National Institutes of Health (NIH)**: Job Vacancies at NIH - NIH Human Resources Services, National Institutes of Health, Bethesda, Maryland 20892. (**http://www.nih.gov**). NIH job vacancies are posted weekly. Proof of U.S. citizenship is required for most jobs.

☤▤⚡️✎☞ **National Rural Health Association (NRHA)** - 521 East 63rd St., Kansas City, MO 64110; 816/756-3140. (**http://www.nrharural.org**) Offers a placement service. Membership consists of physicians, health planners, physician assistants, nurses, nurse midwives, state and national policy-makers, hospital and clinic administrators and others. View job ads online, post your résumé and receiver job alerts by e-mail.

▤⚡️✎☞ **NationJob Network** - 601 SW 9th Street, Suites J & K, Des Moines, IA 50309; 800-292-7731. (**http://www.nationjob.com**). Has sections for computer jobs, nursing and medical/healthcare. Features a Personal Job Scout, which notifies you via email about suitable jobs.

📁☞ **Nelson and Wallery. Ltd** (**http://www.nursinghomeinfo.com** and **http://www.assistedlivinginfo.com**) These two Web sites have databases which provides basic contact information for thousands of nursing homes or assisted living facilities.

⬛📊✍🖱 **Netscape** - (**http://www.netscape.com/**) Search ads in the Careers & Jobs section by category or location. Post your résumé, have job opportunities mailed to you and browse extensive career advice. Install their browser and they can warn you of sites not to be trusted.

📖 *Opportunities in Allied Health Careers* - by Alex Kacen, published by McGraw-Hill, 2005, $11.16, ISBN: 0071438475

📖📄🗂🖱 **Pam Pohly's Net Guide** (**http://www.pohly.com**) Pam Pohly is a healthcare administrator and a recruiter who has an award-winning, incredibly informative and well-organized web site. Job ads are for upper level healthcare, hospital management and executive positions. The abundant career resources are useful for everyone else: links to health care companies and professional associations, directories of medical facilities, advice on handling job interviews, and articles such as "Working with Recruiters" and "Build a Powerful résumé." A book, *The Directory of Healthcare Recruiters*, is available for $39.95.

📖🗂🖱 **Petersons Guides** - Customer Service: 800-338-3282 ext. 5660; (custsvc@petersons.com), (**http://www.petersons.com**). Peterson's books are available at many libraries and bookstores. Just a few of the useful titles: *College and University Almanac 2005, Guide to Career Colleges 2005, College Money Handbook 2006 and Vocational and Technical Schools* (East and West editions). *Peterson's College and Graduate School Planning* has data on over 2100 educational programs, financial aid information and test preparation resources. Also has books on exams such as SAT, GRE, etc.

📖 **Pfizer** - http://www.pfizercareerguides.com/ provides 4 free books in PDF format for nursing, physicians, public health and pharmacy.

📄🖱 **Protouch Staffing** - 17822 Davenport Road, Ste A, Dallas, TX 75252; 972/671-3152 or 888/902-7161. Post your résumé and search for jobs in nursing, information technology, and many allied health professions at: **http://www.protouchstaffing.com**

📖 **Résumés for Health and Medical Careers** by Editors of VGM. McGraw-Hill, ISBN: 0071411542, $9.56. Offers nearly 100 diverse sample résumés and cover letters, plus other advice.

📖 **Résumés That Knock 'Em Dead** - by Martin Yate, published by Adams Media Corporation, 6th edition 2004, ISBN: 159337108X , $10.36.

🖰 **The Riley Guide** (http://www.rileyguide.com/) Employment Opportunities and Job Resources on the Internet, compiled by Margaret Riley Dikel. This award-winning site has career and education guidance, and tips on using the Internet, résumé writing and salary guides.

⚕🖥📁🖰 **Rural Recruitment and Retention Network (3RNet)** - (**http://www.3rnet.org**, info@3rnet.org) 800/787-2512. The 3RNet helps health professionals find employment in rural areas. Professions served include MD, PA, NP, dentist, dental hygienist or pharmacist.   Can provide information on loan repayment programs. Provides links to state offices of rural health and other organizations.

🖥✍📁🖰 **Saludos Web** (**http://www.saludos.com**) Supported by *Saludos Hispanos Magazine* (subscription, $12.00; 800/748-6426), this site promotes careers and education for Latinos. Articles about career fields and financial aid. Search the job listings (special section for health care), find out about internships and view employer profiles.

🖥📁🖰 **State job banks** Every state employment service maintains a state job bank with a web site. To find it, use your search engine and type in the name of your state and the phrase "job bank" (put this term in parentheses) or search: **http://www.acinet.org**.

🖥✍📁🖰 **thingamajob.com** - Allegis Group family of recruiters (**http://www.thingamajob.com**)   Lot of career advice, including transition from the military. Jobs in the U.S. and Canada, not strictly health care, but including information technology. Online résumé, e-mail job alerts.

📖📁 **Thomson Gale** - (**http://www.gale.com**). Publishes *Directories In Print*, 26th edition, lists over 15,000 published directories worldwide. The *Job Hunter's Sourcebook*, 6th edition lists thousands of placement options for 179 specialties. These books are available at many libraries.

⚕✍🖰 **TROA: The Retired Officers Association** - 201 N. Washington Street, Alexandria, VA 22314; 800/245-6622. (**http://www.troa.org**). Membership open to anyone who served as a commissioned officer in any branch of the service including warrants. Offers scholarship (also for members' children), loan, and other information on education and has employment services.

☐✎🖰 **U.S. Administration on Aging** - Department of Health and Human Services, (**http://www.aoa.gov/**). Offers a directory of web sites on aging, both national and state directories. It also has information and an Eldercare Locator (**http://www.eldercare.gov/**) for finding nursing homes and long-term care facilities.

📄✎🖰 **USA Jobs** - (**http://www.usajobs.opm.gov**) The official US Government site for jobs and employment information provided by the United States Office of Personnel Management. Searchable by category or alphabetically, with online application. Create and store your résumé.

🖰 Wall Street Journal - (http://www.careers.wsj.com) Excellent advice on job hunting, résumés and interviewing.

📄✎🖰 **WorkInHealthcare** (**www.workinhealthcare.net**) Post your résumé, search job ads and connect with potential employers. Career Center has information on career development, interviewing, résumés and immigration issues.

📄🎣✎🖰 **WORKsearch** (**http://www.worksearch.gc.ca**) This web site has some great resources for Canadian job hunters.

📖 *The Yale Guide to Careers in Medicine and the Health Professions : Pathways to Medicine in the 21st Century* - by Robert Donaldson (editor), Kathleen Lundgren (editor), Howard Spiro (editor), Publisher: Yale University Press, 2003, ISBN: 0300100299, $19.95.

Chapter
4

HEALTH TECHNOLOGISTS

Debra Burton

Debra Burton, R.T. (R)(M)(CT) always knew she wanted to work in the medical field. After high school, while working at a local hospital in housekeeping, she took an emergency medical technician course. Soon after that, she was hired as a radiology aid. Her supervisors recognized her potential and encouraged her to go to school in radiologic technology.

While attending school full-time, she was able to work week-ends in radiology departments in small hospitals. She graduated from Fort Hays University in Kansas in 1987 with an Associate's degree. After passing the boards, she became a registered radiological technologist.

Debra explained that one can get certified in several different specialties in diagnostic imaging. "There are always opportunities and such a variety of imaging modalities to learn." You can also get raises when

49

you earn a new certification. Currently certified in computerized tomography (CT scans) and mammography, Debra is working towards an additional certification in abdominal sonography.

"There are always opportunities in the field," Debra says. She has worked in several hospitals, sometimes as a supervisor. If you would like to work in a certain specialty, she encourages you to go for it. "If there was a certain area of the state I wanted to live in, I would put my application in, and within six months I would usually get a job offer." Debra adds, "It is a job that every hospital needs, so you can go anywhere: hospitals, clinics—even x-ray mummies at a university."

Working with different types of technologically sophisticated equipment is a favorite aspect of her career. "There is a lot to do with computers and digital technology. More and more of imaging is going into PACS (Picture Archival Computer Systems)" so images will be put onto DVDs instead of film.

Having worked in both large city hospitals and smaller rural hospitals, Debra prefers the smaller ones. Currently she works at the Ellsworth County Medical Center in a town of 2300 in central Kansas. "I have found one of the best things about working in small hospitals is that I have become part of a family in the workplace." Debra feels that she wouldn't enjoy working without that family atmosphere. She also likes rural hospitals because they don't feel as hectic as urban facilities. "You have more control over what you do." The disadvantage in small hospitals is that you are on call more often. "You can get called at 2 AM. When you have kids, you have to have a support system so you can go in to work for emergencies."

Debra really enjoys being a part of the healthcare team. "Radiologic technologists use their skills to greatly assist physicians in diagnosing their patients. A single radiograph can change the course of the way the physician is treating the patient." Much of diagnostic imaging is operator-dependent. In sonography, it is the technologist's responsibility to point out which abnormalities the physician needs to examine.

Debra gets a lot of meaning and satisfaction from working closely with the physicians to assist in diagnosis. She points out, "Most of our job is routine, but in a split second it can turn into a fast-paced emergency situation."

Working in diagnostic imaging is "almost like an artist at times the way you can demonstrate a human body. You learn skills to obtain radiographs without disturbing a broken leg and causing undue pain to a patient." Debra is very enthusiastic about her career. "It is one-on-one work with the patients. You never know what each new day will bring interesting cases, interesting people, and new experiences."

This chapter features health care technologists. The major occupational groups are:

Clinical Lab Technologists	**Nuclear Medicine Technologists**
Clinical Lab Technicians	**Radiologic Technologists**
Cardiovascular technicians	**Diagnostic Medical Sonographers**
Cardiovascular technologists	**Surgical Technologists**

Each specialty is described below. Following each job description is a list of job resources: Associations, Books, Directories, Internet Sites, Job Ads, E-mail Job Notification/Job Hotlines, Job Fairs, and Résumé/ Placement Services with icons to guide you.

CLINICAL LABORATORY TECHNOLOGISTS & TECHNICIANS

OCCUPATIONAL TITLES:

Blood Bank Technologists	**Histotechnicians**
Clinical Chemistry Technologists	**Phlebotomists**
Medical Laboratory Technicians	**Cytotechnologists**
Immunology Technologists	**Medical Technologists**
Microbiology Technologists	

Significant Points
- Faster than average employment growth is expected as the volume of laboratory tests continues to increase with both population growth and the development of new types of tests.
- Clinical laboratory technologists usually have a bachelor's degree with a major in medical technology or in one of the life sciences; clinical laboratory technicians generally need either an associate degree or a certificate.
- Job opportunities are expected to be excellent.

Nature of the Work

Clinical laboratory testing plays a crucial role in the detection, diagnosis, and treatment of disease. Clinical laboratory technologists, also referred to as clinical laboratory scientists or medical technologists, and clinical laboratory technicians, also known as medical technicians or medical laboratory technicians, perform most of these tests.

Clinical laboratory personnel examine and analyze body fluids and cells. They look for bacteria, parasites, and other microorganisms; analyze the chemical content of fluids; match blood for transfusions; and test for drug levels in the blood to show how a patient is responding to treatment. Technologists also prepare specimens for examination, count cells, and look for abnormal cells in blood and body fluids. They use automated equipment and computerized instruments capable of performing a number of tests simultaneously, as well as microscopes, cell counters, and other sophisticated laboratory equipment. Then they analyze the results and relay them to physicians. With increasing automation and the use of computer technology, the work of technologists and technicians has become less hands-on and more analytical.

The complexity of tests performed, the level of judgment needed, and the amount of responsibility workers assume depend largely on the amount of education and experience they have.

Clinical laboratory technologists perform complex chemical, biological, hematological, immunologic, microscopic, and bacteriological tests. Technologists microscopically examine blood and other body fluids. They make cultures of body fluid and tissue samples, to determine the presence of bacteria, fungi, parasites, or other microorganisms. Clinical laboratory technologists analyze samples for chemical content or a chemical reaction and determine concentrations of compounds such as blood glucose and cholesterol levels. They also type and cross match blood samples for transfusions.

Clinical laboratory technologists evaluate test results, develop and modify procedures, and establish and monitor programs, to ensure the accuracy of tests. Some technologists supervise clinical laboratory technicians.

Technologists in small laboratories perform many types of tests, whereas those in large laboratories generally specialize. Technologists who prepare specimens and analyze the chemical and hormonal contents of body fluids are called clinical chemistry technologists. Those who examine and identify bacteria and other microorganisms are microbiology technologists. Blood bank technologists, or immunohematology technologists, collect, type, and prepare blood and its components for transfusions. Immunology technologists examine elements of the human immune system and its response to foreign bodies. Cytotechnologists prepare slides of body cells and examine these cells microscopically for abnormalities that may signal the beginning of a cancerous growth. Molecular biology technologists perform complex protein and nucleic acid testing on cell samples.

Clinical laboratory technicians perform less complex tests and laboratory procedures than technologists perform. Technicians may prepare specimens and operate automated analyzers, for example, or they may perform manual tests in accordance with detailed instructions. Like technologists, they may work in several areas of the clinical laboratory or specialize in just one. Histotechnicians cut and stain tissue specimens for microscopic examination by pathologists, and phlebotomists collect blood samples. They usually work under the supervision of medical and clinical laboratory technologists or laboratory managers.

Working Conditions

Hours and other working conditions of clinical laboratory technologists and technicians vary with the size and type of employment setting. In large hospitals or in independent laboratories that operate continuously, personnel usually work the day, evening, or night shift and may work weekends and holidays. Laboratory personnel in small facilities may work on rotating shifts, rather than on a regular shift. In some facilities, laboratory personnel are on call several nights a week or on weekends, in case of an emergency.

Clinical laboratory personnel are trained to work with infectious specimens. When proper methods of infection control and sterilization are followed, few hazards exist. Protective masks, gloves, and goggles are often necessary to ensure the safety of laboratory personnel.

Laboratories usually are well lighted and clean; however, specimens, solutions, and reagents used in the laboratory sometimes produce fumes. Laboratory workers may spend a great deal of time on their feet.

Training, Other Qualifications, and Advancement

The usual requirement for an entry-level position as a clinical laboratory technologist is a bachelor's degree with a major in medical technology or in one of the life sciences; although it is possible to qualify through a combination of education, on-the-job, and specialized training. Universities and hospitals offer medical technology programs.

Bachelor's degree programs in medical technology include courses in chemistry, biological sciences, microbiology, mathematics, and statistics, as well as specialized courses devoted to knowledge and skills used in the clinical laboratory. Many programs also offer or require courses in management, business, and computer applications. The Clinical Laboratory Improvement Act requires technologists who perform highly complex tests to have at least an associate degree.

Medical and clinical laboratory technicians generally have either an associate degree from a community or junior college or a certificate from a hospital, a vocational or technical school, or one of the U.S. Armed Forces. A few technicians learn their skills on the job.

The National Accrediting Agency for Clinical Laboratory Sciences (NAACLS) fully accredits 469 programs for medical and clinical laboratory technologists, medical and clinical laboratory technicians, histotechnologists and histotechnicians, cytogenetic technologists, and diagnostic molecular scientists. NAACLS also approves 57 programs in phlebotomy and clinical assisting. Other nationally recognized accrediting agencies that accredit specific areas for clinical laboratory workers include the Commission on Accreditation of Allied Health Education Programs and the Accrediting Bureau of Health Education Schools.

Some states require laboratory personnel to be licensed or registered. Information on licensure is available from state departments of health or boards of occupational licensing. Certification is a voluntary process by which a nongovernmental organization, such as a professional society or certifying agency, grants recognition to an individual whose professional competence meets prescribed standards. Widely accepted by employers in the health care industry, certification is a prerequisite for most jobs and often is necessary for advancement. Agencies certifying medical and clinical laboratory technologists and technicians include the Board of Registry of the American Society for Clinical Pathology, the American Medical Technologists, the National Credentialing Agency for Laboratory Personnel, and the Board of Registry of the American Association of Bioanalysts. These agencies have different requirements for certification and different organizational sponsors.

Clinical laboratory personnel need good analytical judgment and the ability to work under pressure. Close attention to detail is essential, because small differences or changes in test substances or numerical readouts can be crucial for patient care. Manual dexterity and normal color vision are highly desirable. With the widespread use of automated laboratory equipment, computer skills are important. In addition, technologists in particular are expected to be good at problem solving.

Technologists may advance to supervisory positions in laboratory work or may become chief medical or clinical laboratory technologists or laboratory managers in hospitals. Manufacturers of home diagnostic testing kits and laboratory equipment and supplies seek experienced technologists to work in product development, marketing, and sales. A graduate degree in medical technology, one of the biological sciences, chemistry, management, or education usually speeds advancement. A doctorate is needed to become a laboratory director; however, federal regulation allows directors of moderately complex laboratories to have either a master's degree or a bachelor's degree, combined with the appropriate amount of training and experience. Technicians can become technologists through additional education and experience.

Employment

Clinical laboratory technologists and technicians held about 302,000 jobs in 2004. More than half of these jobs were in hospitals. Most of the remaining jobs were in offices of physicians and in medical and diagnostic laboratories. A small proportion were in educational services and in all other ambulatory health care services.

Job Outlook

Employment of clinical laboratory workers is expected to grow faster than average for all occupations through the year 2014, as the volume of laboratory tests continues to increase with both population growth and the development of new types of tests.

Technological advances will continue to have two opposing effects on employment. On the one hand, new, increasingly powerful diagnostic tests will encourage additional testing and spur employment. On the other hand, research and development efforts targeted at simplifying routine testing procedures may enhance the ability of non-laboratory personnel—physicians and patients in particular—to perform tests now conducted in laboratories. Although hospitals are expected to continue to be the major employer of clinical laboratory workers, employment is expected to grow faster in medical and diagnostic laboratories, offices of physicians, and all other ambulatory health care services.

Although significant, job growth will not be the only source of opportunities. As in most occupations, many openings will result from the need to replace workers who transfer to other occupations, retire, or stop working for some other reason.

Earnings

Median annual earnings of medical and clinical laboratory technologists were $45,730 in May 2004. The middle 50 percent earned between $38,740 and $54,310. The lowest 10 percent earned less than $32,240, and the highest 10 percent earned more than $63,120. Median annual earnings in the industries employing the largest numbers of medical and clinical laboratory technologists in May 2004 were as follows: General medical and surgical hospitals, $46,020; Medical and diagnostic laboratories, $45,840; Offices of physicians, $41,070.

Median annual earnings of medical and clinical laboratory technicians were $30,840 in May 2004. The middle 50 percent earned between $24,890 and $37,770. The lowest 10 percent earned less than $20,410, and the highest 10 percent earned more than $45,680. Median annual earnings in the industries employing the largest numbers of medical and clinical laboratory technicians in May 2004 were as follows: Colleges, universities, and professional schools, $32,410; General medical and surgical hospitals, $31,830; Offices of physicians, $29,620; Medical and diagnostic laboratories, $29,220; Other ambulatory health care services, $28,130.

According to the American Society for Clinical Pathology, median hourly wages of staff clinical laboratory technologists and technicians in 2003 varied by specialty and laboratory type as follows: Cytotechnoligists, $24.07 to $25.66; Histotechnologists, $19.22 to $20.50; Medical technologists, $19.00 to $20.40; Histotechnicians, $16.13 to $20.00; Medical laboratory technicians, $14.75 to $16.12; Phlebotomists, $10.50 to $11.13.

Related Occupations

Clinical laboratory technologists and technicians analyze body fluids, tissue, and other substances, using a variety of tests. Similar or related procedures are performed by chemists and materials scientists, science technicians, and veterinary technologists and technicians.

RESOURCES FOR CLINICAL LABORATORY TECHNOLOGISTS and TECHNICIANS

Don't forget! Refer to the general resources listed in Chapter Three.

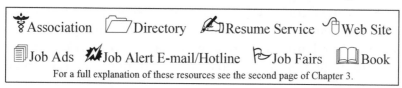

Association   Directory   Resume Service   Web Site

Job Ads   Job Alert E-mail/Hotline   Job Fairs   Book

For a full explanation of these resources see the second page of Chapter 3.

ADVANCE Newsmagazines - 650 Park Avenue West, Box 61556, King of Prussia, PA 19406-0956; 800/355-1088. The web site (**http://www.advanceweb.com/**) is packed with resources. Publishes *ADVANCE for Medical Laboratory Professionals* and *ADVANCE for Administrators of the Laboratory:* free for professionals, many job ads.

American Association of Blood Banks (AABB) - 8101 Glenbrook Road, Bethesda, MD 20814-2749; 301/907-6977. Accredits blood banks and sponsors workshops. Web site allows you to view job ads, post your résumé and receive email job alerts. Provides networking for members through Special Interest Groups. (**http://www.aabb.org**, aabb@aabb.org)

American Association for Clinical Chemistry (AACC) - Suite 202, 2101 L Street NW, Washington, DC 20037; 800/892-1400, 202/857-0717. (**http://www.aacc.org/**, info@aacc.org) Great web site has a job center, career information, email networking and many other excellent resources.

American Association of Bioanalysts (AAB), 906 Olive Street, Suite 1200, Saint Louis, Missouri 63101-1434; 314/241-1445. (**http://www.aab.org/**, aab@aab.org) The AAB has information on certification, and has a job posting center which allows you to view job openings, post your résumé and get job alerts by email.

American Association of Pathologists Assistants (AAPA) - Rosewood Office Plaza, Suite 300N, 1711 W. County Rd. B, Roseville,

MN, 55113; 800/532-2272. The AAPA provides certification. The web site (**http://www.pathologistsassistants.org**) explains the duties of these professionals and list accredited training programs.

☤ 📱🔍 **American Medical Technologists** (**AMT**) - 710 Higgins Rd., Park Ridge, IL 60068, 847/823-5169. (**http://www.amt1.com**) The AMT provides certification for several laboratory careers. The Web site has a career center with job ads, scholarship information and a list of accredited schools.

☤ 📱🏫📁🔍 **American Society for Clinical Laboratory Science** (**ASCLS**), 6701 Democracy Blvd., Suite 300, Bethesda, MD 20817; 301-657-2768. (**http://www.ascls.org/**, ascls@ascls.org) Online Career Center to research information on many laboratory careers, find scholarship information, view job ads, post a résumé or receive email job alerts.

☤ 📱🏫📁🔍 **American Society for Clinical Pathology (ASCP)** - 2100 W. Harrison St., Chicago, IL 60612; 312/738-1336. (**http://www.ascp.org/**, info@ascp.org) The ASCP has certification information. Their web site has career and scholarship information. Post your résumé, view job ads or request email job alerts.

☤ 📱🔍 **American Society for Cytotechnology (ASCT)** - 1500 Sunday Drive, Suite 102, Raleigh, North Carolina 27607; 919/861-5571; 800/948-3947. (**http://www.asct.com/**, info@asct.com) Job ads and links to cytology information on web site.

☤ 📱🏫📁🔍 **American Society of Cytopathology (ASC)** - 400 West 9th Street, Suite 201, Wilmington, Delaware 19801; 302/429-8802. (**http://www.cytopathology.org,** asc@cytopathology.org) Online Career Center lets you view ads, post a résumé or receive email job alerts. Email them for pamphlets, a brochure on the career, and school listings.

☤ 📱🏫📁🔍 **American Society for Microbiology** - 1752 N Street NW, Washington, DC 20036; 202/737-3600. (**http://www.asm.org**). The ASM web site has career information and a minority mentoring program. Online you can read job ads, post a résumé and receive email job alerts.

☤ 📱🏫📁🔍 **Clinical Laboratory Management Association (CLMA)** - 989 Old Eagle School Road, Suite 815, Wayne, Pennsylvania 19087-1704; 610/995-9580. (**http://www.clma.org,** support@clma.org) Career Opportunities section of the web site has job ads for management. technicians and technologists.

Laboratory Jobs on All Healthcare Jobs - Search job ads, post your résumé or receive email job alerts from a link on the main web page at **http://www.allhealthcarejobs.com/**.

National Accrediting Agency for Clinical Laboratory Sciences (NAACLS) - 8410 W. Bryn Mawr Ave., Suite 670, Chicago, IL 60631; 773/714-8880. (**http://www.naacls.org/**, info@naacls.org) Use the web site to find accredited educational programs by type, name, state, or zip code. Links to scholarship information.

National Credentialing Agency for Laboratory Personnel (NCA), P.O. Box 15945-289, Lenexa, Kansas 66285; 913/438-5110, ext. 4647. (**http://www.nca-info.org/**, nca-info@goamp.com) The NCA provides credentialing and their web site has job ads.

National Society for Histotechnology (NSH) - 4201 Northview Drive, Suite 502, Bowie, MD 20716-2604; 301/262-6221. (**http://www.nsh.org**, histo@nsh.org) Employment section of web site lists jobs. Request a free brochure on the profession or rent a video. Online directory of state societies, training programs and scholarship information.

Opportunities in Medical Technology Careers by Karen R. Karni, Hardcover, $14.95. Published by VGM Career Horizons, 1996.

CARDIOVASCULAR TECHNOLOGISTS AND TECHNICIANS

OCCUPATIONAL TITLES

Vascular technologists   Echocardiographers
Cardiographic (EKG) technicians   Cardiology technologists

Significant Points

- About 3 out of 4 jobs were in hospitals.
- The vast majority of cardiovascular technologists and technicians complete a 2-year junior or community college program.
- Employment will grow much faster than the average, but the number of job openings created will be low because the occupation is small.
- Employment of most specialties will grow, but fewer EKG technicians will be needed.

Nature of the Work

Cardiovascular technologists and technicians assist physicians in diagnosing and treating cardiac (heart) and peripheral vascular (blood vessel) ailments. Cardiovascular technologists may specialize in any of three areas of practice: invasive cardiology, echocardiography, and vascular technology. Cardiovascular technicians who specialize in electrocardiograms (EKGs), stress testing, and Holter monitors are known as cardiographic technicians, or EKG technicians.

Cardiovascular technologists specializing in invasive procedures are called cardiology technologists. They assist physicians with cardiac catheterization procedures in which a small tube, or catheter, is threaded through a patient's artery from a spot on the patient's groin to the heart. The procedure can determine whether a blockage exists in the blood vessels that supply the heart muscle. The procedure also can help to diagnose other problems. Part of the procedure may involve balloon angioplasty, which can be used to treat blockages of blood vessels or heart valves without the need for heart surgery. Cardiology technologists assist physicians as they insert a catheter with a balloon on the end to the point of the obstruction.

Technologists prepare patients for cardiac catheterization and balloon angioplasty by first positioning them on an examining table and then shaving, cleaning, and administering anesthesia to the top of their leg near the groin. During the procedures, they monitor patients' blood pressure and heart rate with EKG equipment and notify the physician if something appears to be wrong. Technologists also may prepare and monitor patients during open-heart surgery and during the insertion of pacemakers and stents that open up blockages in arteries to the heart and major blood vessels.

Cardiovascular technologists who specialize in echocardiography or vascular technology often run noninvasive tests using ultrasound instrumentation, such as Doppler ultrasound. Tests are "noninvasive" if they do not require the insertion of probes or other instruments into the patient's body. The ultrasound instrumentation transmits high frequency sound waves into areas of the patient's body and then processes reflected echoes of the sound waves to form an image. Technologists view the ultrasound image on a screen and may record the image on videotape or photograph it for interpretation and diagnosis by a physician. As the instrument scans the image, technologists check the image on the screen for subtle differences between healthy and diseased areas, decide which images to include in the report to the physician, and judge whether the images are satisfactory for diagnostic purposes. They also explain the procedure to patients, record any additional medical history the patient relates, select appropriate equipment settings, and change the patient's position as necessary. (Information about diagnostic medical sonographers is presented later in this chapter.)

Those who assist physicians in the diagnosis of disorders affecting the circulation are known as vascular technologists or vascular sonographers. They perform a medical history, evaluate pulses and assess blood flow in arteries and veins by listening to the vascular flow sounds for abnormalities. Then they perform a noninvasive procedure using ultrasound instrumentation to record vascular information such as vascular blood flow, blood pressure, changes in limb volume, oxygen saturation, cerebral circulation, peripheral circulation, and abdominal circulation. Many of these tests are performed during or immediately after surgery.

Technologists who use ultrasound to examine the heart chambers, valves, and vessels are referred to as cardiac sonographers, or echocardiographers. They use ultrasound instrumentation to create images called echocardiograms. An echocardiogram may be performed while the patient is either resting or physically active. Technologists may administer medication to physically active patients to assess their heart function. Cardiac sonographers also may assist physicians who perform transesophageal echocardiography, which involves placing a tube in the patient's esophagus to obtain ultrasound images.

Cardiovascular technicians who obtain EKGs are known as electro-cardiograph (or EKG) technicians. To take a basic EKG, which traces electrical impulses transmitted by the heart, technicians attach electrodes to the patient's chest, arms, and legs, and then manipulate switches on an EKG machine to obtain a reading. An EKG is printed out for interpretation by the physician. This test is done before most kinds of surgery or as part of a routine physical examination, especially on persons who have reached middle age or who have a history of cardiovascular problems.

EKG technicians with advanced training perform Holter monitor and stress testing. For Holter monitoring, technicians place electrodes on the patient's chest and attach a portable EKG monitor to the patient's belt. Following 24 or more hours of normal activity by the patient, the technician removes a tape from the monitor and places it in a scanner. After checking the quality of the recorded impulses on an electronic screen, the technician usually prints the information from the tape for analysis by a physician. Physicians use the output from the scanner to diagnose heart ailments, such as heart rhythm abnormalities or problems with pacemakers.

For a treadmill stress test, EKG technicians document the patient's medical history, explain the procedure, connect the patient to an EKG monitor, and obtain a baseline reading and resting blood pressure. Next, they monitor the heart's performance while the patient is walking on a treadmill, gradually increasing the treadmill's speed to observe the effect of increased exertion. Like vascular technologists and cardiac sonographers, cardiographic technicians who perform EKG, Holter monitor, and stress tests are known as "noninvasive" technicians.

Some cardiovascular technologists and technicians schedule appointments, type doctors' interpretations, maintain patient files, and care for equipment.

Working Conditions

Technologists and technicians generally work a 5-day, 40-hour week that may include weekends. Those in catheterization laboratories tend to work longer hours and may work evenings. They also may be on call during the night and on weekends.

Cardiovascular technologists and technicians spend a lot of time walking and standing. Heavy lifting may be involved to move equipment or transfer patients. These workers wear heavy protective aprons while conducting some procedures. Those who work in catheterization laboratories may face stressful working conditions because they are in close contact with patients with serious heart ailments. For example, some patients may encounter complications that have life-or-death implications.

Training, Other Qualifications, and Advancement

Although a few cardiovascular technologists, vascular technologists, and cardiac sonographers are currently trained on the job, most receive training in 2- to 4-year programs. The majority of technologists complete a 2-year junior or community college program, but 4-year programs are increasingly available. The first year is dedicated to core courses and is followed by a year of specialized instruction in either invasive, noninvasive cardiovascular, or noninvasive vascular technology. Those who are qualified in an allied health profession need to complete only the year of specialized instruction.

Graduates of the 33 programs accredited by the Joint Review Committee on Education in Cardiovascular Technology are eligible to obtain professional certification in cardiac catheterization, echocardiography, vascular ultrasound, and cardiographic techniques from Cardiovascular Credentialing International. Cardiac sonographers and vascular technologists also may obtain certification from the American Registry of Diagnostic Medical Sonographers.

Most EKG technicians are trained on the job by an EKG supervisor or a cardiologist. On-the-job training usually lasts about 8 to 16 weeks. Most employers prefer to train people already in the health care field—nursing aides, for example. Some EKG technicians are students enrolled in 2-year programs to become technologists, working part time to gain experience and make contact with employers. One-year certification programs exist for basic EKGs, Holter monitoring, and stress testing.

Cardiovascular technologists and technicians must be reliable, have mechanical aptitude, and be able to follow detailed instructions. A pleasant, relaxed manner for putting patients at ease is an asset.

Employment
Cardiovascular technologists and technicians held about 45,000 jobs in 2004. About 3 out 4 jobs were in hospitals (private and government), primarily in cardiology departments. The remaining jobs were mostly in offices of physicians, including cardiologists or in medical and diagnostic laboratories, including diagnostic imaging centers.

Job Outlook
Employment of cardiovascular technologists and technicians is expected to grow much faster than the average for all occupations through the year 2014. Growth will occur as the population ages, because older people have a higher incidence of heart problems and use more diagnostic imaging. Employment of vascular technologists and echocardiographers will grow as advances in vascular technology and sonography reduce the need for more costly and invasive procedures. However, fewer EKG technicians will be needed, as hospitals train nursing aides and others to perform basic EKG procedures. Individuals trained in Holter monitoring and stress testing are expected to have more favorable job prospects than are those who can perform only a basic EKG.

Some job openings for cardiovascular technologists and technicians will arise from replacement needs as individuals transfer to other jobs or leave the labor force. However, job growth and replacement needs will produce relatively few job openings because the occupation is small.

Earnings
Median annual earnings of cardiovascular technologists and technicians were $38,690 in May 2004. The middle 50 percent earned between $27,890 and $50,130. The lowest 10 percent earned less than $21,790, and the highest 10 percent earned more than $59,000. Median annual earnings of cardiovascular technologists and technicians in May 2004 were $36,890 in offices of physicians and $38,150 in general medical and surgical hospitals.

Related Occupations

Cardiovascular technologists and technicians operate sophisticated equipment that helps physicians and other health practitioners to diagnose and treat patients. So do diagnostic medical sonographers, nuclear medicine technologists, radiation therapists, radiologic technologists and technicians, and respiratory therapists.

Resources for Cardiovascular Technologists & Technicians, Nuclear Medicine Technologists, Radiologic Technologists, and Diagnostic Medical Sonographers are combined as most resources serve multiple professions. See the end of the Diagnostic Medical Sonographers section.

NUCLEAR MEDICINE TECHNOLOGISTS

Significant Points

- About 7 out of 10 work in hospitals.
- Nuclear medicine technology programs range in length from 1 to 4 years and lead to a certificate, an associate degree, or a bachelor's degree.
- Faster than average growth will arise from an increase in the number of middle-aged and elderly persons, who are the primary users of diagnostic procedures.
- The number of job openings each year will be relatively low because the occupation is small; technologists who also are trained in other diagnostic methods, such as radiologic technology or diagnostic medical sonography, will have the best prospects.

Nature of the Work

Diagnostic imaging embraces several procedures that aid in diagnosing ailments, the most familiar being the x-ray. Another increasingly common diagnostic imaging method, called magnetic resonance imaging (MRI), uses giant magnets and radio waves, rather than radiation, to create an image. In nuclear medicine, radionuclides—unstable atoms that emit radiation spontaneously—are used to diagnose and treat disease. Radionuclides are purified and com-pounded to form radio-pharmaceuticals. Nuclear medicine technologists administer radio-pharmaceuticals to patients and then monitor the characteristics and functions of tissues or organs in which the drugs localize. Abnormal areas show higher-than-expected or lower-than expected concentrations of radioactivity. Nuclear medicine differs from other diagnostic imaging technologies because it determines the presence of disease on the basis of biological changes rather than changes in organ structure.

Nuclear medicine technologists operate cameras that detect and map the radioactive drug in a patient's body to create diagnostic images. After explaining test procedures to patients, technologists prepare a dosage of the radiopharmaceutical and administer it by mouth, injection, inhalation, or other means. They position patients and start a gamma scintillation camera, or "scanner," which creates images of the distribution of a radiopharmaceutical as it localizes in, and emits signals from, the patient's body. The images are produced on a computer screen or on film for a physician to interpret.

When preparing radiopharmaceuticals, technologists adhere to safety standards that keep the radiation dose to workers and patients as low as possible. Technologists keep patient records and record the amount and type of radionuclides that they receive, use, and discard.

Radiologic technologists and technicians, diagnostic medical sonographers, and cardiovascular technologists and technicians also operate diagnostic imaging equipment, but their equipment creates images by means of a different technology. (See the statements on these occupations elsewhere in this chapter.)

Nuclear medicine technologists also perform radioimmunoassay studies that assess the behavior of a radioactive substance inside the body. For example, technologists may add radioactive substances to blood or serum to determine levels of hormones or of therapeutic drugs in the body. Most nuclear medicine studies, such as cardiac function studies, are processed with the aid of a computer.

Working Conditions

Nuclear medicine technologists generally work a 40-hour week, perhaps including evening or weekend hours, in departments that operate on an extended schedule. Opportunities for part-time and shift work also are available. In addition, technologists in hospitals may have on-call duty on a rotational basis.

Physical stamina is important because technologists are on their feet much of the day and may lift or turn disabled patients.

Although the potential for radiation exposure exists in this field, it is kept to a minimum by the use of shielded syringes, gloves, and other protective devices and by adherence to strict radiation safety guidelines. The amount of radiation in a nuclear medicine procedure is comparable to that received during a diagnostic x-ray procedure. Technologists also wear badges that measure radiation levels. Because of safety programs, badge measurements rarely exceed established safety levels.

Training, Other Qualifications, and Advancement

Many employers and an increasing number of states require certification or licensure. Aspiring nuclear medicine technologists should check the requirements of the state in which they plan to work. Certification is available from the American Registry of Radiologic Technologists and from the Nuclear Medicine Technology Certification Board. Some workers receive certification from both agencies. Nuclear medicine technologists must meet the minimum federal standards on the administration of radioactive drugs and the operation of radiation detection equipment.

Nuclear medicine technology programs range in length from 1 to 4 years and lead to a certificate, an associate degree, or a bachelor's degree. Generally, certificate programs are offered in hospitals, associate degree programs in community colleges, and bachelor's degree programs in 4-year colleges and universities. Courses cover the physical sciences, biological effects of radiation exposure, radiation protection and procedures, the use of radiopharmaceuticals, imaging techniques, and computer applications.

One-year certificate programs are for health professionals who already posses an associate degree—especially radiologic technologists and diagnostic medical sonographers—but who wish to specialize in nuclear medicine. The programs also attract medical technologists, registered nurses, and others who wish to change fields or specialize. Others interested in nuclear medicine technology have three options: a 2-year certificate program, a 2-year associate degree program, or a 4-year bachelor's degree program.

The Joint Review Committee on Education Programs in Nuclear Medicine Technology accredits most formal training programs in nuclear medicine technology. In 2005, there were 100 accredited programs in the continental United states and Puerto Rico.

Nuclear medicine technologists should be sensitive to patients' physical and psychological needs. They must pay attention to detail, follow instructions, and work as part of a team. In addition, operating complicated equipment requires mechanical ability and manual dexterity.

Technologists may advance to supervisor, then to chief technologist, and, finally, to department administrator or director. Some technologists specialize in a clinical area such as nuclear cardiology or computer analysis or leave patient care to take positions in research laboratories. Some become instructors in, or directors of, nuclear medicine technology programs, a step that usually requires a bachelor's or master's degree in the subject. Others leave the occupation to work as sales or training representatives for medical equipment and radiopharmaceutical manufacturing firms or as radiation safety officers in regulatory agencies or hospitals.

Employment

Nuclear medicine technologists held about 18,000 jobs in 2004. About 7 out of 10 were in hospitals—private and government. Most of the rest were in offices of physicians or in medical and diagnostic laboratories, including diagnostic imaging centers.

Job Outlook

Employment of nuclear medicine technologists is expected to grow faster than the average for all occupations through the year 2014. Growth will arise from technological advancement, the development of new nuclear medicine treatments, and an increase in the number of middle-aged and older persons, who are the primary users of diagnostic procedures, including nuclear medicine tests. However, the number of openings each year will be relatively low because the occupation is small. Technologists who also are trained in other diagnostic methods, such as radiologic technology or diagnostic medical sonography, will have the best prospects.

Technological innovations may increase the diagnostic uses of nuclear medicine. One example is the use of radiopharmaceuticals in combination with monoclonal antibodies to detect cancer at far earlier stages than is customary today and without resorting to surgery. Another is the use of radionuclides to examine the heart's ability to pump blood. New nuclear medical imaging technologies, including positron emission tomography (PET) and single photon emission computed tomography (SPECT), are expected to be used increasingly and to contribute further to employment growth. The wider use of nuclear medical imaging to observe metabolic and biochemical changes during neurology, cardiology, and oncology procedures also will spur demand for nuclear medicine technologists.

Nonetheless, cost considerations will affect the speed with which new applications of nuclear medicine grow. Some promising nuclear medicine procedures, such as positron emission tomography, are extremely costly, and hospitals contemplating these procedures will have to consider equipment costs, reimbursement policies, and the number of potential users.

Earnings

Median annual earnings of nuclear medicine technologists were $56,450 in May 2004. The middle 50 percent earned between $48,720 and $67,460. The lowest 10 percent earned less than $41,800, and the highest 10 percent earned more than $80,300. Median annual earnings of nuclear medicine technologists in May 2004 were $54,920 in general medical and surgical hospitals.

Related Occupations

Nuclear medical technologists operate sophisticated equipment to help physicians and other health practitioners diagnose and treat patients. cardiovascular technologists and technicians, clinical laboratory technologists and technicians, diagnostic medical sonographers, radiation therapists, radiologic technologists and technicians, and respiratory therapists perform similar functions.

Resources for Cardiovascular Technologists & Technicians, Nuclear Medicine Technologists, Radiologic Technologists, and Diagnostic Medical Sonographers are combined as most resources serve multiple professions. See the end of the Diagnostic Medical Sonographers section.

RADIOLOGIC TECHNOLOGISTS &TECHNICIANS

OCCUPATIONAL TITLES:

Radiographers   Sonographers
Radiation Therapy Technologists

Significant Points

- Job opportunities are expected to be favorable; some employers report difficulty hiring sufficient numbers of radiologic technologists and technicians.
- Formal training programs in radiography range in length from 1 to 4 years and lead to a certificate, an associate degree, or a bachelor's degree.
- Although hospitals will remain the primary employer, a greater number of new jobs will be found in physicians' offices and diagnostic imaging centers.

Nature of the Work

Radiologic technologists and technicians take x-rays and administer nonradioactive materials into patients' bloodstreams for diagnostic purposes. Some specialize in diagnostic imaging technologies, such as computerized tomography (CT) and magnetic resonance imaging (MRI).

In addition to radiologic technologists and technicians, others who conduct diagnostic imaging procedures include cardiovascular technologists and technicians, diagnostic medical sonographers, and nuclear medicine technologists. (Each is discussed elsewhere in this chapter.)

Radiologic technologists and technicians, also referred to as radiographers, produce x-ray films (radiographs) of parts of the human body for use in diagnosing medical problems. They prepare patients for radiologic examinations by explaining the procedure, removing articles such as jewelry, through which x-rays cannot pass, and positioning patients so that the parts of the body can be appropriately radiographed. To prevent unnecessary exposure to radiation, these workers surround the exposed area with radiation protection devices, such as lead shields, or limit the size of the x-ray beam. Radiographers position radiographic equipment at the correct angle and height over the appropriate area of a patient's body. Using instruments similar to a measuring tape, they may measure the thickness of the section to be radiographed and set controls on the x-ray machine to produce radiographs of the appropriate density, detail, and contrast. They place the x-ray film under the part of the patient's body to be examined and make the exposure. They then remove the film and develop it.

Experienced radiographers may perform more complex imaging procedures. For fluoroscopies, radiographers prepare a solution of contrast medium for the patient to drink, allowing the radiologist (a physician who interprets radiographs) to see soft tissues in the body. Some radiographers, called CT technologists, operate CT scanners to produce cross-sectional images of patients. Radiographers who operate machines that use strong magnets and radio waves, rather than radiation, to create an image are called MRI technologists.

Radiologic technologists and technicians must follow physicians' orders precisely and conform to regulations concerning the use of radiation to protect themselves, their patients, and their coworkers from unnecessary exposure.

In addition to preparing patients and operating equipment, radiologic technologists and technicians keep patient records and adjust and maintain equipment. They also may prepare work schedules, evaluate purchases of equipment, or manage a radiology department.

Working Conditions

Most full-time radiologic technologists and technicians work about 40 hours a week. They may, however, have evening, weekend, or on-call hours. Opportunities for part-time and shift work also are available.

Physical stamina is important, because technologists and technicians are on their feet for long periods and may lift or turn disabled patients. Technologists and technicians work at diagnostic machines, but also may perform some procedures at patients' bedsides. Some travel to patients in large vans equipped with sophisticated diagnostic equipment.

Although radiation hazards exist in this occupation, they are minimized by the use of lead aprons, gloves, and other shielding devices, as well as by instruments monitoring exposure to radiation. Technologists and technicians wear badges measuring radiation levels in the radiation area, and detailed records are kept on their cumulative lifetime dose.

Training, Other Qualifications, and Advancement

Preparation for this profession is offered in hospitals, colleges and universities, vocational-technical institutes, and the U.S. Armed Forces. Hospitals, which employ most radiologic technologists and technicians, prefer to hire those with formal training.

Formal training programs in radiography range in length from 1 to 4 years and lead to a certificate, an associate degree, or a bachelor's degree. Two-year associate degree programs are most prevalent.

Some 1-year certificate programs are available for experienced radiographers or individuals from other health occupations, such as medical technologists and registered nurses, who want to change fields or specialize in CT or MRI. A bachelor's or master's degree in one of the radiologic technologies is desirable for supervisory, administrative, or teaching positions.

The Joint Review Committee on Education in Radiologic Technology accredits most formal training programs for the field. The committee accredited 606 radiography programs in 2005. Radiography programs require, at a minimum, a high school diploma or the equivalent. High school courses in mathematics, physics, chemistry, and biology are helpful. The programs provide both classroom and clinical instruction in anatomy and physiology, patient care procedures, radiation physics, radiation protection, principles of imaging, medical terminology, positioning of patients, medical ethics, radiobiology, and pathology.

Federal legislation protects the public from the hazards of unnecessary exposure to medical and dental radiation by ensuring that operators of radiologic equipment are properly trained. Under this legislation, the federal government sets voluntary standards that the states may use for accrediting training programs and certifying individuals who engage in medical or dental radiography.

In 2005, 38 states certified radiologic technologists and technicians. Certification, which is voluntary, is offered by the American Registry of Radiologic Technologists. To be eligible for certification, technologists generally must graduate from an accredited program and pass an examination. Many employers prefer to hire certified radiographers. To be recertified, radiographers must complete 24 hours of continuing education every two years.

Radiologic technologists and technicians should be sensitive to patients' physical and psychological needs. They must pay attention to detail, follow instructions, and work as part of a team. In addition, operating complicated equipment requires mechanical ability and manual dexterity.

With experience and additional training, staff technologists may become specialists, performing CT scanning, angiography, and magnetic resonance imaging. Experienced technologists also may be promoted to supervisor, chief radiologic technologist, and, ultimately, department administrator or director. Depending on the institution, courses or a master's degree in business or health administration may be necessary for the director's position. Some technologists progress by leaving the occupation to become instructors or directors in radiologic technology programs; others take jobs as sales representatives or instructors with equipment manufacturers.

Employment
Radiologic technologists and technicians held about 182,000 jobs in 2004. More than half of all jobs were in hospitals. Most of the rest were in offices of physicians; medical and diagnostic laboratories, including diagnostic imaging centers; and outpatient care centers.

Job Outlook
Job opportunities are expected to be favorable. Some employers report difficulty hiring sufficient numbers of radiologic technologists and technicians. Imbalances between the demand for, and supply of, radiologic technologists and technicians should spur efforts to attract and retain qualified workers, such as improved compensation and working conditions. Radiologic technologists who also are experienced in more complex diagnostic imaging procedures, such as CT and MRI, will have better employment opportunities, brought about as employers seek to control costs by using multi-skilled employees.

Employment of radiologic technologists and technicians is expected to grow faster than the average for all occupations through 2014, as the population grows and ages, increasing the demand for diagnostic imaging. Although healthcare providers are enthusiastic about the clinical benefits of new technologies, the extent to which they are adopted depends largely on cost and reimbursement considerations. For example, digital imaging technology can improve the quality of the images and the efficiency of the procedure, but remains expensive. Some promising new technologies may not come into widespread use because they are too expensive and third-party payers may not be willing to pay for their use.

Hospitals will remain the principal employer of radiologic technologists and technicians. However, a greater number of new jobs will be found in offices of physicians and diagnostic imaging centers. Health facilities such as these are expected to grow rapidly through 2014, due to the strong shift toward outpatient care, encouraged by third-party payers and made possible by technological advances that permit more procedures to be performed outside the hospital. Some job openings also will arise from the need to replace technologists and technicians who leave the occupation.

Earnings
Median annual earnings of radiologic technologists and technicians were $43,350 in May 2004. The middle 50 percent earned between $36,170 and $52,430. The lowest 10 percent earned less than $30,020, and the highest 10 percent earned more than $60,210. Median annual earnings in the industries employing the largest numbers of radiologic technologists and technicians in May 2004 were: medical and diagnostic laboratories, $46,620; general medical and surgical hospitals, $43,960; and offices of physicians $40,290.

Related Occupations
Radiologic technologists and technicians operate sophisticated equipment to help physicians, dentists, and other health practitioners diagnose and treat patients. Workers in related occupations include cardiovascular technologists and technicians, clinical laboratory technologists and technicians, diagnostic medical sonographers, nuclear medicine technologists, radiation therapists, and respiratory therapists.

Resources for Cardiovascular Technologists & Technicians, Nuclear Medicine Technologists, Radiologic Technologists, and Diagnostic Medical Sonographers are combined as most resources serve multiple professions. See the end of the Diagnostic Medical Sonographers section.

DIAGNOSTIC MEDICAL SONOGRAPHERS

OCCUPATIONAL TITLES
Sonographers (Ultrasonographers)   **Neurosonographers**

Significant Points
- Job opportunities should be favorable, as sonography becomes an increasingly attractive alternative to radiologic procedures.
- About 6 out of 10 sonographers were employed by hospitals, and most of the rest worked in offices of physicians or in medical and diagnostic laboratories, including diagnostic imaging centers.
- Sonographers may train in hospitals, vocational-technical institutions, colleges and universities, and the Armed Forces.

Nature of the Work
Diagnostic imaging embraces several procedures that aid in diagnosing ailments. Besides the familiar x-ray, another common diagnostic imaging method is magnetic resonance imaging, which uses giant magnets that create radio waves, rather than radiation, to form an image. Not all imaging technologies use ionizing radiation or radio waves, however. Sonography, or ultrasonography, is the use of sound waves to generate an image for the assessment and diagnosis of various medical conditions. Sonography usually is associated with obstetrics and the use of ultrasound imaging during pregnancy, but this technology has many other applications in the diagnosis and treatment of medical conditions.

Diagnostic medical sonographers, also known as ultrasonographers, use special equipment to direct nonionizing, high frequency sound waves into areas of the patient's body. Sonographers operate the equipment, which collects reflected echoes and forms an image that may be videotaped, transmitted, or photographed for interpretation and diagnosis by a physician.

Sonographers begin by explaining the procedure to the patient and recording any medical history that may be relevant to the condition being viewed. They then select appropriate equipment settings and direct the patient to move into positions that will provide the best view. To perform the exam, sonographers use a transducer, which transmits sound waves in a cone- or rectangle-shaped beam. Although techniques vary with the area being examined, sonographers usually spread a special gel on the skin to aid the transmission of sound waves.

Viewing the screen during the scan, sonographers look for subtle visual cues that contrast healthy areas with unhealthy ones. They decide whether the images are satisfactory for diagnostic purposes and select which ones to show to the physician. Sonographers take measurements, calculate values, and analyze the results in preliminary reports for the physicians.

Diagnostic medical sonographers may specialize in obstetric and gynecologic sonography (the female reproductive system), abdominal sonography (the liver, kidneys, gallbladder, spleen, and pancreas), neurosonography (the brain), or breast sonography. In addition, sonographers may specialize in vascular technology or echocardiography. (Vascular technologists and echocardiographers are covered in the section on cardiovascular technologists and technicians.)

Obstetric and gynecologic sonographers specialize in the study of the female reproductive system. Included in the discipline is one of the more well-known uses of sonography: examining the fetus of a pregnant woman to track the baby's growth and health.

Abdominal sonographers inspect a patient's abdominal cavity to help diagnose and treat conditions primarily involving the gallbladder, bile ducts, kidneys, liver, pancreas, and spleen. Abdominal sonographers also are able to scan parts of the chest, although studies of the heart using sonography usually are done by echocardiographers.

Neurosonographers focus on the nervous system, including the brain. In neonatal care, neurosonographers study and diagnose neurological and nervous system disorders in premature infants. They also may scan blood vessels to check for abnormalities indicating a stroke in infants diagnosed with sickle-cell anemia. Like other sonographers, neurosonographers operate transducers to perform the sonogram, but use frequencies and beam shapes different from those used by obstetric and abdominal sonographers.

Breast sonographers use sonography to study the disease in breasts. Sonography aids mammography in the detection of breast cancer. Breast sonography can also track tumors, blood supply conditions, and assist in the accurate biopsy of breast tissue. Breast sonographers use high-frequency transducers, made exclusively to study breast tissue.

In addition to working directly with patients, diagnostic medical sonographers keep patient records and adjust and maintain equipment. They also may prepare work schedules, evaluate equipment purchases, or manage a sonography or diagnostic imaging department.

Working Conditions

Most full-time sonographers work about 40 hours a week. Hospital-based sonographers may have evening and weekend hours and times when they are on call and must be ready to report to work on short notice.

Sonographers typically work in healthcare facilities that are clean and well lighted. Some travel to patients in large vans equipped with sophisticated diagnostic equipment. A growing number of sonographers work as contract employees and may perform tests at a number of different hospitals. Sonographers are on their feet for long periods and may have to lift or turn disabled patients. They work at diagnostic imaging machines, but also may perform some procedures at patients' bedsides.

Training, Other Qualifications, and Advancement

There are several avenues for entry into the field of diagnostic medical sonography. Sonographers may train in hospitals, vocational technical institutions, colleges and universities, and the Armed Forces. Some training programs prefer applicants with a background in science or experience in other healthcare professions, but also will consider high school graduates with courses in mathematics and science, as well as applicants with liberal arts backgrounds.

Colleges and universities offer formal training in both 2- and 4-year programs, culminating in an associate or a bachelor's degree. Two-year programs are most prevalent. Course work includes classes in anatomy, physiology, instrumentation, basic physics, patient care, and medical ethics. The Commission on Accreditation for Allied Health Education Programs accredits most formal training programs—132 programs in 2005.

Some healthcare workers, such as obstetric nurses and radiologic technologists, increase their marketability by seeking training in fields such as sonography. This usually requires completion of an additional 1-year program that may result in a certificate. In addition, sonographers specializing in one particular discipline often seek competency in others; for example, obstetric sonographers might seek training in abdominal sonography to broaden their opportunities.

Although no state requires licensure in diagnostic medical sonography, organizations such as the American Registry for Diagnostic Medical Sonography (ARDMS) certify the competency of sonographers through registration. Because registration provides an independent, objective measure of an individual's professional standing, many employers prefer to hire registered sonographers. Registration with ARDMS requires passing a general physical principles and instrumentation examination, in addition to passing an exam in a specialty such as obstetric and gynecologic sonography, abdominal sonography, or neurosonography. To keep their registration current, sonographers must complete continuing education to stay abreast of technological advances related to the occupation.

Sonographers need good communication and interpersonal skills because they must be able to explain technical procedures and results to their patients, some of whom may be nervous about the exam or the problems it may reveal. Sonographers also should have a background in mathematics and science.

Employment

Diagnostic medical sonographers held about 42,000 jobs in 2004. About 6 out of 10 sonographer jobs were in hospitals—public and private. Most of the rest were in offices of physicians or in medical and diagnostic laboratories, including diagnostic imaging centers.

Job Outlook

Employment of diagnostic medical sonographers is expected to grow much faster than the average for all occupations through 2014 as the population grows and ages, increasing the demand for diagnostic imaging and therapeutic technology. In addition to job openings from growth, some job openings will arise from the need to replace sonographers who leave the occupation permanently.

Opportunities should be favorable because sonography is becoming an increasingly attractive alternative to radiologic procedures, as patients seek safer treatment methods. Unlike most diagnostic imaging methods, sonography does not involve radiation, so harmful side effects and complications from repeated use are rarer for both the patient and the sonographer. Sonographic technology is expected to evolve rapidly and to spawn many new sonography procedures, such as 3D - and 4D - sonography for use in obstetric and ophthalmologic diagnosis. However, high costs may limit the rate at which some promising new technologies are adopted.

Hospitals will remain the principal employer of diagnostic medical sonographers. However, employment is expected to grow more rapidly in offices of physicians and in medical and diagnostic laboratories, including diagnostic imaging centers. Healthcare facilities such as these are expected to grow very rapidly through 2014 because of the strong shift toward outpatient care, encouraged by third-party payers and made possible by technological advances that permit more procedures to be performed outside the hospital.

Earnings

Median annual earnings of diagnostic medical sonographers were $52,490 in May 2004. The middle 50 percent earned between $44,720 and $61,360 a year. The lowest 10 percent earned less than $37,800, and the highest 10 percent earned more than $72,230. Median annual earnings of diagnostic medical sonographers in May 2004 were $53,790 in offices of physicians and $51,860 in general medical and surgical hospitals.

Related Occupations

Diagnostic medical sonographers operate sophisticated equipment to help physicians and other health practitioners diagnose and treat patients. Workers in related occupations include cardiovascular technologists and technicians, clinical laboratory technologists and technicians, nuclear medicine technologists, radiologic technologists and technicians, and respiratory therapists.

DIAGNOSTIC IMAGING CAREER RESOURCES: CARDIOVASCULAR TECHNOLOGISTS AND TECHNICIANS, NUCLEAR MEDICINE TECHNICIANS, RADIOLOGIC TECHNICIANS, AND DIAGNOSTIC MEDICAL SONOGRAPHERS

Don't forget! Refer to the general resources listed in Chapter Three.

ADVANCE Newsmagazines - 2900 Horizon Drive, King of Prussia, PA 19406-0956; 800/355-5627. **(http://www.advanceweb.com/)** Publishes *ADVANCE for Imaging and Radiation Therapy Professionals* and *ADVANCE for Imaging and Oncology Administrators,* available free for professionals. The web site is an excellent source of job ads to search by state or career. Online access job fair information and to "Talking to Talent" surveys of allied health professionals.

All Healthcare Jobs - **(http://www.allhealthcarejobs.com/)** Search job ads, post your résumé or receive email job alerts on sites specific for CT technologists, cardiac cath techs, Radiology techs, mammography, MRI technologists, nuclear medicine, PET, radiologic technologists and ultrasound.

Alliance of Cardiovascular Professionals (ACVP) - Thalia Landing Offices, Bldg. 2, 4356 Bonney Road, #103, Virginia Beach, VA 23452-1200; 757/497-1225. For all specialties in cardiovascular service. Provides credentialing. Web site has career information and a message board for networking. Job Board has ads and allows you to post your résumé. **(http://www.acp-online.org/**, peggymcelgunn@comcast.net)

American College of Radiology - 1891 Preston White Dr, Reston, VA 20191, 703/648-8900. **(http://www.acr.org/)** Members are MDs. Search for accredited facilities by imaging modality and state.

American Heart Association CareerMatch - Post your résumé, view company profiles and job ads by location or profession at **http://aha.medcareers.com/seeker/**.

American Healthcare Radiology Administrators (AHRA) - 490B Boston Post Road #101, Sudbury, MA 01776; 800/334-AHRA or 978/443-7591. **(http://www.ahra.com/**, info@ahraonline.org) Contact the AHRA for a free career information brochure. The web site has job openings by region, a directory of radiology consultants and a List Server for networking. Free sample issue of *Link* newsletter has job ads.

American Institute of Ultrasound in Medicine (AIUM) - 14750 Sweitzer Lane, Suite 100, Laurel, Maryland 20707; 301/498-4100. (**http://www.aium.org**, membership@aium.org) Web site has information on scholarships, a sonographers' Listserv and a Job Board.

American Nuclear Society (ANS) - 555 North Kensington Ave., La Grange Park, IL 60526; 708/352-6611. (**http://www.ans.org**) Members may post résumés and search ads online. Students can find information on nuclear careers and scholarships.

American Registry for Diagnostic Medical Sonography (ARDMS) - 51 Monroe St., Plaza East One, Rockville, Maryland 20850-2400; 301/738-8401. (**http://www.ardms.org/**, admin@ardms.org) The ARDMS awards credentials in diagnostic medical sonography, diagnostic cardiac sonography and vascular technology. You can view job ads, post a résumé, get email job alerts and search a directory of employers.

American Registry of Radiologic Technologists (ARRT), 1255 Northland Drive, Saint Paul, MN 55120-1155; 651/687-0048. (**http://www.arrt.org/**) The web site has a section for radiologist assistants with career and certification information, and a directory of educational programs for radiography, nuclear medicine technology, radiation therapy, and sonography.

American Society of Echocardiography (ASE) - 1500 Sunday Drive, Suite102, Raleigh, North Carolina 27607; 919/861-5574. (**http://www.asecho.org/**, webstaff@asecho.org) Web site has career information and a directories of education programs and local societies. Their Job Marketplace is for members only.

American Society of Radiologic Technologists (ASRT) - 15000 Central Ave. SE, Albuquerque, NM 87123-3917; 800/444-2778 or 505/298-4500. (**http://www.asrt.org/**, customerinfo@asrt.org) ASRT has a Student Intern Program and directory of state and local societies. The online Job Bank lets you post a résumé, view ads and receive email job alerts. Ask about scholarships and student loans.

Cardiovascular Credentialing International (CCI) - 1500 Sunday Drive, Suite 102, Raleigh, NC 27607; 800/326-0268. Credentialing information, online job listings and links to educational programs. (**http://www.cci-online.org/**)

Careers in Nuclear Medicine - http://www.cnmt.com, customerservice@cnmt.com) Offers an employment news letter for medical technologists. Search jobs database, post your résumé or have job email alerts sent to you. Phone number 866/266-8776.

CathLab.com - (http://www.cathlab.com) Classified section has job ads for cardiovascular technologists. Heart2Heart section lists over 2,000 cath labs and has a chat room.

Commission on Accreditation of Allied Health Education Programs (CAAHEP) - 1361 Park St., Clearwater, FL 33756; 727/210-2350. **(http://www.caahep.org)**. Online find information on accredited educational programs for 22 careers.

Hot Radiology Jobs - (http://www.hotradiologyjobs.com/) Job listings for administrators and technologists sorted by specialty. Post your résumé. Search jobs then click on link to employers' URLs.

Intersocietal Commission for the Accreditation of Echocardiography Laboratories (ICAEL) - 8830 Stanford Boulevard, Suite 306, Columbia, MD 21045; or 800/838-2110. **(http://www.icael.org)**. The web site has a directory of accredited echocardiography laboratories.

Joint Review Committee on Education in Cardiovascular Technology (JRC-CVT) - 1248 Harwood Rd, Bedford, Texas 76021-4244; 214/206-3117. **(http://www.jrccvt.org/)** Web site has a directory of accredited education institutions.

Joint Review Committee On Education in Diagnostic Medical Sonography (JRC-DMS) - 2025 Woodlane Drive, St. Paul, MN 55125-2998; 651/731-1582. **(http://www.jrcdms.org/**, jrc-dms@jcahpo.org) Online list of accredited educational programs.

Medical Workers.com - Search for jobs and view details about employers, apply for jobs online. You can also post your résumé at **http://www.medicalworkers.com/Radiology/**

Nuclear Medicine Technology Certification Board - 2970 Clairmont Rd., Suite 935, Atlanta, GA 30329; 404/315-1739. **(http://www.nmtcb.org)** Certifies technologists. The web site has a presentation "Introduction to Nuclear Medicine" and links to job ads.

RadCareers.com - (http://www.radcareers.com) Search job ads by state, post a résumé or receive email job alerts.

📋🖱 *Radiology Today* - (**http://www.radiologytoday.net**) Free e-newsletter with career opportunities from Great Valley Publishing.

📋📁🖱 **Radworking.com** - (**http://www.radworking.com**) Job listings for rad techs, radiation therapists, ultrasound techs, nuclear medicine techs, and jobs in MRI and mammography. Post your résumé and view their detailed directory of health care facilities.

📋 *RT Image* - Valley Forge Press, 1041 Chesterfield Parkway, Suite 100, Malvern, PA 19355; 610/854-3770, 800/983-7737. Bi-weekly publication. Has pages of employment ads for radiologic science professionals, educators, and administrators. Professionals may call for free subscriptions and/or place "position wanted" ads. Their job ad site is (**http://www.MedHealthJobs.com**).

⚕🖱 **Society of Diagnostic Medical Sonography (SDMS)** - 2745 Dallas Parkway Suite 350, Plano, TX 75093-8730; 214/473-8057; 800/229-9506. (**http://www.sdms.org**, info@sdms.org) Online networking for members. Web site has information about the career and scholarships.

⚕🖱 **The Society of Invasive Cardiovascular Professionals (SICP)** - 1500 Sunday Drive, Suite 102, Raleigh, NC 27607; 919/861-4546. (**http://www.sicp.com**, membership@sicp.com) Subscription to *Cath-Lab Digest*, for the non-physician cardiac catheterization lab professional, is free to qualified personnel. No jobs on the web site.

⚕📋📁🖱 **Society of Nuclear Medicine (SNM)** - 1850 Samuel Morse Drive, Reston, VA 22090; 703/708-9000. (**http://www.snm.org**). The web site has information about nuclear medicine, scholarships, certification/licensure and resources for students, including networking and a directory of accredited education programs. The online job bank gives you the URL of the employers.

⚕📋🖱 **Society for Vascular Ultrasound (SVU)** - 4601 Presidents Drive, Suite 260, Lanham, MD 20706; 301/459-7550. (**http://www.svunet.org/**, svuinfo@svunet.org) Represents vascular technologists, vascular surgeons, vascular lab managers, nurses, and other allied medical ultrasound professionals. Web site has career information, discussion groups for networking, job listings, a page for students to post profiles for prospective employers.

SURGICAL TECHNOLOGISTS

Significant Points
- Employment is expected to grow much faster than the average for all occupations through the year 2014.
- Job opportunities are expected to be good.
- Training programs last 9 to 24 months and lead to a certificate, diploma, or associate degree.
- Hospitals will continue to be the primary employer, although much faster employment growth is expected in offices of physicians and in outpatient care centers, including ambulatory surgical centers.

Nature of the Work
Surgical technologists, also called scrubs and surgical or operating room technicians, assist in surgical operations under the supervision of surgeons, registered nurses, or other surgical personnel. Surgical technologists are members of operating room teams, which most commonly include surgeons, anesthesiologists, and circulating nurses. Before an operation, surgical technologists help prepare the operating room by setting up surgical instruments and equipment, sterile drapes, and sterile solutions. They assemble both sterile and nonsterile equipment, as well as adjust and check it to ensure it is working properly. Technologists also get patients ready for surgery by washing, shaving, and disinfecting incision sites. They transport patients to the operating room, help position them on the operating table, and cover them with sterile surgical "drapes." Technologists also observe patients' vital signs, check charts, and assist the surgical team with putting on sterile gowns and gloves.

During surgery, technologists pass instruments and other sterile supplies to surgeons and surgeon assistants. They may hold retractors, cut sutures, and help count sponges, needles, supplies, and instruments. Surgical technologists help prepare, care for, and dispose of specimens taken for laboratory analysis and help apply dressings. Some operate sterilizers, lights, or suction machines, and help operate diagnostic equipment.

After an operation, surgical technologists may help transfer patients to the recovery room and clean and restock the operating room.

Working Conditions

Surgical technologists work in clean, well-lighted, cool environments. They must stand for long periods and remain alert during operations. At times they may be exposed to communicable diseases and unpleasant sights, odors, and materials.

Most surgical technologists work a regular 40-hour week, although they may be on call or work nights, weekends, and holidays on a rotating basis.

Training, Other Qualifications, and Advancement

Surgical technologists receive their training in formal programs offered by community and junior colleges, vocational schools, universities, hospitals, and the military. In 2005, the Commission on Accreditation of Allied Health Education Programs (CAAHEP) recog-nized more than 400 accredited programs. Programs last from 9 to 24 months and lead to a certificate, diploma, or associate degree. High school graduation normally is required for admission. Recommended high school courses include health, biology, chemistry, and mathematics.

Programs provide classroom education and supervised clinical experience. Students take courses in anatomy, physiology, microbiology, pharmacology, professional ethics, and medical terminology. Other studies cover the care and safety of patients during surgery, sterile techniques, and surgical procedures. Students also learn to sterilize instruments; prevent and control infection; and handle special drugs, solutions, supplies, and equipment.

Most employers prefer to hire certified technologists. Technologists may obtain voluntary professional certification from the Liaison Council on Certification for the Surgical Technologist by graduating from a CAAHEP-accredited program and passing a national certification examination. They may then use the Certified Surgical Technologist (CST) designation. Continuing education or reexamination is required to maintain certification, which must be renewed every 4 years.

Certification also may be obtained from the National Center for Competency Testing. To qualify to take the exam, candidates follow one of three paths: complete an accredited training program; undergo a 2-year hospital on-the-job training program; or acquire seven years of experience working in the field. After passing the exam, individuals may use the designation Tech in Surgery-Certified, TS-C (NCCT). This certification may be renewed every 5 years through either continuing education or reexamination.

Surgical technologists need manual dexterity to handle instruments quickly. They also must be conscientious, orderly, and emotionally stable to handle the demands of the operating room environment. Technologists must respond quickly and must be familiar with operating procedures in order to have instruments ready for surgeons without having to be told. They are expected to keep abreast of new developments in the field.

Technologists advance by specializing in a particular area of surgery, such as neurosurgery or open heart surgery. They also may work as circulating technologists. A circulating technologist is the "unsterile" member of the surgical team who prepares patients; helps with anesthesia; obtains and opens packages for the "sterile" persons to remove the sterile contents during the procedure; interviews the patient before surgery; keeps a written account of the surgical procedure; and answers the surgeon's questions about the patient during the surgery. With additional training, some technologists advance to first assistants, who help with retracting, sponging, suturing, cauterizing bleeders, and closing and treating wounds. Some surgical technologists manage central supply departments in hospitals, or take positions with insurance companies, sterile supply services, and operating equipment firms.

Employment
Surgical technologists held about 84,000 jobs in 2004. About 7 out of 10 jobs for surgical technologists were in hospitals, mainly in operating and delivery rooms. Other jobs were in offices of physicians or dentists who perform outpatient surgery and in outpatient care centers, including ambulatory surgical centers. A few, known as private scrubs, are employed directly by surgeons who have special surgical teams, like those for liver transplants.

Job Outlook
Employment of surgical technologists is expected to grow much faster than average for all occupations through the year 2014 as the volume of surgery increases. Job opportunities are expected to be good. The number of surgical procedures is expected to rise as the population grows and ages. The number of older people, including the baby boom generation, who generally require more surgical procedures, will ac-

count for a larger portion of the general population. Technological advances, such as fiber optics and laser technology, will permit an increasing number of new surgical procedures to be performed and also will allow surgical technologists to assist with a greater number of procedures.

Hospitals will continue to be the primary employer of surgical technologists, although much faster employment growth is expected in offices of physicians and in outpatient care centers, including ambulatory surgical centers.

Earnings

Median annual earnings of surgical technologists were $34,010 in May 2004. The middle 50 percent earned between $28,560 and $40,750. The lowest 10 percent earned less than $23,940, and the highest 10 percent earned more than $45,990. Median hourly earnings in the industries employing the largest numbers of surgical technologists in May 2004 were: Offices of dentists, $37,510; Offices of physicians, $36,570; General medical and surgical hospitals, $33,130.

Related Occupations

Other health occupations requiring approximately 1 year of training after high school include dental assistants, licensed practical and licensed vocational nurses, clinical laboratory technologists and technicians, and medical assistants.

SURGICAL TECHNOLOGISTS RESOURCES

Don't forget! Refer to the general resources listed in Chapter Three.

☤Association	▱Directory	✐Resume Service	⌲Web Site
▤Job Ads	✍Job Alert E-mail/Hotline	☞Job Fairs	▭Book

For a full explanation of these resources see the second page of Chapter 3.

☤ ▱ ⌲ **Accreditation Review Committee on Education in Surgical Technology (ARC-ST) - (http://www.arcst.org/)** The web site has a directory of accredited educational programs.

American Society of Extra-Corporeal Technology (AMSECT) - 2209 Dickens Road, PO Box 11086, Richmond, VA 23230; 804/565-6363. Members are perfusionists, technologists, physicians and nurses that apply extracorporeal technology, the use of heart-lung machines. (http://www.amsect.org, president@amsect.org) The web site has information on the profession, scholarships and offers a Student Job Kit. *AmSECT Today* newsletter has job ads and members may send their résumés to the national office for their placement service.

Association of Surgical Technologists (AST) - 6 W Dry Creek Circle, Littleton, CO 80120; 303/694-9130. (http://www.ast.org, membership@ast.org) Student membership benefits ($45/yr) include *The Surgical Technologist* (with job ads) and a discount on the study guide and certification test. The web site has information on education and scholarships, with career description on the Profession web page. Jobs online are by region or members may call 800/637-7433 for help finding employment.

Liaison Council on Certification for the Surgical Technologist (LCC-ST) - 6 West Dry Creek Circle, Suite 100, Littleton, CO 80120; 800/707-0057. (http://www.lcc-st.org/) Contact for information on certification.

Protouch Staffing - 17822 Davenport Road, Ste A, Dallas, TX 75252; 972/671-3152 or 888/902-7161. Post your résumé and search for allied health jobs at: http://www.protouchstaffing.com

Chapter
5

HEALTH TECHNICIANS

Stacey Langston

Stacey Langston has been an optician for more than 13 years. At first he worked fitting conventional glasses, but now most of his work is fitting and pre-testing high-tech eyewear devices for patients who are visually impaired or legally blind.

An ABO-certified optician currently working for Envision, Stacey did much of his training on his own, combined with on-the-job training in Wichita, Kansas. He says that some states require certification, but even if it is not required, it is probably an advantage in finding a job in the field. He says employers are looking for experienced workers and for workers they know will be in the career for a number of years. Stacey believes certification shows an employer you are serious about the career. He has noticed that more men are getting into the field now.

"One disadvantage of the career is that you hit the promotion ceiling pretty quickly," Stacey said, but added, "Employers pay more for additional experience." He also thinks they pay more for certified workers. Another factor that can increase your salary is advanced technical skills. Stacey sees a growing need for opticians who are skilled in devices such as bioptics and prisms. A bioptic is a type of telescope that can be mounted in a lens. It is used for people who have conditions such as pinhole vision or limited peripheral vision or macular degeneration. Prisms mainly help people who have blind spots in central vision. They redirect vision to a more healthy area of the retina.

He says that society is much more aware of low vision problems and macular degeneration, now that the population is aging. "The prescriptions we are getting now are very different than the glasses we fit in the past." Not every company makes and fits the high tech glasses though. Stacey says, "It's pretty exciting to build something for someone – to completely customize eyewear" to fit special needs.

One of the favorite aspects of his career is working with people. "People rely on you to know all the latest products and need you on several different levels. You need to talk to them, to listen to them, so you know what they need and expect."

He says you need to consider your work a career, rather than a job for just a few months or years. "Maybe you can do the job in four or five months, the basics anyway, but you are not a good optician until you have done this work a few years." Stacey adds, "You really need to know the products and what a patient needs."

Stacey says he learns something everyday because every person he helps is an individual. "Like most jobs, it is what you put into it. You need to enjoy people. That's what keeps me happy."

This chapter features health care technicians. The major occupational groups are:

Dental Hygienists
Dental Assistants
Dispensing Opticians
Emergency Medical Technicians and Paramedics
Medical, Dental, and Ophthalmic Laboratory Technicians

The following other technicians are grouped with the related technologist occupations in Chapter 3: Cardiovascular Technicians, Clinical Laboratory Technicians and Radiologic Technicians. Health Information Technicians are grouped with Medical Records Technicians in Chapter 10.

Each specialty is described below. Occupational groups are divided into primary and related occupations so that individuals can investigate other fields for additional job opportunities.

Following each job description are job resource lists: Associations, Books, Directories, Internet Sites, Job Ads, E-mail Job Notification/Job Hotlines, Job Fairs, and Résumé/Placement Services.

DENTAL HYGIENISTS

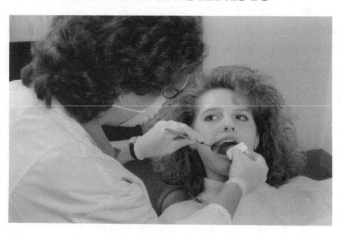

Registered dental hygienist performing an oral exam.
The American Dental Hygienist' Association

Significant Points

- Most dental hygiene programs grant an associate degree; others offer a certificate, a bachelor's degree, or a master's degree.
- Dental hygienists rank among the fastest growing occupations.
- Job prospects are expected to remain excellent.
- More than half work part time, and flexible scheduling is a distinctive feature of this job.

Nature of the Work

Dental hygienists remove soft and hard deposits from teeth, teach patients how to practice good oral hygiene, and provide other preventive dental care. Hygienists examine patients' teeth and gums, recording the presence of diseases or abnormalities. They remove calculus, stains, and plaque from teeth; perform root planing as a periodontal therapy; take and develop dental x-rays; and apply cavity-preventive agents such as fluorides and pit and fissure sealants. In some states, hygienists administer anesthetics; place and carve filling materials, temporary fillings, and periodontal dressings; remove sutures; and smooth and polish metal restorations. Although hygienists may not diagnose diseases, they can prepare clinical and laboratory diagnostic tests for the dentist to interpret. Hygienists sometimes work chairside with the dentist during treatment.

Dental hygienists also help patients develop and maintain good oral health. For example, they may explain the relationship between diet and oral health or inform patients how to select toothbrushes and show them how to brush and floss their teeth.

Dental hygienists use hand and rotary instruments and ultrasonics to clean and polish teeth, x-ray machines to take dental pictures, syringes with needles to administer local anesthetics, and models of teeth to explain oral hygiene.

Working Conditions

Flexible scheduling is a distinctive feature of this job. Full-time, part-time, evening, and weekend schedules are widely available. Dentists frequently hire hygienists to work only 2 or 3 days a week, so hygienists may hold jobs in more than one dental office.

Dental hygienists work in clean, well-lighted offices. Important health safeguards include strict adherence to proper radiological procedures and the use of appropriate protective devices when administering anesthetic gas. Dental hygienists also wear safety glasses, surgical masks, and gloves to protect themselves and patients from infectious diseases.

Training, Other Qualifications, and Advancement

Dental hygienists must be licensed by the state in which they practice. To qualify for licensure in nearly all states, a candidate must graduate from an accredited dental hygiene school and pass both a written and clinical examination. The American Dental Association's Joint Commission on National Dental Examinations administers the written examination, which is accepted by all states and the District of Columbia. State or regional testing agencies administer the clinical examination. In addition, most states require an examination on the legal aspects of dental hygiene practice. Alabama allows candidates to take its examinations if they have been trained through a state-regulated on-the-job program in a dentist's office.

In 2004, the Commission on Dental Accreditation accredited 266 programs in dental hygiene. Most dental hygiene programs grant an associate degree, although some also offer a certificate, a bachelor's degree, or a master's degree. A minimum of an associate degree or certificate in dental hygiene is generally required for practice in a private dental office. A bachelor's or master's degree usually is required for research, teaching, or clinical practice in public or school health programs.

A high school diploma and college entrance test scores are usually required for admission to a dental hygiene program. Also, some dental hygiene programs prefer applicants who have completed at least 1 year of college. Requirements vary from one school to another. Schools offer laboratory, clinical, and classroom instruction in subjects such as anatomy, physiology, chemistry, microbiology, pharmacology, nutrition, radiography, histology (the study of tissue structure), periodontology (the study of gum diseases), pathology, dental materials, clinical dental hygiene, and social and behavioral sciences.

Dental hygienists should work well with others and must have good manual dexterity, because they use dental instruments within a patient's mouth, with little room for error. High school students interested in becoming a dental hygienist should take courses in biology, chemistry, and mathematics.

Employment
Dental hygienists held about 158,000 jobs in 2004. Because multiple job-holding is common in this field, the number of jobs exceeds the number of hygienists. More than half of all dental hygienists worked part time—less than 35 hours a week. Almost all jobs for dental hygienists were in offices of dentists. A very small number worked for employment services or in offices of physicians.

Job Outlook

Employment of dental hygienists is expected to grow much faster than average for all occupations through 2014, ranking among the fastest growing occupations, in response to increasing demand for dental care and the greater utilization of hygienists to perform services previously performed by dentists. Job prospects are expected to remain excellent.

Population growth and greater retention of natural teeth will stimulate demand for dental hygienists. Older dentists, who have been less likely to employ dental hygienists, are leaving the occupation and will be replaced by recent graduates, who are more likely to employ one or even two hygienists. In addition, as dentists' workloads increase, they are expected to hire more hygienists to perform preventive dental care, such as cleaning, so that they may devote their own time to more profitable procedures.

Earnings

Median hourly earnings of dental hygienists were $28.05 in May 2004. The middle 50 percent earned between $22.72 and $33.82 an hour. The lowest 10 percent earned less than $18.05, and the highest 10 percent earned more than $40.70 an hour.

Earnings vary by geographic location, employment setting, and years of experience. Dental hygienists may be paid on an hourly, daily, salary, or commission basis.

Benefits vary substantially by practice setting and may be contingent upon full-time employment. According to the American Dental Association (ADA), almost all full-time dental hygienists employed by private practitioners received paid vacation. The ADA also found that 9 out of 10 full-time and part-time dental hygienists received dental coverage. Dental hygienists who work for school systems, public health agencies, the federal government, or state agencies usually have substantial benefits.

Related Occupations

Other workers supporting health practitioners in an office setting include dental assistants, medical assistants, occupational therapist assistants and aides, physical therapist assistants and aides, physician assistants, and registered nurses.

Resources for Dental Hygienists, Dental Assistants, & Dental Laboratory Technicians are combined. See the end of the Dental Assistants section.

DENTAL ASSISTANTS

Dental assistants perform a variety of patient care, office, and laboratory duties. They work chair side as dentists examine and treat patients. They make patients as comfortable as possible in the dental chair, prepare them for treatment, and obtain their dental records. Assistants hand instruments and materials to dentists and keep patients' mouths dry and clear by using suction or other devices. Assistants also sterilize and disinfect instruments and equipment, prepare trays of instruments for dental procedures, and instruct patients on post-operative and general oral health care. Those with laboratory duties make casts of the teeth and mouth from impressions, clean and polish removable appliances, and make temporary crowns. Dental assistants with office duties schedule and confirm appointments, receive patients, keep treatment records, send bills, receive payments, and order dental supplies and materials.

Job prospects should be excellent. Dentists are expected to hire more assistants to perform routine tasks so that they may devote their own time to more complex procedures. Most assistants learn their skills on the job, although an increasing number are trained in dental-assisting programs offered by community and junior colleges, trade schools, technical institutes, or the Armed Forces; most programs take 1 year or less to complete. Assistants must be a second pair of hands for a dentist; therefore, dentists look for people who are reliable, work well with others, and have good manual dexterity. Most states regulate the duties that dental assistants are allowed to perform through licensure or registration. Licensure or registration may require passing a written or practical examination.

Certification is available through DANB and is recognized or required in more than 30 states. Median hourly earnings of dental assistants were $13.62 in May 2004. More information on this profession can be found at *Occupational Outlook Handbook, 2006-07 Edition*, Dental Assistants, on the Internet at **http://www.bls.gov/oco/ocos163.htm**.

DENTAL HYGIENISTS, DENTAL ASSISTANTS & DENTAL LABORATORY TECHNICIANS RESOURCES

Don't forget! Refer to the general resources listed in Chapter Three. Check the dentists resources section in Chapter 9 for more directories.

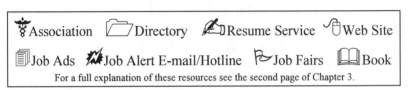

For a full explanation of these resources see the second page of Chapter 3.

🦷📁🖱 **American Academy of Dental Group Practice (AADGP)** - 2525 E. Arizona Biltmore Circle, Suite 127 , Phoenix, AZ 85016; 602/381-1185. **(http://www.aadgp.org,** info@aadgp.org) Members comprised of dentists and dental group practices. Publishes membership directory, $50 to nonmembers.

🦷📁🖱 **American Academy of Pediatric Dentistry (AAPD)** - 211 E. Chicago Avenue, Suite 700, Chicago, Illinois 60611-2663; 312/337-2169. **(http://www.aapd.org)** AAPD's *Find a Pediatric Dentist* service, online, provides names and addresses for over 4,600 pediatric dentists.

🦷📋📁🖱 **American Association of Public Health Dentistry (AAPHD)** - P.O. Box 7536, Springfield, IL 62791-7536; 217/391-0218. **(http://www.aaphd.org,** natoff@aaphd.org) Organization of dentists and dental hygienists. Membership directory online for members only. Job postings open to public on web. Student membership $40. Extensive collection of links.

🦷📋📁🖊🖱 **American Dental Assistants Association (ADAA)** - 35 East Wacker Drive, Suite 1730, Chicago, IL 60601-2211; 312/541-1550. **(http://dentalassistant.org,** adaa1@aol.com) Student membership is $25. Web site has career information and links to state associations. Partner site **http://www.dentalworkers.com/** has extensive online posting of job ads and résumés. (Site is being updated; there may be a fee.)

🦷📁🖱 **American Dental Association (ADA)** - 211 E. Chicago Ave., Chicago, IL 60611; 312/440-2500. **(http://www.ada.org)** The web page **http://www.ada.org/public/education/index.asp** lists career mentoring resources from 20 area dental associations for students K-16 and brochures for all dental related jobs. Inquiries about this program can be sent to skoogb@ada.org. *American Dental Directory* lists over 141,000 dentists. Web site lists dental associations by state and has excellent links to dental organizations (including the Commission on Dental Accreditation) and to Internet search engines.

American Dental Hygienists' Association (ADHA) - 444 N. Michigan Ave., Suite 3400, Chicago, Illinois 60611; 312/440-8900. **(http://www.adha.org,** mail@adha.net) Student membership, $45 includes student liability insurance and two journals. Web site has information on job hunting and links to placement services and schools.

DentalGlobe (http://dentalglobe.com) This Web site has information on education, student resources and job ads at no charge for dentists and dental hygienists with phone and E-mail addresses for employers. It also has links to dental labs, schools, associations, publications and companies. Provides bulletin boards/chat.

Dental Assisting National Board (DANB) - 676 North Saint Clair St., Suite 1880, Chicago, IL 60611; 312/642-3368 or 800/FOR-DANB. **(http://www.danb.org/)** Contact for information on becoming a Certified Dental Assistant and a list of state boards of dentistry and information on DAMB exams.

DentalLogic.com - (http://www.dentallogic.com) Created and maintained by: Stephen J. Charnitski D.M.D. and Robert W. Beadle D.D.S., this site lists dental schools, laboratories and manufacturers, and employment ads. Includes joke page.

DentalPower International, Inc. - 100 Park Avenue, Ste. 205, Rockville, Maryland 20850; 301/340-9600. **(www.dentalpower.com,** jobs@dentalpower.com) Job site for temporary and permanent positions. Place résumé on web site, or visit local office links nationwide.

Dental Related Internet Resources - List of dental educational institutions, and information about specific dental issues. Their URL is **(http://www.dental-resources.com).**

The Dental Site - (http://www.dentalsite.com) Excellent site for dental patients, dentists, dental assistants, dental hygienists, dental technicians and dental vendors. It has a directory of dental laboratories, links to education, publications, directories, job sources.

📁⌐ **Dentist Directory** - (http://www.dentistdirectory.com) A search engine to locate dentists nationwide.

📑📁🔑⌐ **Dentistinfo.com** - 853 Sanders Road, Suite 252, Northbrook, IL 60062; 847/564-5329. (**http://www.dentistinfo.com**, drtooth@dentistinfo.com) Operated by Ronald R. Widen, D.D.S., web site has Find a Dentist section and a Job Search section for dentists, hygienists, assistants and sales reps, where you can place a "position wanted" ad free.

📖 **Exploring Careers in Dentistry** by Jessica A. Rickert. $25.25. Published by The Rosen Publishing Group, Inc., 29 East 21st St., New York, NY, 10010; 800/237-9932, Available through used book sellers.

⌐ **Guide to Careers in Dentistry** - Provided by the University of North Carolina at Chapel Hill School of Dentistry. Visit their web site located at (**http://www.dent.unc.edu/careers/index.htm**).

⚕ **National Association of Dental Assistants** - 900 South Washington St., Suite G-13, Falls Church, VA 22046; 703/237-8616. This association has information about continuing education courses.

⚕📑📁⌐ **National Association of Dental Laboratories (NADL)** - 325 John Knox Rd L103, Tallahassee, Florida 32303; (800) 950-1150. (**http:\\www.nadl.org**, nadl@nadl.org) Organization comprised of state associations representing over 3100 dental laboratories. Sponsors National Board for Certification which certifies labs and technicians. *Journal of Dental Technology* classifieds are online.

⚕⌐ **National Board for Certification in Dental Technology (NBC)**, 325 John Knox Road #L103, Tallahassee, Florida 32303; 800/684-5310. (**http://www.nbccert.org**, adrienne@nbccert.org) Contact for information on requirements for certification.

⚕ **National Dental Assistants Association (NDAA)** - This is an auxiliary that serves minority Dental Assistants. Contact Christine Wright, President, at christine.wright@chsys.org or fax: 205/939-9796.

📁⌐ **University of Pittsburgh** - This is an excellent starting point for an Internet search involving the dental profession. The Internet site (**http://www.hsls.pitt.edu/intres/health/dental.html**) contains links to many dental information sites.

📃📁✍️🖱️ **WebDental (http://www.webdental.com)** Links to Web sites of colleges, laboratories, equipment suppliers, publications, and professional organizations. Classified section allows you to view job ads or post jobs wanted.

DISPENSING OPTICIANS

Significant Points
- Most dispensing opticians receive training on the job or through apprenticeships lasting 2 or more years; however, some employers seek graduates of post-secondary training programs in opticianry.
- About 20 states require a license.
- Projected average employment growth reflects the steady demand for corrective lenses and eyeglass frames that are in fashion.

Nature of the Work
Dispensing opticians fit eyeglasses and contact lenses, following prescriptions written by ophthalmologists or optometrists. (The work of optometrists is described in Chapter 10. See the statement in Chapter 10 on physicians and surgeons for information about ophthalmologists.)

Dispensing opticians examine written prescriptions to determine the specifications of lenses. They recommend eyeglass frames, lenses, and lens coatings after considering the prescription and the customer's occupation, habits, and facial features. Dispensing opticians measure clients' eyes, including the distance between the centers of the pupils and the distance between the ocular surface and the lens. For customers without prescriptions, dispensing opticians may use a focimeter to record eyeglass measurements in order to duplicate the eyeglasses. They also may obtain a customer's previous record to remake eyeglasses or contact lenses, or they may verify a prescription with the examining optometrist or ophthalmologist.

Dispensing opticians prepare work orders that give ophthalmic laboratory technicians information needed to grind and insert lenses into a frame. The work order includes prescriptions for lenses and information on their size, material, color, and style. Some dispensing opticians grind and insert lenses themselves. After the glasses are made, dispensing opticians verify that the lenses have been ground to specifications. Then they may reshape or bend the frame, by hand or using pliers, so that the eyeglasses fit the customer properly and comfortably. Some also fix, adjust, and refit broken frames. They instruct clients about adapting to, wearing, or caring for eyeglasses.

Some dispensing opticians, after additional education and training, specialize in fitting contacts, artificial eyes, or cosmetic shells to cover blemished eyes.

To fit contact lenses, dispensing opticians measure the shape and size of the eye, select the type of contact lens material, and prepare work orders specifying the prescription and lens size. Fitting contact lenses requires considerable skill, care, and patience. Dispensing opticians observe customers' eyes, corneas, lids, and contact lenses with specialized instruments and microscopes. During several follow-up visits, opticians teach proper insertion, removal, and care of contact lenses. Opticians do all this to ensure that the fit is correct.

Dispensing opticians keep records on customers' prescriptions, work orders, and payments; track inventory and sales; and perform other administrative duties.

Working Conditions

Dispensing opticians work indoors in attractive, well-lighted, and well-ventilated surroundings. They may work in medical offices or small stores where customers are served one at a time. Some work in large stores where several dispensing opticians serve a number of customers at once. Opticians spend a fair amount of time on their feet. If they prepare lenses, they need to take precautions against the hazards associated with glass cutting, chemicals, and machinery.

Most dispensing opticians work about 40 hours a week, although a few work longer hours. Those in retail stores may work evenings and weekends. Some work part time.

Training, Other Qualifications, and Advancement

Employers usually hire individuals with no background as an optician or as an ophthalmic laboratory technician. (See the statement on ophthalmic laboratory technicians in this chapter.) The employers then provide the required training. Most dispensing opticians receive training on the job or through apprenticeships lasting 2 or more years. Some employers, however, seek people with post-secondary training in the field.

Knowledge of physics, basic anatomy, algebra, and trigonometry as well as experience with computers is particularly valuable, because training usually includes instruction in optical mathematics, optical physics, and the use of precision measuring instruments and other machinery and tools. Dispensing opticians deal directly with the public, so they should be tactful, pleasant, and communicate well. Manual dexterity and the ability to do precision work are essential.

Large employers usually offer structured apprenticeship programs; small employers provide more informal, on-the-job training. About 20 states require dispensing opticians to be licensed. States may require individuals to pass one of more of the following for licensure: a state practical examination, a state written examination, and certification examinations offered by the American Board of Opticianry (ABO) and the National Contact Lens Examiners (NCLE). To qualify for the examinations, states often require applicants to complete postsecondary training or work from 2 to 4 years as apprentices. Continuing education is commonly required for licensure renewal. Information about specific licensing requirements is available from the state board of occupational licensing. Apprenticeships or formal training programs are offered in other states as well.

Apprentices receive technical training and learn office management and sales. Under the supervision of an experienced optician, optometrist, or ophthalmologist, apprentices work directly with patients, fitting eyeglasses and contact lenses.

Formal training in the field is offered in community colleges and a few colleges and universities. In 2004, the Commission on Opticianry Accreditation accredited 24 programs that awarded 2-year associate degrees. There also are shorter programs of 1 year or less. Some states that offer a license to dispensing opticians allow graduates to take the licensure exam immediately upon graduation; others require a few months to a year of experience.

Dispensing opticians may apply to the ABO and the NCLE for certification of their skills. All applicants age 18 or older with a high school diploma or equivalent are eligible for the exam; however, some state licensing boards have additional eligibility requirements. Certification must be renewed every 3 years through continuing education. Those licensed in states where licensure renewal requirements include continuing education credits may use proof of their renewed state license to meet the re-certification requirements of the ABO. Likewise, the NCLE will accept proof of renewal from any state that has contact lens requirements.

Many experienced dispensing opticians open their own optical stores. Others become managers of optical stores or sales representatives for wholesalers or manufacturers of eyeglasses or lenses.

Employment

Dispensing opticians held about 66,000 jobs in 2004. Nearly one-third worked in health and personal care stores, including optical goods stores. Many of these stores offer one-stop shopping. Customers may have their eyes examined, choose frames, and have glasses made on the spot. About 30 percent of dispensing opticians worked in offices of other health practitioners, including offices of optometrists. Over 10 percent worked in offices of physicians, including ophthalmologists who sell glasses directly to patients. Some work in optical departments of department stores or other general merchandise stores, such as warehouse clubs and superstores. Nearly 6 percent are self-employed and run their own unincorporated businesses.

Job Outlook

Employment of dispensing opticians is expected to grow about as fast as average for all occupations through 2014 as demand grows for corrective lenses. The number of middle-aged and elderly persons is projected to increase rapidly. Middle age is a time when many individuals use corrective lenses for the first time, and elderly persons generally require more vision care than others. Fashion also influences demand. Frames come in a growing variety of styles and colors — encouraging people to buy more than one pair.

Increasing awareness of laser surgery that corrects some vision problems will have an impact on demand for eyewear. Although the surgery remains relatively more expensive than eyewear, patients who successfully undergo this surgery may not require glasses or contact lenses for several years.

The need to replace those who leave the occupation will result in additional job openings. Nevertheless, the number of job openings will be limited because the occupation is small. Dispensing opticians are vulnerable to changes in the business cycle, because eyewear purchases often can be deferred for a time.

Earnings

Median annual earnings of dispensing opticians were $27,950 in May 2004. The middle 50 percent earned between $21,360 and $35,940. The lowest 10 percent earned less than $17,390, and the highest 10 percent earned more than $45,340. Median annual earnings in the industries employing the largest numbers of dispensing opticians in May 2004 were: Health and personal care stores, $30,890; Offices of physicians, $30,560; Offices of other health practitioners, $26,970.

Related Occupations

Other workers who deal with customers and perform delicate work include jewelers and precious stone and metal workers, locksmiths and safe repairers, orthotists and prosthetists, and precision instrument and equipment repairers.

DISPENSING OPTICIANS & OPHTHALMIC LABORATORY TECHNICIANS RESOURCES

Don't forget! Refer to the general resources listed in Chapter Three.

Association   Directory   Resume Service   Web Site
Job Ads   Job Alert E-mail/Hotline   Job Fairs   Book
For a full explanation of these resources see the second page of Chapter 3.

American Board of Opticianry (ABO) and **National Contact Lens Examiners (NCLE)** - 6506 Loisdale Rd., Suite 209, Springfield, VA 22150; 703/719-5800. (**http://www.abo.org**) The ABO and NCLE are national not-for-profit organizations for the voluntary certification of ophthalmic dispensers. The ABO certifies opticians.

Association of Technical Personnel in Ophthalmology (ATPO) - 2025 Woodlane Drive, Saint Paul, MN, 55125; call 800/482-4858. (**http://www.atpo.org**, ATPOmembership@jcahpo.org) Member organization allied with The Joint Commission on Allied Health Personnel in Ophthalmology. Has extensive job listings by region on web, open to public. Student membership $20. Promotes educational opportunities for allied health personnel in ophthalmology.

♈ ↻ **Commission on Opticianry Accreditation** - 8665 Sudley Road, #341, Manassas, VA 20110; 703/ 941- 9110. Accrediting organization for optician programs. (**http://www.coaccreditation.com**)

▭╱↻ **Consortium of Ophthalmic Training Programs (COTP)** (**http://www.cotpweb.org**, info@cotpweb.org) Organization of post-secondary educational institutions with an online directory educational programs for ophthalmic medical assistants, ophthalmic medical technicians, and ophthalmic medical technologists.

♈ ↻ **The Joint Commission on Allied Health Personnel in Ophthalmology (JCAHPO)** - 2025 Woodlane Drive, St. Paul, MN 55125-2995; 651/731-2944 or 800/284-3937.Certification agency for all allied health professionals in ophthalmology. Has home study courses for assistants. (**http://www.jcahpo.org**, jcahpo@jcahpo.org)

♈▤✍↻ National Academy of Opticianry (NAO) - 8401 Corporate Dr., Suite 605, Landover, Maryland 20785; 301/577-4828 or 800/229-4828. (**http://www.nao.org**, info@nao.org) Web site has a job bank and résumé upload service.

♈▭╱↻ **National Federation of Opticianry Schools (NFOS)** 1238 Robinson Point Road, Mountain Home, Arkansas 72653; 870/492-6623. Their Web site at (**http://www.nfos.org**) lists education programs by state, colleges offering opticianry degrees through distance education, and has extensive links to eye care organizations and journals.

▢ **Opportunities in Eye Care Careers** by Kathleen Belikoff, 2003, paperback. $12.95. Published by McGraw-Hill. ISBN: 007141150X.

♈▭╱↻ **Optical Laboratories Association (OLA)** - 11096 Lee Highway, Suite A-101, Fairfax, VA 22030-5039; 800-477-5652, 703/ 359-2830. Their Web site at (**http://www.ola-labs.org**, ola@ola-labs.org) includes summer student internship information and allows searches for OLA member laboratories by name, state or country.

♈▤▭✍↻ Opticians Association of America (OAA) - 441 Carlisle Drive, Herndon Virginia 20170; 703/437-8780. (**http://www.oaa.org**, oaa@oaa.org) Members consist of dispensing opticians, state opticians' associations, and retail optical companies. Web site has job listings and résumé upload service.

MEDICAL, DENTAL, AND OPHTHALMIC LABORATORY TECHNICIANS

Significant Points

- Around 3 out of 5 salaried jobs were in medical equipment and supply manufacturing laboratories, which usually are small, privately owned businesses with fewer than 5 employees.
- Most medical, dental, and ophthalmic laboratory technicians learn their craft on the job; however, many employers prefer to hire those with formal training in a related field.
- Slower-than-average employment growth is expected for dental and ophthalmic laboratory technicians, while average employment growth is expected for medical appliance technicians.
- Job opportunities should be favorable as employers have difficulty filling trainee positions.

Nature of the Work

When patients require a special appliance to see clearly, chew and speak well, or walk, their health care providers send requests to medical, dental, and ophthalmic laboratory technicians. These technicians produce a wide variety of appliances to help patients.

Medical appliance technicians construct, fit, maintain, and repair braces, artificial limbs, joints, arch supports, and other surgical and medical appliances. They read prescriptions or detailed information from orthotists, podiatrists, or prosthetists. Orthotists treat patients who need braces, supports, or corrective shoes. Podiatrists are doctors who treat foot problems and request the same appliances as orthotists. Prosthetists work with patients who need a replacement limb, such as an arm, leg, hand, or foot, due to a birth defect or an accident. The appliances are called orthoses and prostheses. Medical appliance technicians are also referred to as orthotic and prosthetic technicians.

For orthoses such as arch supports, technicians first make a wax or plastic impression of the patient's foot. Then they bend and form a material so that it conforms to prescribed contours required to fabricate structural components. If a support is mainly required to correct the balance of a patient with legs of different lengths, a rigid material is used. If the support is primarily intended to protect those with arthritic or diabetic feet, a soft material is used. Supports and braces are polished with grinding and buffing wheels. Technicians may cover arch supports with felt to make them more comfortable.

For prostheses, technicians construct or receive a plaster cast of the patient's limb to use as a pattern. Then, they lay out parts and use precision measuring instruments to measure them. Technicians may use wood, plastic, metal, or other material for the parts of the artificial limb. Next, they carve, cut, or grind the material using hand or power tools. Then, they drill holes for rivets and glue, rivet, or weld the parts together. They are able to do very precise work using common tools. Next, technicians use grinding and buffing wheels to smooth and polish artificial limbs. Lastly, they may cover or pad the limbs with rubber, leather, felt, plastic, or another material. Also, technicians may mix pigments according to formulas to match the patient's skin color and apply the mixture to the artificial limb.

After fabrication, medical appliance technicians test devices for proper alignment, movement, and biomechanical stability using meters and alignment fixtures. They also may fit the appliance on the patient and adjust them as necessary. Over time the appliance will wear down, so technicians must repair and maintain the device. They also may service and repair the machinery used for the fabrication of orthotic and prosthetic devices.

Dental laboratory technicians fill prescriptions from dentists for crowns, bridges, dentures, and other dental prosthetics. First, dentists send a specification of the item to be manufactured, along with an impression (mold) of the patient's mouth or teeth. Then, dental laboratory technicians, also called dental technicians, create a model of the patient's mouth by pouring plaster into the impression and allowing it to set. Next, they place the model on an apparatus that mimics the bite and movement of the patient's jaw. The model serves as the basis of the prosthetic device. Technicians examine the model, noting the size and shape of the adjacent teeth, as well as gaps within the gumline. Based upon these observations and the dentist's specifications, technicians build and shape a wax tooth or teeth model, using small hand instruments called wax spatulas and wax carvers. They use this wax model to cast the metal framework for the prosthetic device.

After the wax tooth has been formed, dental technicians pour the cast and form the metal and, using small hand-held tools, prepare the surface to allow the metal and porcelain to bond. They then apply porcelain in layers, to arrive at the precise shape and color of a tooth. Technicians place the tooth in a porcelain furnace to bake the porcelain onto the metal framework, and then adjust the shape and color, with subsequent grinding and addition of porcelain to achieve a sealed finish. The final product is a nearly exact replica of the lost tooth or teeth.

In some laboratories, technicians perform all stages of the work, whereas, in other labs, each technician does only a few. Dental laboratory technicians can specialize in 1 of 5 areas: orthodontic appliances, crowns and bridges, complete dentures, partial dentures, or ceramics. Job titles reflect specialization in these areas. For example, technicians who make porcelain and acrylic restorations are called dental ceramists.

Ophthalmic laboratory technicians—also known as manufacturing opticians, optical mechanics, or optical goods workers—make prescription eyeglass or contact lenses. Prescription lenses are curved in such a way that light is correctly focused onto the retina of the patient's eye, improving his or her vision. Some ophthalmic laboratory technicians manufacture lenses for other optical instruments, such as telescopes and binoculars. Ophthalmic laboratory technicians cut, grind, edge, and finish lenses according to specifications provided by dispensing opticians, optometrists, or ophthalmologists and may insert lenses into frames to produce finished glasses. Although some lenses still are produced by hand, technicians are increasingly using automated equipment to make lenses.

Ophthalmic laboratory technicians should not be confused with workers in other vision care occupations. Ophthalmologists and optometrists are "eye doctors" who examine eyes, diagnose and treat vision problems, and prescribe corrective lenses. Ophthalmologists are physicians who perform eye surgery. Dispensing opticians, who also may do the work of ophthalmic laboratory technicians, help patients select frames and lenses, and adjust finished eyeglasses. (See the statements in Chapter 10 on optometrists and on physicians and surgeons, which includes ophthalmologists, as well as the statements on and dispensing opticians above.)

Ophthalmic laboratory technicians read prescription specifications, select standard glass or plastic lens blanks, and then mark them to indicate where the curves specified on the prescription should be ground. They place the lens in the lens grinder, set the dials for the prescribed curvature, and start the machine. After a minute or so, the lens is ready to be "finished" by a machine that rotates it against a fine abrasive, to grind it and smooth out rough edges. The lens is then placed in a polishing machine with an even finer abrasive, to polish it to a smooth, bright finish.

Next, the technician examines the lens through a lensometer, an instrument similar in shape to a microscope, to make sure that the degree and placement of the curve are correct. The technician then cuts the lenses and bevels the edges to fit the frame, dips each lens into dye if the prescription calls for tinted or coated lenses, polishes the edges, and assembles the lenses and frame parts into a finished pair of glasses.

In small laboratories, technicians usually handle every phase of the operation. In large ones, in which virtually every phase of the operation is automated, technicians may be responsible for operating computerized equipment. Technicians also inspect the final product for quality and accuracy.

Working Conditions

Medical, dental, and ophthalmic laboratory technicians generally work in clean, well-lighted, and well-ventilated laboratories. They have limited contact with the public. Salaried laboratory technicians usually work 40 hours a week, but some work part time. At times, technicians wear goggles to protect their eyes, gloves to handle hot objects, or masks to avoid inhaling dust. They may spend a great deal of time standing.

Dental technicians usually have their own workbenches, which can be equipped with Bunsen burners, grinding and polishing equipment, and hand instruments, such as wax spatulas and wax carvers. Some dental technicians have computer-aided milling equipment to assist them with creating artificial teeth.

Training, Other Qualifications, and Advancement

Most medical, dental, and ophthalmic laboratory technicians learn their craft on the job; however, many employers prefer to hire those with formal training in a related field.

Medical appliance technicians begin as a helper and gradually learn new skills as they gain experience. Formal training is also available. There are currently 4 programs actively accredited by the National Commission on Orthotic and Prosthetic Education (NCOPE). These programs offer either an associate degree for orthotics and prosthetic technicians or one-year certificate for orthotic technicians or prosthetic technicians. The programs instruct students on human anatomy and physiology, orthotic and prosthetic equipment and materials, and applied biomechanical principles to customize orthoses or prostheses. The programs also include clinical rotations to provide hands-on experience.

Voluntary certification is available through the American Board for Certification in Orthotics and Prosthetics (ABC). Applicants are eligible for an exam after completing a program accredited by NCOPE or obtaining two years of experience as a technician under the direct supervision of an ABC-certified practitioner. After successfully passing the appropriate exam, technicians receive the Registered Orthotic Technician, Registered Prosthetic Technician, or Registered Prosthetic-Orthotic Technician credential.

High school students interested in becoming medical appliance technicians should take mathematics, metal and wood shop, and drafting. With additional formal education, medical appliance technicians can advance to become orthotists or prosthetists.

Dental laboratory technicians begin with simple tasks, such as pouring plaster into an impression, and progress to more complex procedures, such as making porcelain crowns and bridges. Becoming a fully trained technician requires an average of 3 to 4 years, depending upon the individual's aptitude and ambition, but it may take a few years more to become an accomplished technician.

Training in dental laboratory technology also is available through community and junior colleges, vocational-technical institutes, and the U.S. Armed Forces. Formal training programs vary greatly both in length and in the level of skill they impart.

In 2004, 25 programs in dental laboratory technology were approved (accredited) by the Commission on Dental Accreditation in conjunction with the American Dental Association (ADA). These programs provide classroom instruction in dental materials science, oral anatomy, fabrication procedures, ethics, and related subjects. In addition, each student is given supervised practical experience in a school or an associated dental laboratory. Accredited programs normally take 2 years to complete and lead to an associate degree. A few programs take about 4 years to complete and offer a bachelor's degree.

Graduates of 2-year training programs need additional hands-on experience to become fully qualified. Each dental laboratory owner operates in a different way, and classroom instruction does not necessarily expose students to techniques and procedures favored by individual laboratory owners. Students who have taken enough courses to learn the basics of the craft usually are considered good candidates for training, regardless of whether they have completed a formal program. Many employers will train someone without any classroom experience.

The National Board for Certification, an independent board established by the National Association of Dental Laboratories, offers certification in dental laboratory technology. Certification, which is voluntary, can be obtained in five specialty areas: crowns and bridges, ceramics, partial dentures, complete dentures, and orthodontic appliances.

In large dental laboratories, technicians may become supervisors or managers. Experienced technicians may teach or may take jobs with dental suppliers in such areas as product development, marketing, and sales. Still, for most technicians, opening one's own laboratory is the way toward advancement and higher earnings.

A high degree of manual dexterity, good vision, and the ability to recognize very fine color shadings and variations in shape are necessary. An artistic aptitude for detailed and precise work also is important. High school students interested in becoming dental laboratory technicians should take courses in art, metal and wood shop, drafting, and sciences. Courses in management and business may help those wishing to operate their own laboratories.

Ophthalmic laboratory technicians start on simple tasks if they are trained to produce lenses by hand. They may begin with marking or blocking lenses for grinding; then, they progress to grinding, cutting, edging, and beveling lenses; finally, they are trained in assembling the eyeglasses. Depending on individual aptitude, it may take up to 6 months to become proficient in all phases of the work.

Employers filling trainee jobs prefer applicants who are high school graduates. Courses in science, mathematics, and computers are valuable; manual dexterity and the ability to do precision work are essential. Technicians using automated systems will find computer skills valuable.

A very small number of ophthalmic laboratory technicians learn their trade in the Armed Forces or in the few programs in optical technology offered by vocational-technical institutes or trade schools. These programs have classes in optical theory, surfacing and lens finishing, and the reading and applying of prescriptions. Programs vary in length from 6 months to 1 year and award certificates or diplomas.

Ophthalmic laboratory technicians can become supervisors and managers. Some become dispensing opticians, although further education or training generally is required in that occupation.

Employment

Medical, dental, and ophthalmic laboratory technicians held about 87,000 jobs in 2004. Around 3 out of 5 salaried jobs were in medical equipment and supply manufacturing laboratories, which usually are small, privately owned businesses with fewer than five employees. However, some laboratories are large; a few employ more than 1,000 workers. Employment by detailed occupation is presented in the following tabulation:

Dental laboratory technicians	50,000
Ophthalmic laboratory technicians	25,000
Medical appliance technicians	11,000

Some medical appliance technicians work in health and personal care stores, while others work in public and private hospitals, professional and commercial equipment and supplies merchant wholesalers, offices of physicians, or consumer goods rental centers. Some are self-employed.

Some dental laboratory technicians work in offices of dentists. Others work for hospitals providing dental services, including U.S. Department of Veterans Affairs hospitals. Some technicians open their own offices or work in dental laboratories in their homes.

Around 30 percent of ophthalmic laboratory technicians work in health and personal care stores, such as optical goods stores that manufacture and sell prescription glasses and contact lenses. Some are in offices of optometrists or ophthalmologists. Others work at professional and commercial equipment and supplies merchant wholesalers. A few work in commercial and service industry machine manufacturing firms that produce lenses for other optical instruments, such as telescopes and binoculars.

Job Outlook

Job opportunities for medical, dental, and ophthalmic laboratory technicians should be favorable, despite expected slower-than-average growth in overall employment through the year 2014. Employers have difficulty filling trainee positions, probably because entry-level salaries are relatively low and because the public is not familiar with these occupations. Most job openings will arise from replacing technicians who transfer to other occupations or who leave the labor force.

Medical appliance technicians will grow faster than dental and ophthalmic laboratory technicians, with employment projected to increase about as fast as the average for all occupations, due to the increasing prevalence of the two leading causes of limb loss—diabetes and cardiovascular disease. Advances in technology may spur demand for prostheses that allow for greater movement.

During the last few years, demand has arisen from an aging public that is growing increasingly interested in cosmetic prostheses. For example, many dental laboratories are filling orders for composite fillings that are the same shade of white as natural teeth to replace older, less attractive fillings. However, job growth for dental laboratory technicians will be limited. The overall dental health of the population has improved because of fluoridation of drinking water, which has reduced the incidence of dental cavities, and greater emphasis on preventive dental care since the early 1960s. As a result, full dentures will be less common, as most people will need only a bridge or crown.

Demographic trends also make it likely that many more Americans will need vision care in the years ahead. Not only will the population grow, but also, the proportion of middle-aged and older adults is projected to increase rapidly. Middle age is a time when many people use corrective lenses for the first time, and elderly persons usually require more vision care than others. However, the increasing use of automated machinery will limit job growth for ophthalmic laboratory technicians.

Earnings

Median hourly earnings of medical appliance technicians were $13.38 in May 2004. The middle 50 percent earned between $10.46 and $18.22 an hour. The lowest 10 percent earned less than $8.21, and the highest 10 percent earned more than $23.66 an hour. Median hourly earnings of medical appliance technicians in May 2004 were $13.00 in medical equipment and supplies manufacturing.

Median hourly earnings of dental laboratory technicians were $14.93 in May 2004. The middle 50 percent earned between $11.18 and $19.71 an hour. The lowest 10 percent earned less than $8.86, and the highest 10 percent earned more than $25.48 an hour. Median hourly earnings of dental laboratory technicians in May 2004 were $15.95 in offices of dentists and $14.40 in medical equipment and supplies manufacturing.

Dental technicians in large laboratories tend to specialize in a few procedures and, therefore, tend to be paid a lower wage than those employed in small laboratories who perform a variety of tasks.

Median hourly earnings of ophthalmic laboratory technicians were $11.40 in May 2004. The middle 50 percent earned between $9.33 and $14.67 an hour. The lowest 10 percent earned less than $7.89, and the highest 10 percent earned more than $17.61 an hour. Median hourly earnings of ophthalmic laboratory technicians in May 2004 were $10.88 in health and personal care stores and $10.79 in medical equipment and supplies manufacturing.

Related Occupations

Medical, dental, and ophthalmic laboratory technicians manufacture a variety of health implements, such as artificial limbs, corrective lenses, and artificial teeth, following specifications and instructions provided by health care practitioners. Other workers who make and repair medical devices or other items include dispensing opticians, orthotists and prosthetists, and precision instrument and equipment repairers.

MEDICAL LABORATORY TECHNICIANS

Resources for Dental Laboratory Technicians are combined with Dental Hygienists & Dental Assistants as most resources serve all three professions. See the end of the Dental Assistants section.

Resources for Ophthalmic Laboratory Technicians are combined with Dispensing Opticians as most resources serve both professions. See the end of the Dispensing Opticians section.

Don't forget! Refer to the general resources listed in Chapter Three.

☤Association   ⌷Directory   ✍Resume Service   ✇Web Site

▤Job Ads   ⚡Job Alert E-mail/Hotline   ☞Job Fairs   📖Book

For a full explanation of these resources see the second page of Chapter 3.

☤ ⌷ ✇ **American Academy of Orthotists and Prosthetists (AAOP)**-
526 King Street, Suite 201, Alexandria, Virginia 22314; 703/836-0788.
(**http://www.opcareers.org/**, careers@oandp.org) Information on careers
and directory of education programs in orthotics and prosthetics.

☤ ⌷ ✇ **National Commission on Orthotic and Prosthetic Education**
(NCOPE) - 330 John Carlyle St., Suite 200, Alexandria, Virginia 22314;
703/836-7114. (**http://www.ncope.org/**, info@ncope.org) Student section
of web site has a list of accredited programs for orthotic and prosthetic
technicians.

EMERGENCY MEDICAL TECHNICIANS
and PARAMEDICS

Significant Points
- Because emergency services function 24 hours a day, emergency
  medical technicians and paramedics have irregular working hours.
- Emergency medical technicians and paramedics need formal training
  and certification, but requirements vary by state.
- Employment is projected to grow much faster than average as paid
  emergency medical technician positions replace unpaid volunteers.
- Competition will be greater for jobs in local fire, police, and rescue
  squad departments than in private ambulance services; opportunities will be best for those who have advanced certification.

Nature of the Work
People's lives often depend on the quick reaction and competent
care of emergency medical technicians (EMTs) and paramedics—EMTs
with additional advanced training to perform more difficult prehospital
medical procedures. Incidents such as automobile accidents, heart attacks, drownings, childbirth, and gunshot wounds all require immediate
medical attention. EMTs and paramedics provide this attention as they
care for and transport the sick or injured to a medical facility.

In an emergency, EMTs and paramedics typically are dispatched to the scene by a 911 operator, and often work with police and fire department personnel. Once they arrive, they determine the nature and extent of the patient's condition while trying to ascertain whether the patient has preexisting medical problems. Following strict rules and guidelines, they give appropriate emergency care and, when necessary, transport the patient. Some paramedics are trained to treat patients with minor injuries on the scene of an accident or at their home without transporting them to a medical facility. Emergency treatment for more complicated problems is carried out under the direction of medical doctors by radio preceding or during transport.

EMTs and paramedics may use special equipment, such as backboards, to immobilize patients before placing them on stretchers and securing them in the ambulance for transport to a medical facility. Usually, one EMT or paramedic drives while the other monitors the patient's vital signs and gives additional care as needed. Some EMTs work as part of the flight crew of helicopters that transport critically ill or injured patients to hospital trauma centers.

At the medical facility, EMTs and paramedics help transfer patients to the emergency department, report their observations and actions to emergency room staff, and may provide additional emergency treatment. After each run, EMTs and paramedics replace used supplies and check equipment. If a transported patient had a contagious disease, EMTs and paramedics decontaminate the interior of the ambulance and report cases to the proper authorities.

Beyond these general duties, the specific responsibilities of EMTs and paramedics depend on their level of qualification and training. To determine this, the National Registry of Emergency Medical Technicians (NREMT) registers emergency medical service (EMS) providers at four levels: First Responder, EMT-Basic, EMT-Intermediate, and EMT- Paramedic. Some states, however, do their own certification and use numeric ratings from 1 to 4 to distinguish levels of proficiency.

The lowest-level workers—First Responders—are trained to provide basic emergency medical care because they tend to be the first persons to arrive at the scene of an incident. Many firefighters, police officers, and other emergency workers have this level of training. The EMT-Basic, also known as EMT-1, represents the first component of the emergency medical technician system. An EMT-1 is trained to care for patients at the accident and while transporting patients to the hospital under medical direction. The EMT-1 has the emergency skills to assess patient conditions, manage respiratory, cardiac, and trauma emergencies.

The EMT-Intermediate (EMT-2 and EMT-3) has more advanced training that allows the administration of intravenous fluids, the use of manual defibrillators to give lifesaving shocks to a stopped heart, and the application of advanced airway techniques and equipment to assist patients experiencing respiratory emergencies. EMT-Paramedics (EMT-4) provide the most extensive prehospital care. In addition to carrying out these procedures, paramedics may administer drugs orally and intravenously, interpret electrocardiograms (EKGs), perform endotracheal intubations, and use monitors and other complex equipment.

Working Conditions

EMTs and paramedics work both indoors and outdoors, in all types of weather. They are required to do considerable kneeling, bending, and heavy lifting. These workers risk noise-induced hearing loss from sirens and back injuries from lifting patients. In addition, EMTs and paramedics may be exposed to diseases such as hepatitis-B and AIDS, as well as violence from drug overdose victims or mentally unstable patients. The work is not only physically strenuous, but can be stressful, sometimes involving life-or-death situations and suffering patients. None the less, many people find the work exciting and challenging and enjoy the opportunity to help others.

EMTs and paramedics employed by fire departments work about 50 hours a week. Those employed by hospitals frequently work between 45 and 60 hours a week, and those in private ambulance services, between 45 and 50 hours. Some of these workers, especially those in police and fire departments, are on call for extended periods. Because emergency services function 24 hours a day, EMTs and paramedics have irregular working hours.

Training, Other Qualifications, and Advancement

Formal training and certification is needed to become an EMT or paramedic. A high school diploma is typically required to enter a formal training program. Some programs offer an associate degree along with the formal EMT training. All 50 states have a certification procedure. In most states and the District of Columbia, registration with the NREMT is required at some or all levels of certification. Other states administer their own certification examination or provide the option of taking the NREMT examination. To maintain certification, EMTs and paramedics must re-register, usually every 2 years. In order to reregister, an individual must be working as an EMT or paramedic and meet a continuing education requirement.

Training is offered at progressive levels: EMT-Basic, also known as EMT-1; EMT-Intermediate, or EMT-2 and EMT-3; and EMT-Paramedic, or EMT-4. EMT-Basic course-work typically emphasizes emergency skills, such as managing respiratory, trauma, and cardiac emergencies, and patient assessment. Formal courses are often combined with time in an emergency room or ambulance. The program also provides instruction and practice in dealing with bleeding, fractures, airway obstruction, cardiac arrest, and emergency childbirth. Students learn how to use and maintain common emergency equipment, such as backboards, suction devices, splints, oxygen delivery systems, and stretchers. Graduates of approved EMT basic training programs who pass a written and practical examination administered by the state certifying agency or the NREMT earn the title "Registered EMT-Basic." The course also is a prerequisite for EMT-Intermediate and EMT-Paramedic training.

EMT-Intermediate training requirements vary from state to state. Applicants can opt to receive training in EMT-Shock Trauma, wherein the caregiver learns to start intravenous fluids and give certain medications, or in EMT-Cardiac, which includes learning heart rhythms and administering advanced medications. Training commonly includes 35 to 55 hours of additional instruction beyond EMT-Basic coursework, and covers patient assessment as well as the use of advanced airway devices and intravenous fluids. Prerequisites for taking the EMT- Intermediate examination include registration as an EMT-Basic, required classroom work, and a specified amount of clinical experience.

The most advanced level of training for this occupation is EMT-Paramedic. At this level, the caregiver receives additional training in body function and learns more advanced skills. The Technology program usually lasts up to 2 years and results in an associate degree in applied science. Such education prepares the graduate to take the NREMT examination and become certified as an EMT-Paramedic. Extensive related coursework and clinical and field experience is required. Because of the longer training requirement, almost all EMT-Paramedics are in paid positions, rather than being volunteers. Refresher courses and continuing education are available for EMTs and paramedics at all levels.

EMTs and paramedics should be emotionally stable, have good dexterity, agility, and physical coordination, and be able to lift and carry heavy loads. They also need good eyesight (corrective lenses may be used) with accurate color vision.

Advancement beyond the EMT-Paramedic level usually means leaving fieldwork. An EMT-Paramedic can become a supervisor, operations manager, administrative director, or executive director of emergency services. Some EMTs and paramedics become instructors, dispatchers, or physician assistants, while others move into sales or marketing of emergency medical equipment. A number of people become EMTs and paramedics to assess their interest in health care, and then decide to return to school and become registered nurses, physicians, or other health workers.

Employment

EMTs and paramedics held about 192,000 jobs in 2004. Most career EMTs and paramedics work in metropolitan areas. Volunteer EMTs and paramedics are more common in small cities, towns, and rural areas. These individuals volunteer for fire departments, emergency medical services (EMS), or hospitals, and may respond to only a few calls for service per month or may answer the majority of calls, especially in smaller communities. EMTs and paramedics work closely with firefighters, who often are certified as EMTs as well and act as first responders. A large number of EMTs or paramedics belong to a union.

Full-time and part-time paid EMTs and paramedics were employed in a number of industries. About 4 out of 10 worked as employees of private ambulance services. About 3 out of 10 worked in local government for fire departments, public ambulance services, and EMS. Another 2 out of 10 were found in hospitals, working full time within the medical facility or responding to calls in ambulances or helicopters to transport critically ill or injured patients. The remainder worked in various industries providing emergency services.

Job Outlook

Employment of emergency medical technicians and paramedics is expected to grow much faster than the average for all occupations through 2014, as full-time paid EMTs and paramedics replace unpaid volunteers. As population and urbanization increase, and as a large segment of the population—aging baby boomers—becomes more likely to have medical emergencies, demand will increase for EMTs and paramedics. There will still be demand for part-time, volunteer EMTs and paramedics in rural areas and smaller metropolitan areas. In addition to jobs arising from growth, openings will occur because of replacement needs; turnover is relatively high in this occupation because of the limited potential for advancement and the modest pay and benefits in private-sector jobs.

Job opportunities should be best in private ambulance services. Competition will be greater for jobs in local government, including fire, police, and independent third-service rescue squad departments, in which salaries and benefits tend to be slightly better. EMTs and paramedics who have advanced certifications, such as EMT-Intermediate and EMT-Paramedic, should enjoy the most favorable job prospects as clients and patients demand higher levels of care before arriving at the hospital.

Earnings

Earnings of EMTs and paramedics depend on the employment setting and geographic location as well as the individual's training and experience. Median annual earnings of EMTs and paramedics were $25,310 in May 2004. The middle 50 percent earned between $19,970 and $33,210. The lowest 10 percent earned less than $16,090, and the highest 10 percent earned more than $43,240. Median annual earnings in the industries employing the largest numbers of EMTs and paramedics in May 2004 were: Local government, $27,710; General medical and surgical hospitals, $26,590; Other ambulatory health care services, $23,130.

Those in emergency medical services who are part of fire or police departments receive the same benefits as firefighters or police officers. For example, many are covered by pension plans that provide retirement at half pay after 20 or 25 years of service or if the worker is disabled in the line of duty.

Related Occupations

Other workers in occupations that require quick and level-headed reactions to life-or-death situations are air traffic controllers, firefighting occupations, physician assistants, police and detectives, and registered nurses.

EMERGENCY MEDICAL TECHNICIANS RESOURCES

Don't forget! Refer to the general resources listed in Chapter Three.

⚕Association   📁Directory   📇Resume Service   💾Web Site

📑Job Ads   📰Job Alert E-mail/Hotline   📖Job Fairs   📖Book

For a full explanation of these resources see the second page of Chapter 3.

📖 **EMT Career Starter, 2nd Edition** - LearningExpress, 2001, $15.95. 223 pages, ISBN: 1576853667. This book has a description of the job, financial aid information, and suggests resources for job opportunities.

⚕📑💾 **International Association of Flight Paramedics (IAFP)** - 4835 Riveredge Cove, Snellville, Georgia 30039; 770/979-6372. The web site **(http://www.flightparamedic.org)** has job ads and links to other job sites.

📑💾 **JEMS (Journal of Emergency Medical Services)** - JEMS Communications; 800/266-JEMS. **(http://www.jems.com)** Job s listed on line by state. Check college library stacks for this.

📑💾 **MERGInet** - **(http://www.merginet.com)** Resources for emergency, fire and rescue professionals include an EMS classified ads.

📁 **Municipal/County Executive Directory** - Carroll Publishing Company, 4701 Sangamore Road, #S-155, Bethesda, MD 20816; 800/336-4240. **(http://www.carrollpub.com)** Published twice a year, the municipal directory lists 7,900 municipalities and their officials; the county directory lists all the more than 3,000 counties and their officials. Check your local library; the contact information is not on the web.

⚕📑📁💾 **National Association of Emergency Medical Technicians (NAEMT)** - 132-A East Northside Drive, Clinton, MS 39056; 800/34-NAEMT, 601/924-7744. **(http://www.naemt.org**, info@naemt.org) Membership is for nationally registered or state certified EMTs. A few jobs currently listed on web site. Directory on web of locations of refresher courses by state, internationally and for the military.

⚕📑📁💾 **National Registry of Emergency Medical Technicians (NREMT)** - Rocco V. Morando Bldg., 6610 Busch Blvd., P.O. Box 29233, Columbus, OH 43229; 614/888-4484. **(http://www.nremt.org/)** Web site has information about education and exams with links to state offices and to other EMT web sites. Job ads online.

Chapter
6

DIETETICS, PHARMACY and THERAPY OCCUPATIONS

Tamara Theodore

Tamara Theodore is a private practice pediatric occupational therapist in Encino, California. "I always wanted to do something in the health field and originally considered being a pediatrician. However, I wanted a family someday and didn't think I could devote time to both. I had a blind date once, which turned out to be a man who was going to be an occupational therapist. He told me that it was a field in which the course of study was a blend of art, psychology, and medicine. That really intrigued me and so I began to pursue it."

She graduated from the University of Southern California in 1972 with a B. S. Degree. "After college, I took two required internships, one in mental health and one in physical disabilities. These were full time positions and, in the second one, I specialized in pediatrics at Children's Hospital of Los Angeles."

When asked for advice to people just starting out, Tamara replied, "Decide what area you want to work in and put your mind to it! When I started school, there were lots of jobs available. When I graduated there were very few. I decided I wanted to work in pediatrics, which was the hardest to get into. I volunteered after my internship was over until they created a position for me." Later, she needed field work experience for a Master's Program. "I went to a special school for children who could not be handled in the regular public school and asked for a volunteer position. They offered me a position as Director of Sensory Integration Therapy because I was an O.T. trained in this specialty. So hang in there!"

Currently, Tamara explains, the job market for occupational therapists is excellent. "The field is wide open, gives professional status, good income and plenty of challenge and variety. The thing that is great about this field is that there are never two days the same. One can create almost any kind of job environment they want, but the premise is always the same: helping people to develop, maintain or achieve maximum function for their developmental level."

The great variety in employment possibilities makes this career especially appealing. Tamara explains, "This job usually includes working closely with nursing and doing a lot of parent training and education. There are Early Intervention Programs across the nation for birth to three that are educationally based and state funded. These programs provide assistance to families with special needs children to help them to learn and develop in areas that are deficient in gross and fine motor skills, cognitive skills, language skills, social and emotional skills. Occupational therapists work with all types of people, ages and problems from premature infants to geriatrics and everything inbetween."

"I have been in this field for 30 years and really love it as much today as I did when I first started. I love working with small children. I love the mix of psychology, medicine and art. I love the opportunity to be creative. In 30 years of continuous learning, I still have so much more to learn." Tamara emphasizes the personality traits needed for success in this field. "I think it is important to want to help people and to have a genuine interest in their well being and a true caring for humankind to be a success in this field. Therapists have to be 'adaptive' and creative and need to enjoy problem solving. If you are that kind of person, go for it! The possibilities are almost endless; thus one can change jobs within the field, keeping it interesting and varied."

This chapter features health care dietetics, pharmacy, and therapy occupations. The major occupational groups are:

Dietitians and Nutritionists	**Recreational Therapists**
Occupational Therapists	**Respiratory Therapists**
Pharmacists	**Audiologists**
Physical Therapists	**Speech-Language Pathologists**

Each specialty is described below. Occupational groups are divided into primary and related occupations so that individuals can investigate other fields for additional job opportunities.

Following each job description are job resource lists: Associations, Books, Directories, Internet Sites, Job Ads, E-mail Job Notification/Job Hotlines, Job Fairs, and Résumé/Placement Services. Job sources are listed alphabetically with the larger sources underlined.

DIETITIANS AND NUTRITIONISTS

Significant Points
- Most jobs are in hospitals, nursing care facilities, and offices of physicians or other health practitioners.
- Dietitians and nutritionists need at least a bachelor's degree in dietetics, foods and nutrition, food service systems management, or a related area.
- Faster than average employment growth is expected; however, growth may be constrained if employers substitute other workers for dietitians and if limitations are placed on insurance reimbursement for dietetic services.
- Those who have specialized training in renal or diabetic diets or have a master's degree should experience good employment opportunities.

Nature of the Work
Dietitians and nutritionists plan food and nutrition programs and supervise the preparation and serving of meals. They help to prevent and treat illnesses by promoting healthy eating habits and recommending dietary modifications, such as the use of less salt for those with

high blood pressure or the reduction of fat and sugar intake for those who are overweight.

Dietitians manage food service systems for institutions such as hospitals and schools, promote sound eating habits through education, and conduct research. Major areas of practice include clinical, community, management, and consultant dietetics.

Clinical dietitians provide nutritional services for patients in institutions such as hospitals and nursing care facilities. They assess patients' nutritional needs, develop and implement nutrition programs, and evaluate and report the results. They also confer with doctors and other health care professionals to coordinate medical and nutritional needs. Some clinical dietitians specialize in the management of overweight patients or in the care of critically ill or renal (kidney) and diabetic patients. In addition, clinical dietitians in nursing care facilities, small hospitals, or correctional facilities may manage the food service department.

Community dietitians counsel individuals and groups on nutritional practices designed to prevent disease and promote health. Working in places such as public health clinics, home health agencies, and health maintenance organizations, community dietitians evaluate individual needs, develop nutritional care plans, and instruct individuals and their families. Dietitians working in home health agencies provide instruction on grocery shopping and food preparation to the elderly, individuals with special needs, and children.

Increased public interest in nutrition has led to job opportunities in food manufacturing, advertising, and marketing. In these areas, dietitians analyze foods, prepare literature for distribution, or report on issues such as the nutritional content of recipes, dietary fiber, or vitamin supplements.

Management dietitians oversee large-scale meal planning and preparation in health care facilities, company cafeterias, prisons, and schools. They hire, train, and direct other dietitians and food service workers; budget for and purchase food, equipment, and supplies; enforce sanitary and safety regulations; and prepare records and reports.

Consultant dietitians work under contract with health care facilities or in their own private practice. They perform nutrition screenings for their clients and offer advice on diet-related concerns such as weight loss and cholesterol reduction. Some work for wellness programs, sports teams, supermarkets, and other nutrition-related businesses. They may consult with food service managers, providing expertise in sanitation, safety procedures, menu development, budgeting, and planning.

Working Conditions

Most full-time dietitians and nutritionists work a regular 40-hour week, although some work weekends. About 1 in 4 worked part time in 2004. Dietitians and nutritionists usually work in clean, well-lighted, and well-ventilated areas. However, some dietitians work in warm, congested kitchens. Many dietitians and nutritionists are on their feet for much of the workday.

Training, Other Qualifications, and Advancement

High school students interested in becoming a dietitian or nutritionist should take courses in biology, chemistry, mathematics, health, and communications. Dietitians and nutritionists need at least a bachelor's degree in dietetics, foods and nutrition, food service systems management, or a related area. College students in these majors take courses in foods, nutrition, institution management, chemistry, biochemistry, biology, microbiology, and physiology. Other suggested courses include business, mathematics, statistics, computer science, psychology, sociology, and economics.

Of the 46 states and jurisdictions with laws governing dietetics, 31 require licensure, 14 require certification, and 1 requires registration. Requirements vary by state. As a result, interested candidates should determine the requirements of the state in which they want to work before sitting for any exam. Although not required, the Commission on Dietetic Registration of the American Dietetic Association (ADA) awards the Registered Dietitian credential to those who pass an exam after completing their academic coursework and supervised experience.

As of 2004, there were about 227 bachelor's and master's degree programs approved by the ADA's Commission on Accreditation for Dietetics Education (CADE).

Supervised practice experience can be acquired in two ways. The first requires the completion of a CADE-accredited program. As of 2004, there were more than 50 accredited programs, which combined academic and supervised practice experience and generally lasted 4 to 5 years. The second option requires the completion of 900 hours of supervised practice experience in any of the 265 CADE-accredited internships. These internships may be full-time programs lasting 6 to 12 months or part-time programs lasting 2 years. To maintain a registered dietitian status, at least 75 credit hours in approved continuing education classes are required every 5 years.

Students interested in research, advanced clinical positions, or public health may need an advanced degree.

Experienced dietitians may advance to management positions, such as assistant director, associate director, or director of a dietetic department, or may become self-employed. Some dietitians specialize in areas such as renal, diabetic, cardiovascular, or pediatric dietetics. Others may leave the occupation to become sales representatives for equipment, pharmaceutical, or food manufacturers.

Employment

Dietitians and nutritionists held about 50,000 jobs in 2004. More than half of all jobs were in hospitals, nursing care facilities, outpatient care centers, or offices of physicians and other health practitioners. State and local government agencies provided about 1 job in 5—mostly in correctional facilities, health departments, and other public health related areas. Some dietitians and nutritionists were employed in special food services, an industry made up of firms providing food services on contract to facilities such as colleges and universities, airlines, correctional facilities, and company cafeterias. Other jobs were in public and private educational services, community care facilities for the elderly (which includes assisted-living facilities), individual and family services, home health care services, and the federal government—mostly in the U.S. Department of Veterans Affairs.

Some dietitians were self-employed, working as consultants to facilities such as hospitals and nursing care facilities or providing dietary counseling to individuals.

Job Outlook

Employment of dietitians is expected to grow faster than the average for all occupations through 2014 as a result of increasing emphasis on disease prevention through improved dietary habits. A growing and aging population will boost the demand for meals and nutritional counseling in hospitals, residential care facilities, schools, prisons, community health programs, and home health care agencies.

Public interest in nutrition and increased emphasis on health education and prudent lifestyles also will spur demand, especially in management. In addition to employment growth, job openings will result from the need to replace experienced workers who leave the occupation.

The number of dietitian positions in nursing care facilities and in state government hospitals is expected to decline, as these establishments continue to contract with outside agencies for food services. However, employment is expected to grow rapidly in contract providers of food services, in outpatient care centers, and in offices of physicians and other health practitioners. With increased public awareness of obesity and diabetes, Medicare coverage may be expanded to include medical nutrition therapy for renal and diabetic patients. As a result, dietitians who have specialized training in renal or diabetic diets or have a master's degree should experience good employment opportunities.

Dietitian and nutritionist employment growth may be constrained if some employers substitute other workers, such as health educators, food service managers, and dietetic technicians. Growth also may be curbed by limitations on insurance reimbursement for dietetic services.

Earnings

Median annual earnings of dietitians and nutritionists were $43,630 in May 2004. The middle 50 percent earned between $35,940 and $53,370. The lowest 10 percent earned less than $27,500, and the highest 10 percent earned more than $63,760. In May 2004, median annual earnings in general medical and surgical hospitals, the industry employing the largest number of dietitians and nutritionists, were $44,050.

According to the American Dietetic Association, median annualized wages for registered dietitians in 2005 varied by practice area as follows: $53,800 in consultation and business; $60,000 in food and nutrition management; $60,200 in education and research; $48,800 in clinical nutrition/ambulatory care; $50,000 in clinical nutrition/long-term care; $44,800 in community nutrition; and $45,000 in clinical nutrition/acute care. Salaries also vary by years in practice, education level, geographic region, and size of the community.

Related Occupations

Workers in other occupations who may apply the principles of dietetics include food service managers, health educators, dietetic technicians, and registered nurses.

DIETICIANS & NUTRITIONISTS RESOURCES

Don't forget! Refer to the general resources listed in Chapter Three.

☤Association   ☐Directory   ✍Resume Service   ⌖Web Site

☐Job Ads   ⚡Job Alert E-mail/Hotline   ⚑Job Fairs   📖Book

For a full explanation of these resources see the second page of Chapter 3.

☤☐⌖ **The American Dietetic Association (ADA)** - 120 South Riverside Plaza, Suite 2000, Chicago, Illinois 60606-6995; 800/877-1600. (**http://www.eatright.org**, education@eatright.org) An organization of food and nutrition professionals, with nearly 65,000 members. The membership includes dietitians, dietetic technicians, students and others. Web site has listing by state of accredited education programs, listing of state associations, and link to HealtheCareers web site for job listings. Student membership $43/yr gives access to information about dietetic internships and financial aid opportunities—including scholarships offered only to ADA members.

☤☐⌖ **School Nutrition Association (SNA)** - 700 South Washington St., Suite 300, Alexandria, VA 22314; 703/739-3900. (servicecenter@ choolnutrition.org, **www.schoolnutrition.org**). Association of school food service professionals has a voluntary certification program for its members. Has a Credentialing Exam Study Guide to help members study for the credentialing exam, and online education courses. Provides regulatory information, scholarship assistance for professional development and to pass the GED. Job bank allows job search by job category.

⌖ **Arbor Nutrition Guide** - (**http://www.arborcom**). Sponsored by Dr. Tony Helman, this site is a search engine for information on diet and dietetics.

⌖ **The Blonz Guide, Nutrition, Food & Health Resources** - (http://www.blonz.com) Written by Edward Blonz, a science journalist. Links to web pages on many nutrition topics. The "It's Academic" area of the web site at has an alphabetical list of nutrition schools and departments.

California Dietetic Association (CDA) - 7740 Manchester Ave., Suite 102, Playa del Rey, CA 90293-8499; or call 310/822-0177. Visit their web site at **(www.dietitian.org**, bridget@dietitian.org). Open job ad listings, scholarship program, and mentoring program for members.

Careers In Nutrition - by Linda Bickerstaff, Rosen Publishing Group, 2005. ISBN: 1404202498 Most recent book on jobs in the field. Discusses job qualifications, possibilities, and education.

Dietitians of Canada - **(www.dietitians.ca)** National accrediting body for training programs credentialing dietitians in Canada. Information on accredited educational programs, internships and becoming accredited as a dietitian in Canada. (centralinfo@dietitians.ca)

Food and Nutrition Information Center of the USDA - Click on their site at **(http://www.nalusda.gov/fnic)** for "Topics A-Z". This section of the web site has links to associations and colleges, directories, and electronic publications.

Institute of Food Technologists - 525 W. Van Buren, Ste. 1000, Chicago, IL 60607; 312/782-8424, 800/234-0270. **(http://www.ift.org**, info@ift.org) Education section of web site lists both undergraduate and graduate programs, and gives information on scholarships. Employment/Career Center allows upload of résumé s and has job listings.

Nutritionjobs - **(http://www.nutritionjobs.com)** Employment service free to applicant. Post job résumé or search for jobs by state. Sign up for e-newsletter or view job hunting advice.

Opportunities in Nutrition Careers - by Carol Coles Caldwell, McGraw-Hill, 1999. ISBN: 0844232408. Describes the career and gives aids in finding a job.

Society for Nutrition Education (SNE) - 7150 Winton Drive, Suite 300, Indianapolis, Indiana 46268; 317/328-4627 or 800/235-6690. **(http://www.sne.org/)** Association of nutrition educators. Jobs are posted on the web site and members can receive job notices by email. The web site has information on careers in human Nutrition/Dietetics.

PHARMACISTS

OCCUPATIONAL TITLES:

Nutrition support pharmacists   Pharmacotherapists
Pharmacists   Radiopharmacists

Significant Points

- Very good employment opportunities are expected for pharmacists.
- Earnings are high, but some pharmacists work long hours, nights, weekends, and holidays.
- Pharmacists are becoming more involved in making decisions regarding drug therapy and in counseling patients.
- A license is required; the prospective pharmacist must graduate from an accredited college of pharmacy and pass a state examination.

Nature of the Work

Pharmacists distribute drugs prescribed by physicians and other health practitioners and provide information to patients about medications and their use. They advise physicians and other health practitioners on the selection, dosages, interactions, and side effects of medications. Pharmacists also monitor the health and progress of patients in response to drug therapy to ensure the safe and effective use of medication. Pharmacists must understand the use, clinical effects, and composition of drugs, including their chemical, biological, and physical properties. Compounding—the actual mixing of ingredients to form powders, tablets, capsules, ointments, and solutions—is a small part of a pharmacist's practice, because most medicines are produced by pharmaceutical companies in a standard dosage and drug delivery form. Most pharmacists work in a community setting, such as a retail drugstore, or in a health care facility, such as a hospital, nursing home, mental health institution, or neighborhood health clinic.

Pharmacists in community and retail pharmacies counsel patients and answer questions about prescription drugs, including questions regarding possible side effects or interactions among various drugs. They provide information about over-the-counter drugs and make recommendations after talking with the patient. They also may give advice about the patient's diet, exercise, or stress management or about durable medical equipment and home health care supplies. In addition, they also may complete third-party insurance forms and other paper-work. Those who own or manage community pharmacies may sell non-health-related merchandise, hire and supervise personnel, and oversee the general operation of the pharmacy. Some community pharmacists provide specialized services to help patients manage conditions such as diabetes, asthma, smoking cessation, or high blood pressure. Some community pharmacists also are trained to administer vaccinations.

Pharmacists in health care facilities dispense medications and advise the medical staff on the selection and effects of drugs. They may make sterile solutions to be administered intravenously. They also assess, plan, and monitor drug programs or regimens. Pharmacists counsel hospitalized patients on the use of drugs and on their use at home when the patients are discharged. Pharmacists also may evaluate drug-use patterns and outcomes for patients in hospitals or managed care organizations.

Pharmacists who work in home health care monitor drug therapy and prepare infusions—solutions that are injected into patients—and other medications for use in the home.

Some pharmacists specialize in specific drug therapy areas, such as intravenous nutrition support, oncology (cancer), nuclear pharmacy (used for chemotherapy), geriatric pharmacy, and psychopharmacotherapy (the treatment of mental disorders by means of drugs).

Most pharmacists keep confidential computerized records of patients' drug therapies to prevent harmful drug interactions. Pharmacists are responsible for the accuracy of every prescription that is filled, but they often rely upon pharmacy technicians and pharmacy aides to assist them in the dispensing process. Thus, the pharmacist may delegate prescription-filling and administrative tasks and supervise their completion. Pharmacists also frequently oversee pharmacy students serving as interns in preparation for graduation and licensure.

Increasingly, pharmacists are pursuing nontraditional pharmacy work. Some are involved in research for pharmaceutical manufacturers, developing new drugs and therapies and testing their effects on people. Others work in marketing or sales, providing expertise to clients on a drug's use, effectiveness, and possible side effects. Some pharmacists work for health insurance companies, developing pharmacy benefit packages and carrying out cost-benefit analyses on certain drugs. Other pharmacists work for the government, public health care services, the armed services, and pharmacy associations. Finally, some pharmacists are employed full time or part time as college faculty, teaching classes and performing research in a wide range of areas.

Working Conditions

Pharmacists work in clean, well-lighted, and well-ventilated areas. Many pharmacists spend most of their workday on their feet. When working with sterile or dangerous pharmaceutical products, pharmacists wear gloves and masks and work with other special protective equipment. Many community and hospital pharmacies are open for extended hours or around the clock, so pharmacists may work nights, weekends, and holidays. Consultant pharmacists may travel to nursing homes or other facilities to monitor patients' drug therapy.

About 21 percent of pharmacists worked part time in 2004. Most full-time salaried pharmacists worked approximately 40 hours a week. Some, including many self-employed pharmacists, worked more than 50 hours a week.

Training, Other Qualifications, and Advancement

A license to practice pharmacy is required in all states, the District of Columbia, and all U.S. territories. To obtain a license, the prospective pharmacist must graduate from a college of pharmacy that is accredited by the Accreditation Council for Pharmacy Education (ACPE) and pass an examination. All states require the North American Pharmacist Licensure Exam (NAPLEX), which tests pharmacy skills and knowledge, and 43 states and the District of Columbia require the Multistate Pharmacy Jurisprudence Exam (MPJE), which tests pharmacy law. Both exams are administered by the National Association of Boards of Pharmacy. Pharmacists in the eight states that do not require the MJPE must pass a state-specific exam that is similar to the MJPE. In addition to the NAPLEX and MPJE, some states require additional exams unique to their state. All states except California currently grant a license without extensive reexamination to qualified pharmacists who already are licensed by another state. In Florida, reexamination is not required if a pharmacist has passed the NAPLEX and MPJE within 12 years of his or her application for a license transfer. Many pharmacists are licensed to practice in more than one state. Most states require continuing education for license renewal. Persons interested in a career as a pharmacist should check with individual state boards of pharmacy for details on examination requirements, license renewal requirements, and license transfer procedures.

In 2004, 89 colleges of pharmacy were accredited to confer degrees by the Accreditation Council for Pharmacy Education. Pharmacy programs grant the degree of Doctor of Pharmacy (Pharm.D.), which requires at least 6 years of postsecondary study and the passing of a state board of pharmacy's licensure examination. Courses offered at colleges of pharmacy are designed to teach students about all aspects of drug therapy. In addition, schools teach students how to communicate with patients and other health care providers about drug information and patient care. Students also learn professional ethics, how to develop and manage medication distribution systems, and concepts of public health. In addition to receiving classroom instruction, students in Pharm.D. programs spend about one-fourth of their time learning in a variety of pharmacy practice settings under the supervision of licensed pharmacists. The Pharm.D. degree has replaced the Bachelor of Pharmacy (B.Pharm.) degree, which is no longer being awarded.

The Pharm.D. is a 4-year program that requires at least 2 years of college study prior to admittance, although most applicants have completed 3 years. Entry requirements usually include courses in mathematics and natural sciences, such as chemistry, biology, and physics, as well as courses in the humanities and social sciences. Approximately two-thirds of all colleges require applicants to take the Pharmacy College Admissions Test (PCAT).

In 2003, the American Association of Colleges of Pharmacy (AACP) launched the Pharmacy College Application Service, also known as PharmCAS, for students who are interested in applying to schools and colleges of pharmacy. This centralized service allows applicants to use a single Web-based application and one set of transcripts to apply to multiple schools of pharmacy. A total of 43 schools participated in 2003.

In the 2003–04 academic year, 67 colleges of pharmacy awarded the master-of-science degree or the Ph.D. degree. Both degrees are awarded after the completion of a Pharm.D. degree and are designed for those who want more laboratory and research experience. Many master's and Ph.D. degree holders do research for a drug company or teach at a university. Other options for pharmacy graduates who are interested in further training include 1-year or 2-year residency programs or fellowships. Pharmacy residencies are postgraduate training programs in pharmacy practice and usually require the completion of a research study. There currently are more than 700 residency training programs nationwide. Pharmacy fellowships are highly individualized programs that are designed to prepare participants to work in a specialized area of pharmacy, such clinical practice or research laboratories. Some pharmacists who run their own pharmacy obtain a master's degree in business administration (MBA). Others may obtain a degree in public administration or public health.

Areas of graduate study include pharmaceutics and pharmaceutical chemistry (physical and chemical properties of drugs and dosage forms), pharmacology (effects of drugs on the body), toxicology and pharmacy administration.

Prospective pharmacists should have scientific aptitude, good communication skills, and a desire to help others. They also must be conscientious and pay close attention to detail, because the decisions they make affect human lives.

In community pharmacies, pharmacists usually begin at the staff level. In independent pharmacies, after they gain experience and secure the necessary capital, some become owners or part owners of pharmacies. Pharmacists in chain drugstores may be promoted to pharmacy supervisor or manager at the store level, then to manager at the district or regional level, and later to an executive position within the chain's headquarters.

Hospital pharmacists may advance to supervisory or administrative positions. Pharmacists in the pharmaceutical industry may advance in marketing, sales, research, quality control, production, packaging, or other areas.

Employment
Pharmacists held about 230,000 jobs in 2004. About 61 percent work in community pharmacies that are either independently owned or part of a drugstore chain, grocery store, department store, or mass merchandiser. Most community pharmacists are salaried employees, but some are self-employed owners. About 24 percent of salaried pharmacists work in hospitals. Others work in clinics, mail-order pharmacies, pharmaceutical wholesalers, home health care agencies, or the federal government.

Job Outlook

Very good employment opportunities are expected for pharmacists over the 2004–14 period because the number of job openings created by employment growth and the need to replace pharmacists who leave the occupation or retire are expected to exceed the number of degrees granted in pharmacy. Enrollments in pharmacy programs are rising as more students are attracted by high salaries and good job prospects. Despite this increase in enrollments, job openings should still be more numerous than those seeking employment.

Employment of pharmacists is expected to grow faster than the average for all occupations through the year 2014, because of the increasing demand for pharmaceuticals, particularly from the growing elderly population. The increasing numbers of middle-aged and elderly people—who use more prescription drugs than younger people—will continue to spur demand for pharmacists in all employment settings. Other factors likely to increase the demand for pharmacists include scientific advances that will make more drug products available, new developments in genome research and medication distribution systems, increasingly sophisticated consumers seeking more information about drugs, and coverage of prescription drugs by a greater number of health insurance plans and Medicare.

Community pharmacies are taking steps to manage an increasing volume of prescriptions. Automation of drug dispensing and greater employment of pharmacy technicians and pharmacy aides will help these establishments to dispense more prescriptions.

With its emphasis on cost control, managed care encourages the use of lower cost prescription drug distributors, such as mail-order firms and online pharmacies, for purchases of certain medications. Prescriptions ordered through the mail and via the Internet are filled in a central location and shipped to the patient at a lower cost. Mail-order and online pharmacies typically use automated technology to dispense medication and employ fewer pharmacists. If the utilization of mail-order pharmacies increases rapidly, job growth among pharmacists could be limited.

Employment of pharmacists will not grow as fast in hospitals as in other industries, because hospitals are reducing inpatient stays, downsizing, and consolidating departments. The number of outpatient surgeries is increasing, so more patients are being discharged and purchasing their medications through retail, supermarket, or mail-order pharmacies, rather than through hospitals. An aging population means that more pharmacy services will be required in nursing homes, assisted-living facilities, and home care settings. The most rapid job growth among pharmacists is expected in these 3 settings.

New opportunities are emerging for pharmacists in managed care organizations where they analyze trends and patterns in medication use, and in pharmacoeconomics—the cost and benefit analysis of different drug therapies. Opportunities also are emerging for pharmacists trained in research and disease management—the development of new methods for curing and controlling diseases. Pharmacists also are finding jobs in research and development and in sales and marketing for pharmaceutical manufacturing firms. Biotechnology breakthroughs will increase the potential for drugs to treat diseases and expand opportunities for pharmacists to conduct research and sell medications. In addition, pharmacists are finding employment opportunities in pharmacy informatics, which uses information technology to improve patient care.

Job opportunities for pharmacists in patient care will arise as cost-conscious insurers and health systems continue to emphasize the role of pharmacists in primary and preventive health care. Health insurance companies realize that the expense of using medication to treat diseases and various health conditions often is considerably less than the costs for patients whose conditions go untreated. Pharmacists also can reduce the expenses resulting from unexpected complications due to allergic reactions or interactions among medications.

Earnings

Median annual wage and salary earnings of pharmacists in May 2004 were $84,900. The middle 50 percent earned between $75,720 and $94,850 a year. The lowest 10 percent earned less than $61,200, and the highest 10 percent earned more than $109,850 a year. Median annual earnings in the industries employing the largest numbers of pharmacists in May 2004 were: Department stores, $86,720; Grocery stores, $85,680; Health and personal care stores, $85,380; General medical and surgical hospitals, $84,560; Other general merchandise stores, $84,170.

RELATED OCCUPATIONS

Pharmacy Technicians and Aides

Pharmacy technicians and assistants help licensed pharmacists provide medication and other health care products to patients. Technicians usually perform routine tasks to help prepare prescribed medication for patients, such as counting and labeling. Pharmacy aides help licensed pharmacists with administrative duties in running a pharmacy. Aides often are clerks or cashiers who primarily answer telephones, handle money, stock shelves, and perform other clerical duties. They work closely with pharmacy technicians. Opportunities for pharmacy technicians and aides are expected to be good, especially for those with formal training or related work experience. Although most pharmacy technicians receive informal on-the-job training, employers favor those who have completed formal training and certification. Most pharmacy aides receive informal on-the-job training, but employers favor those with at least a high school diploma. In May 2004 median hourly earnings of pharmacy technicians were $11.37 and of pharmacy aides were $8.86. Certified technicians may earn more. For information, contact the Pharmacy Technician Certification Board, 2215 Constitution Ave. NW., Washington DC 20037, 800/363-8012 (**http://www.ptcb.org**) and check the resource section for pharmacists below. Pharmacy Technician careers can be found at **http://www.bls.gov/oco/ocos252.htm**, while Pharmacy Aides are described at **www.bls.gov/oco/ocos274.htm.**

PHARMACISTS RESOURCES

Don't forget! Refer to the general resources listed in Chapter Three.

Association   Directory   Resume Service   Web Site

Job Ads   Job Alert E-mail/Hotline   Job Fairs   Book

For a full explanation of these resources see the second page of Chapter 3.

Academy of Managed Care Pharmacy (AMCP) - 100 N. Pitt Street, Suite 400, Alexandria, VA 22314; 800/827-2627, 703/683-8416. (**www.amcp.org**) Job listings in Career Center. Information about residencies, internships, and listing of schools in the U. S.

American Association of Colleges of Pharmacy (AACP) - 1426 Prince St., Alexandria, VA 22314; 703/739-2330. (**http://www.aacp.org**, mail@aacp.org) Student page has article on "Is Pharmacy for You?", listing of pharmacy colleges and schools, and financial aid information.

 ☺▤☞✻☌⌐ **American Pharmacists Association (APhA)** - 2215 Constitution Avenue NW, Washington, DC 20037; 202/628-4410; 800/237-2742. (**www.aphanet.org,** Education@aphanet.org) Includes practicing pharmacists, pharmaceutical scientists, student pharmacists, and pharmacy technicians. The pharmacist.com career center has job listings, a résumé service, information about the Employment Exchange job fair that is held in conjunction with the association's annual convention, job seeker support, and a Career Pathway Evaluation Program.

 ☺▤☞☌⌐ **American Society of Health-System Pharmacists (ASHP)** - 7272 Wisconsin Avenue, Bethesda, MD 20814; 301/657-3000. (**http://www.ashp.com,** info@ashp.org) Student Forum has Pharmacy Jobs page with information about the job fairs at ASHP meetings, information on writing résumés and handling job interviews, and a place to upload résumés, and view job openings. Their **CareerPharm** site at **http://www.careerpharm.com/** offers help in finding jobs, residencies, or fellowships. There is also a technician section.

 ☺▤✻☌⌐ **California Pharmacists Association (CphA)** - 4030 Lennane Drive, Sacramento, CA 95834; 916/ 779-1400, 800/444-3851. (**http://www.cpha.com,** cpha@cpha.com) The career center has job ads, uploading of résumés, and job alerts emailed to you that fit your criteria.

 ☺▤☐☌⌐ **International Society for Pharmaceutical Engineering (ISPE)** - 3109 W. Dr. Martin Luther King, Jr. Blvd., Suite 250, Tampa, FL 33607; 813/960-2105. (**www.ispe.org,** customerservice@ispe.org) Organization of pharmaceutical engineers. Web site has job ads and information about Communities of Practice, groups of engineers that get together to work on emerging technologies.

 ☺☐☌⌐ **National Association of Chain Drug Stores (NACDS)** - 413 N. Lee St., PO Box 1417, Alexandria, VA 22313. (**http://www.nacds.org**) Pharmacy tab of the web site has student section with information on the profession, directory of programs, and scholarship, internship, and student loan information.

 ☺☌⌐ **National Association of Boards of Pharmacy (NABP)** - 1600 Feehanville Drive, Mount Prospect, IL 60056; 847/391-4406. (**http://www.nabp.net,** custserv@nabp.net) Association of State Boards that acts a coordinator between individual state licensing programs. Writes and administers the North American Pharmacist Licensure Examination™ (NAPLEX®) and the Multistate Pharmacy Jurisprudence

Exam (MPJE) used by the state boards of pharmacy as part of their assessment of competence to practice pharmacy.

National Community Pharmacists Association (NCPA) - 100 Daingerfield Road, Alexandria, VA 22314; 703/683-8200, 800/544-7447. (**http://www.ncpanet.org**) Organization of independent pharmacists and owners of independent pharmacies. Student section has career guide, information on scholarships and student loans, and a program of virtual mentors for learning about pharmacy ownership.

National Pharmaceutical Association (NPhA) - 107 Kilmayne Drive, Suite C, Cary, NC 27511; 800/944-NPHA. (**http://www.npha.net/**, TVbbamc@aol.com) Association of minority pharmacists.

National Pharmacy Technician Association (NPTA) - 3707 FM 1960 RD W, Suite #460, Houston , TX 77068; 888/247-8700, 281/866-7900. (**http://www.pharmacytechnician.org**) Under the jobs tab, about employment links to information about certification requirements in each State and salary and benefits estimates. Free online continuing education credits for members.

Pharmacy Technician Certification Board (PTCB) - 2215 Constitution Avenue North West, Washington, DC 20037; 800/363-8012. (**http://www.ptcb.org**) Pharmacy technicians assist in pharmacy activities not requiring the professional judgement of a pharmacist. Voluntary certifying group for pharmacy technicians. Their Guidebook to Certification in the *About PTCB* tab has information on certification, and on studying for the certification exam. The *Pharmacy Technicians* tab has info on education, advantages of certification , and income. It also has an outline for studying for the certification exam. The *PTCB exam* tab has information on taking the exam. The *CphT services* tab has links to the state Pharmacy Boards, so you can see what the requirements are in your jurisdiction.

Pharmacy Times - 241 Forsgate Drive, Jamesburg, N.J. 08831; 732/656-1140. (**http://www.pharmacytimes.com**) The web site has continuing education, free subscriptions for students, career information and classified job ads, as well asa link to the AbsolutelyHealthCare job site.

PharmWeb - (**http://www.pharmweb.net**) Directories of schools, people, and information.

U.S. Pharmacist - Jobson Publishing, 1515 Broad Street, Bloom-field, NJ 07003; 973/954-9300. (http://www.uspharmacist.com) This site has lots of continuing education, and a classified ads area which has a few jobs ads.

OCCUPATIONAL THERAPISTS

Significant Points
- Employment is projected to increase much faster than the average, as rapid growth in the number of middle-aged and elderly individuals increases the demand for therapeutic services.
- Beginning in 2007, a master's degree or higher in occupational therapy will be the minimum educational requirement.
- Occupational therapists are increasingly taking on supervisory roles, allowing assistants and aides to work more closely with clients under the guidance of a therapist, in an effort to reduce the cost of therapy.
- More than a quarter of occupational therapists work part time.

Nature of the Work
Occupational therapists (OTs) help people improve their ability to perform tasks in their daily living and working environments. They work with individuals who have conditions that are mentally, physically, developmentally, or emotionally disabling. They also help them to develop, recover, or maintain daily living and work skills. Occupational therapists help clients not only to improve their basic motor functions and reasoning abilities, but also to compensate for permanent loss of function. Their goal is to help clients have independent, productive, and satisfying lives.

Occupational therapists assist clients in performing activities of all types, ranging from using a computer to caring for daily needs such as dressing, cooking, and eating. Physical exercises may be used to increase strength and dexterity, while other activities may be chosen to improve visual acuity and the ability to discern patterns. For example, a client with short-term memory loss might be encouraged to make lists to aid recall, and a person with coordination problems might be assigned exercises to improve hand-eye coordination. Occupational therapists also use computer programs to help clients improve decision making, abstract-reasoning, problem-solving, and perceptual skills, as well as memory, sequencing, and coordination—all of which are important for independent living.

Therapists instruct those with permanent disabilities, such as spinal cord injuries, cerebral palsy, or muscular dystrophy, in the use of adaptive equipment, including wheelchairs, orthotics, and aids for eating and dressing. They also design or make special equipment needed at home or at work. Therapists develop computer-aided adaptive equipment and teach clients with severe limitations how to use that equipment in order to communicate better and control various aspects of their environment.

Some occupational therapists treat individuals whose ability to function in a work environment has been impaired. These practitioners arrange employment, evaluate the work environment, plan work activities, and assess the client's progress. Therapists also may collaborate with the client and the employer to modify the work environment so that the work can be successfully completed.

Occupational therapists may work exclusively with individuals in a particular age group or with particular disabilities. In schools, for example, they evaluate children's abilities, recommend and provide therapy, modify classroom equipment, and help children participate as fully as possible in school programs and activities. A therapist may work with children individually, lead small groups in the classroom, consult with a teacher, or serve on a curriculum or other administrative committee. Early intervention therapy services are provided to infants and toddlers who have, or are at risk of having, developmental delays. Specific therapies may include facilitating the use of the hands, promoting skills for listening and following directions, fostering social play skills, or teaching dressing and grooming skills.

Occupational therapy also is beneficial to the elderly population. Therapists help the elderly lead more productive, active, and independent lives through a variety of methods, including the use of adaptive equipment. Therapists with specialized training in driver rehabilitation assess an individual's ability to drive using both clinical and on-the-road tests. The evaluations allow the therapist to make recommendations for adaptive equipment, training to prolong driving independence, and alternative transportation options. Occupational therapists also work with the client to assess the home for hazards and to identify environmental factors that contribute to falls.

Occupational therapists in mental health settings treat individuals who are mentally ill, mentally retarded, or emotionally disturbed. To treat these problems, therapists choose activities that help people learn to engage in and cope with daily life. Activities include time management skills, budgeting, shopping, homemaking, and the use of public transportation. Occupational therapists also may work with individuals who are dealing with alcoholism, drug abuse, depression, eating disorders, or stress-related disorders.

Assessing and recording a client's activities and progress is an important part of an occupational therapist's job. Accurate records are essential for evaluating clients, for billing, and for reporting to physicians and other health care providers.

Working Conditions

Occupational therapists in hospitals and other health care and community settings usually work a 40-hour week. Those in schools may participate in other activities during and after the school day. In 2004, more than a quarter of occupational therapists worked part time.

In large rehabilitation centers, therapists may work in spacious rooms equipped with machines, tools, and other devices generating noise. The work can be tiring, because therapists are on their feet much of the time. Those providing home health care services may spend time driving from appointment to appointment. Therapists also face hazards such as back strain from lifting and moving clients and equipment.

Therapists increasingly are taking on supervisory roles. Because of rising health care costs, third-party payers are beginning to encourage occupational therapist assistants and aides to take more hands-on responsibility. The cost of therapy should decline if assistants and aides work more closely with clients under the guidance of a therapist.

Training, Other Qualifications, and Advancement

Currently, a bachelor's degree in occupational therapy is the minimum requirement for entry into the field. Beginning in 2007, however, a master's degree or higher will be the minimum educational requirement. As a result, students in bachelor's-level programs must complete their coursework and fieldwork before 2007. All states, Puerto Rico, Guam, and the District of Columbia regulate the practice of occupational therapy. To obtain a license, applicants must graduate from an accredited educational program and pass a national certification examination. Those who pass the exam are awarded the title "Occupational Therapist Registered (OTR)." Some states have additional requirements for therapists who work in schools or early intervention programs. These requirements may include classes, an education practice certificate, or early intervention certification requirements.

In 2005, 122 master's degree programs offered entry-level education, 65 programs offered a combined bachelor's and master's degree, and 5 offered an entry-level doctoral degree. Most schools have full-time programs, although a growing number are offering weekend or part-time programs as well. Bachelor's degree programs in occupational therapy are no longer offered because of the requirement for a master's degree or higher beginning in 2007. In addition, post baccalaureate certificate programs for students with a degree other than occupational therapy are no longer offered.

Occupational therapy coursework includes the physical, biological, and behavioral sciences and the application of occupational therapy theory and skills. The completion of 6 months of supervised fieldwork also is required.

Persons considering this profession should take high school courses in biology, chemistry, physics, health, art, and the social sciences. College admissions offices also look favorably at paid or volunteer experience in the health care field. Relevant undergraduate majors include biology, psychology, sociology, anthropology, liberal arts, and anatomy.

Occupational therapists need patience and strong interpersonal skills to inspire trust and respect in their clients. Patience is necessary because many clients may not show rapid improvement. Ingenuity and imagination in adapting activities to individual needs are assets. Those working in home health care services must be able to adapt to a variety of settings.

Employment

Occupational therapists held about 92,000 jobs in 2004. About 1 in 10 occupational therapists held more than one job. The largest number of jobs were in hospitals. Other major employers were offices of other health practitioners (including offices of occupational therapists), public and private educational services, and nursing care facilities. Some occupational therapists were employed by home health care services, outpatient care centers, offices of physicians, individual and family services, community care facilities for the elderly, and government agencies.

A small number of occupational therapists were self-employed in private practice. These practitioners saw clients referred by physicians or other health professionals or provided contract or consulting services to nursing care facilities, schools, adult day care programs, and home health care agencies.

Job Outlook

Employment of occupational therapists is expected to increase much faster than the average for all occupations through 2014. The impact of proposed federal legislation imposing limits on reimbursement for therapy services may adversely affect the job market for occupational therapists in the short run. However, over the long run, the demand for occupational therapists should continue to rise as a result of growth in the number of individuals with disabilities or limited function who require therapy services. The baby-boom generation's movement into middle age, a period when the incidence of heart attack and stroke increases, will spur demand for therapeutic services. Growth in the population 75 years and older—an age group that suffers from high incidences of disabling conditions—also will increase demand for therapeutic services. Driver rehabilitation and fall-prevention training for the elderly are emerging practice areas for occupational therapy. In addition, medical advances now enable more patients with critical problems to survive—patients who ultimately may need extensive therapy.

Hospitals will continue to employ a large number of occupational therapists to provide therapy services to acutely ill inpatients. Hospitals also will need occupational therapists to staff their outpatient rehabilitation programs.

Employment growth in schools will result from the expansion of the school-age population, the extension of services for disabled students, and an increasing prevalence of sensory disorders in children. Therapists will be needed to help children with disabilities prepare to enter special education programs.

Earnings

Median annual earnings of occupational therapists were $54,660 in May 2004. The middle 50 percent earned between $45,690 and $67,010.

The lowest 10 percent earned less than $37,430, and the highest 10 percent earned more than $81,600. Median annual earnings in the industries employing the largest numbers of occupational therapists in May 2004 were: Home health care services, $58,720; Offices of other health practitioners, $56,620; Nursing care facilities, $56,570; General medical and surgical hospitals, $55,710; Elementary and secondary schools, $48,580.

RELATED OCCUPATIONS

Occupational Therapy Assistants and Aides

Occupational therapy assistants and aides work under the direction of occupational therapists to provide rehabilitative services to persons with mental, physical, emotional, or developmental impairments. Occupational therapy assistants help clients with rehabilitative activities and exercises outlined in a treatment plan developed in collaboration with an occupational therapist. Occupational therapy aides typically prepare materials and assemble equipment used during treatment and are responsible for a range of clerical tasks. An associate degree or a certificate from an accredited community college or technical school is generally required to qualify for occupational therapist assistant jobs. In contrast, occupational therapist aides usually receive most of their training on the job. Employment is projected to increase much faster than the average, reflecting growth in the number of individuals with disabilities or limited function who require therapeutic services. Median annual earnings of occupational therapy assistants and aides were $38,430 in 2004. Information on a career as an occupational therapy assistant or aide can be found at **http://www.bls.gov/oco/ocos166.htm** or from the American Occupational Therapy Association below.

Resources for occupational therapists and physical therapists are combined as many resources serve both professions. See the end of the Physical Therapist section.

PHYSICAL THERAPISTS

Significant Points

- Employment is expected to increase much faster than the average, as growth in the number of individuals with disabilities or limited functioning spurs demand for therapy services.
- Job opportunities should be particularly good in acute hospital, rehabilitation, and orthopedic settings.

- After graduating from an accredited physical therapist educational program, therapists must pass a licensure exam before they can practice.
- Nearly 6 out of 10 physical therapists work in hospitals or in offices of physical therapists.

Nature of the Work

Physical therapists provide services that help restore function, improve mobility, relieve pain, and prevent or limit permanent physical disabilities of patients suffering from injuries or disease. They restore, maintain, and promote overall fitness and health. Their patients include accident victims and individuals with disabling conditions such as low back pain, arthritis, heart disease, fractures, head injuries, and cerebral palsy.

Therapists examine patients' medical histories and then test and measure the patients' strength, range of motion, balance and coordination, posture, muscle performance, respiration, and motor function. They also determine patients' ability to be independent and reintegrate into the community or workplace after injury or illness. Next, physical therapists develop plans describing a treatment strategy, its purpose, and its anticipated outcome. Physical therapist assistants, under the direction and supervision of a physical therapist, may be involved in implementing treatment plans with patients. Physical therapist aides perform routine support tasks, as directed by the therapist. (Physical therapist assistants and aides are discussed at the end of this section.)

Treatment often includes exercise for patients who have been immobilized and lack flexibility, strength, or endurance. Physical therapists encourage patients to use their own muscles to increase their flexibility and range of motion before finally advancing to other exercises that improve strength, balance, coordination, and endurance. The goal is to improve how an individual functions at work and at home.

Physical therapists also use electrical stimulation, hot packs or cold compresses, and ultrasound to relieve pain and reduce swelling. They may use traction or deep-tissue massage to relieve pain. Therapists also teach patients to use assistive and adaptive devices, such as crutches, prostheses, and wheelchairs. They also may show patients exercises to do at home to expedite their recovery.

As treatment continues, physical therapists document the patient's progress, conduct periodic examinations, and modify treatments when necessary. Besides tracking the patient's progress, such documentation identifies areas requiring more or less attention.

Physical therapists often consult and practice with a variety of other professionals, such as physicians, dentists, nurses, educators, social workers, occupational therapists, speech-language pathologists, and audiologists.

Some physical therapists treat a wide range of ailments; others specialize in areas such as pediatrics, geriatrics, orthopedics, sports medicine, neurology, and cardiopulmonary physical therapy.

Working Conditions

Physical therapists practice in hospitals, clinics, and private offices that have specially equipped facilities, or they treat patients in hospital rooms, homes, or schools.

In 2004, most full-time physical therapists worked a 40-hour week; some worked evenings and weekends to fit their patients' schedules. About 1 in 4 physical therapists worked part time. The job can be physically demanding because therapists often have to stoop, kneel, crouch, lift, and stand for long periods. In addition, physical therapists move heavy equipment and lift patients or help them turn, stand, or walk.

Training, Other Qualifications, and Advancement

All states require physical therapists to pass a licensure exam before they can practice, after graduating from an accredited physical therapist educational program.

According to the American Physical Therapy Association, there were 205 accredited physical therapist programs in 2004. Of the accredited programs, 94 offered master's degrees, and 111 offered doctoral degrees. All physical therapist programs seeking accreditation are required to offer degrees at the master's degree level and above, in accordance with the Commission on Accreditation in Physical Therapy Education.

Physical therapist programs start with basic science courses such as biology, chemistry, and physics and then introduce specialized courses, including biomechanics, neuroanatomy, human growth and development, manifestations of disease, examination techniques, and therapeutic procedures. Besides getting classroom and laboratory instruction, students receive supervised clinical experience. Among the courses that are useful when one applies to a physical therapist educational program are anatomy, biology, chemistry, social science, mathematics, and physics. Before granting admission, many professional education programs require experience as a volunteer in a physical therapy department of a hospital or clinic. For high school students, volunteering with the school athletic trainer is a good way to gain experience.

Physical therapists should have strong interpersonal skills in order to be able to educate patients about their physical therapy treatments. Physical therapists also should be compassionate and possess a desire to help patients. Similar traits are needed to interact with the patient's family.

Physical therapists are expected to continue their professional development by participating in continuing education courses and workshops. In fact, a number of states require continuing education as a condition of maintaining licensure.

Employment

Physical therapists held about 155,000 jobs in 2004. The number of jobs is greater than the number of practicing physical therapists, because some physical therapists hold two or more jobs. Some may work in a private practice, but also work part time in another health care facility.

Nearly 6 out of 10 physical therapists worked in hospitals or in offices of physical therapists. Other jobs were in home health care services, nursing care, outpatient care centers, and physician offices.

Some physical therapists were self-employed in private practices, seeing individual patients and contracting to provide services in hospitals, rehabilitation centers, nursing care facilities, home health care agencies, adult day care programs, and schools. Physical therapists also teach in academic institutions and conduct research.

Job Outlook

Employment of physical therapists is expected to grow much faster than the average for all occupations through 2014. The impact of proposed federal legislation imposing limits on reimbursement for therapy services may adversely affect the short-term job outlook for physical therapists. However, over the long run, the demand for physical therapists should continue to rise as growth in the number of individuals with disabilities or limited function spurs demand for therapy services. Job opportunities should be particularly good in acute hospital, rehabilitation, and orthopedic settings, because the elderly receive the most treatment in these settings. The growing elderly population is particularly vulnerable to chronic and debilitating conditions that require therapeutic services. Also, the baby-boom generation is entering the prime age for heart attacks and strokes, increasing the demand for cardiac and physical rehabilitation. Further, young people will need physical therapy as technological advances save the lives of a larger proportion of newborns with severe birth defects.

Future medical developments also should permit a higher percentage of trauma victims to survive, creating additional demand for rehabilitative care. In addition, growth may result from advances in medical technology that could permit the treatment of more disabling conditions.

Widespread interest in health promotion also should increase demand for physical therapy services. A growing number of employers are using physical therapists to evaluate worksites, develop exercise programs, and teach safe work habits to employees in the hope of reducing injuries in the workplace.

Earnings

Median annual earnings of physical therapists were $60,180 in May 2004. The middle 50 percent earned between $50,330 and $71,760. The lowest 10 percent earned less than $42,010, and the highest 10 percent earned more than $88,580. Median annual earnings in the industries employing the largest numbers of physical therapists in May 2004 were: Home health care services, $64,650; Nursing care facilities, $61,720; Offices of physicians, $61,270; General medical and surgical hospitals, $60,350; Offices of other health practitioners, $60,130.

RELATED OCCUPATIONS

Physical Therapist Assistants and Aides

Physical therapist assistants and aides perform components of physical therapy procedures and related tasks selected by a supervising physical therapist. Physical therapist assistants perform a variety of tasks. Components of treatment procedures performed by these workers involve exercises, massages, electrical stimulation, paraffin baths, hot and cold packs, traction, and ultrasound. Physical therapist assistants record the patient's responses to treatment and report the outcome of each treatment to the physical therapist. Physical therapist aides usually are responsible for keeping the treatment area clean and organized and for preparing for each patient's therapy. Physical therapist aides are trained on the job, but physical therapist assistants typically earn an associate degree from an accredited physical therapist assistant program. Employment is projected to increase much faster than average; physical therapist aides may face keen competition from the large pool of qualified applicants. Median annual earnings of physical therapist assistants and aides were $37,890 in 2004. Information on a career as a physical therapist assistant and a list of accredited schools can be obtained from The American Physical Therapy Association, listed in the resources section and at **http://www.bls.gov/oco/ocos167.htm**.

OCCUPATIONAL THERAPISTS, PHYSICAL THERAPISTS, and OT/PT ASSISTANTS & AIDES RESOURCES

Don't forget! Refer to the general resources listed in Chapter Three and the Home Health Care Chapter.

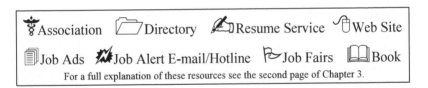

Association 　　 Directory 　　 Resume Service 　　 Web Site

Job Ads 　　 Job Alert E-mail/Hotline 　　 Job Fairs 　　 Book

For a full explanation of these resources see the second page of Chapter 3.

ADVANCE Newsmagazines - 2900 Horizon Drive, Box 61556, King of Prussia, Pa 19406-0956; 610/ 278-1400. (**http://www.merion.com**) *ADVANCE for Physical Therapists and PT Assistants, ADVANCE for Directors in Rehabilitation,* and *ADVANCE for Occupational Therapy Practitioners,* have extensive classified ads searchable by specialty or by state on the web. They hold job fairs around the US . Dates and locations also on web.

American Massage Therapy Association (AMTA) - 500 Davis St., Suite 900, Evanston, IL 60201; 847/864-0123, 877/905-2700. (**http://www.amtamassage.org**, info@amtamassage.org) Web site has career, school and certification information. Career Center lists positions available, searchable by state, city and/or specialty. Members can post resumes on the Job Network for free, nonmembers are charged.

American Occupational Therapy Association (AOTA) - 4720 Montgomery Lane, P.O. Box 31220, Bethesda, MD 20824; 800/377-8555, 301/652-2682. (**http://www.aota.org**) Students section has listings of schools and certification information. OT Job Link has jobs available searchable by state and city. Members can put résumés on web, and get emails on new jobs available that meet their criteria.

American Society of Hand Therapists (ASHT) - 401 North Michigan Ave., Chicago, IL 60611; 312/321-6866. (**http://www.asht.org**) One job ad in Employment Network at time of publication.

Commission on Rehabilitation Counselor Certification (CRCC) - 1835 Rohlwing Road, Suite E, Rolling Meadows, Illinois 60008; 847/394-2104. (**http://www.crccertification.com**) Certification organization for rehabilitation counselors in the US and Canada. Certification information and directory of members on web site.

Hand Therapy Certification Commission (HTCC) - 11160 Sun Center Drive, Suite B, Rancho Cordova, CA 95670; 800/860-7097. (**http://www.htcc.org**, info@htcc.org) Certification agency for hand therapists. Job listings both for Occupational Therapists in training for hand therapy and Certified Hand Therapists under Certification page of web site.

Jobs in Therapy - **http://www.jobsintherapy.com/** U.S. job openings for therapy fields including physical, occupational, speech, respiratory, radiation, recreation and massage. Résumé posting is required before job searches and recruiting services offered.

National Clearinghouse of Rehabilitation Training Materials (NCRTM) 6524 Old Main Hill, Logan UT 84322; 866/821-5355. (**ncrtm.ed.usu.edu**) A federally funded information service currently being moved from Oklahoma State University to Utah State University. Has a major free job bank where both job seekers can list their résumés and employers can list their job openings.

National Rehabilitation Association (NRA) - 633 S. Washington Street, Alexandria, VA 22314; 703/836-0850. (**www.nationalrehab.org/**, info@nationalrehab.org) This group has regional and state chapters for networking. Student membership is $35.

National Rehabilitation Counseling Association (NRCA) - PO Box 4480, Manassas, VA 20108; 703/361-2077. (**http://nrca-net.org/**, NRCAOFFICE@aol.com) Recently independent from the National Rehabilitation Association, NRCA is the major association of rehabilitation counselors. Employment web page lists job openings.

National Strength and Conditioning Association (NSCA) - 1885 Bob Johnson Drive, Colorado Springs, CO 80906; 719/632-6722, 800/815-6826. (**http://www.nsca-lift.org/menu.asp**, nsca@ nsca-lift.org) Recognizes education programs, and certifies trainers. The NSCA Career Center online, available to members only, currently has 102 job ads. Student membership $80. On-site Career Fair available at annual conferences.

Medrise. (**www.occupationalTherapist.com**) Check both listings and jobs. Jobs link takes you to the Midrise home site listings, where you can choose occupational therapist listings, and Listings link takes you directly to different listings for occupational therapists. Also has links for other job search sites. Includes a directory of schools.

Opportunities in Occupational Therapy Careers by Zona R. Weeks ISBN: B000063Y61 and Opportunities in Physical Therapy Careers by Bernice R. Krumhansl ISBN: B000062UHL are published by McGraw Hill. Both include training and education requirements, salary statistics, and professional and Internet resources.

Physical Therapy Web Space - (**http://automailer.com/tws**) Offers great resources for Canadian and U.S. physical therapists and PT students. Has RSS feeds of jobs available in the US, Canada, and other areas of the world, as well as links to other job sites. Links to both distance and residential learning institutions, listed by state, articles on becoming a PT, directory of PT organizations, and other PT sites listing everything from equipment and software, to recruiters and management services.

PTJobs.com - **http://www.PTJobs.com/** Job listings for physical therapists and assistants. Job seekers are required to sign in to post résumés and apply for jobs.

RehabCareer.com - **http://www.rehabcareer.com/** Web site for physical, occupational and speech therapy jobs.

Rehabjobsonline.com - **http://www.rehabjobsonline.com/**

Nationwide jobs for physical, occupational and speech therapists, assistants. Post résumés and receive email from employers.

📄🖊️ **rehaboptions.com** - Call or email about unadvertised jobs for physical and occupational therapists and assistants. Also link to Health Care's more than 275,000 health care job listings.

📖 **SLACK Incorporated** - 6900 Grove Road, Thorofare, NJ 08086; 856/848-1000. (http://www.slackbooks.com). Publishes many books on health care, including *OT Student Primer: A Guide to College Success.*

RECREATIONAL THERAPISTS

Significant Points
- Overall employment of recreational therapists is expected to grow more slowly than the average for all occupations, but employment of therapists who work in community care facilities for the elderly and in residential mental retardation, mental health, and substance abuse facilities should grow faster than the average.
- Opportunities should be best for persons with a bachelor's degree in therapeutic recreation, or in recreation with a concentration in therapeutic recreation.
- Recreational therapists should be comfortable working with persons who are ill or who have disabilities.

ADDITIONAL OCCUPATIONAL TITLES

Art Therapists	**Dance Therapists**
Drama Therapists	**Music Therapists**

Nature of the Work
Recreational therapists, also referred to as therapeutic recreation specialists, provide treatment services and recreation activities to individuals with disabilities or illnesses. Using a variety of techniques, including arts and crafts, animals, sports, games, dance and movement, drama, music, and community outings, therapists treat and maintain the physical, mental, and emotional well-being of their clients. Therapists help individuals reduce depression, stress, and anxiety; recover basic motor functioning and reasoning abilities; build confidence; and socialize effectively so that they can enjoy greater independence, as well as reduce or eliminate the effects of their illness or disability. In addition, therapists

help integrate people with disabilities into the community by teaching them how to use community resources and recreational activities. Recreational therapists should not be confused with recreation workers, who organize recreational activities primarily for enjoyment.

In acute health care settings, such as hospitals and rehabilitation centers, recreational therapists treat and rehabilitate individuals with specific health conditions, usually in conjunction or collaboration with physicians, nurses, psychologists, social workers, and physical and occupational therapists. In long-term and residential care facilities, recreational therapists use leisure activities—especially structured group programs—to improve and maintain their clients' general health and well-being. They also may provide interventions to prevent the client from suffering further medical problems and complications related to illnesses and disabilities.

Recreational therapists assess clients on the basis of information the therapists learn from standardized assessments, observations, medical records, the medical staff, the clients' families, and the clients themselves. They then develop and carry out therapeutic interventions consistent with the clients' needs and interests. For example, clients who are isolated from others or who have limited social skills may be encouraged to play games with others, and right-handed persons with right-side paralysis may be instructed in how to adapt to using their unaffected left side to throw a ball or swing a racket. Recreational therapists may instruct patients in relaxation techniques to reduce stress and tension, stretching and limbering exercises, proper body mechanics for participation in recreational activities, pacing and energy conservation techniques, and individual as well as team activities. In addition, therapists observe and document a patient's participation, reactions, and progress.

Community-based recreational therapists may work in park and recreation departments, special-education programs for school districts, or programs for older adults and people with disabilities. Included in the last group are programs and facilities such as assisted-living, adult day care, and substance abuse rehabilitation centers. In these programs, therapists use interventions to develop specific skills, while providing opportunities for exercise, mental stimulation, creativity, and fun. Although most therapists are employed in other areas, those who work in schools help counselors, teachers, and parents address the special needs of students, including easing disabled students' transition into adult life.

Working Conditions

Recreational therapists provide services in special activity rooms, but also plan activities and prepare documentation in offices. When working with clients during community integration programs, they may travel locally to instruct the clients regarding the accessibility of public transportation and other public areas, such as parks, playgrounds, swimming pools, restaurants, and theaters.

Therapists often lift and carry equipment, as well as lead recreational activities. Recreational therapists generally work a 40-hour week that may include some evenings, weekends, and holidays.

Training, Other Qualifications, and Advancement

A bachelor's degree in therapeutic recreation, or in recreation with a concentration in therapeutic recreation, is the usual requirement for entry-level positions. Persons may qualify for paraprofessional positions with an associate degree in therapeutic recreation or a health care related field. An associate degree in recreational therapy; training in art, drama, or music therapy; or qualifying work experience may be sufficient for activity director positions in nursing homes.

Approximately 150 programs prepare students to become recreational therapists. Most offer bachelor's degrees, although some also offer associate, master's, or doctoral degrees. Programs include courses in assessment, treatment and program planning, intervention design, and evaluation. Students also study human anatomy, physiology, abnormal psychology, medical and psychiatric terminology, characteristics of illnesses and disabilities, professional ethics, and the use of assistive devices and technology.

Although certification is usually voluntary, most employers prefer to hire candidates who are certified therapeutic recreation specialists. The National Council for Therapeutic Recreation Certification is the certificatory agency. To become certified, specialists must have a bachelor's degree, pass a written certification examination, and complete an internship of at least 480 hours. Additional requirements apply in order to maintain certification and to recertify. Some States require licensure or certification to practice recreational therapy.

Recreational therapists should be comfortable working with persons who are ill or who have disabilities. Therapists must be patient, tactful, and persuasive when working with people who have a variety of special needs. Ingenuity, a sense of humor, and imagination are needed to adapt activities to individual needs, and good physical coordination is necessary to demonstrate or participate in recreational activities.

Therapists may advance to supervisory or administrative positions. Some teach, conduct research, or consult for health or social services agencies.

Employment
Recreational therapists held about 24,000 jobs in 2004. About 6 out of 10 were in nursing care facilities and hospitals. Others worked in state and local government agencies and in community care facilities for the elderly, including assisted-living facilities. The rest worked primarily in residential mental retardation, mental health, and substance abuse facilities; individual and family services; federal government agencies; educational services; and outpatient care centers. Only a small number of therapists were self-employed, generally contracting with long-term care facilities or community agencies to develop and oversee programs.

Job Outlook
Overall employment of recreational therapists is expected to grow more slowly than the average for all occupations through the year 2014. In nursing care facilities—the largest industry employing recreational therapists—employment will grow slightly faster than the occupation as a whole as the number of older adults continues to grow. Employment is expected to decline, however, in hospitals as services shift to outpatient settings and employers emphasize cost containment. Fast employment growth is expected in the residential and outpatient settings that serve disabled persons, the elderly, or those diagnosed with mental retardation, mental illness, or substance abuse problems. Among these settings are community care facilities for the elderly (including assisted-living facilities); residential mental retardation, mental health, and substance abuse facilities; and facilities that provide individual and family services (such as day care centers for disabled persons and the elderly). Opportunities should be best for persons with a bachelor's degree in therapeutic recreation or in recreation with an option in therapeutic recreation. Opportunities also should be good for therapists who hold

specialized certifications, for example, in, aquatic therapy, meditation, or crisis intervention.

Health care facilities will support a growing number of jobs in adult day care and outpatient programs offering short-term mental health and alcohol or drug abuse services. Rehabilitation, home health care, and transitional programs will provide additional jobs.

The rapidly growing number of older adults is expected to spur job growth for recreational therapy professionals and paraprofessionals in assisted-living facilities, adult day care programs, and other social assistance agencies. Continued growth also is expected in community residential care facilities, as well as in day care programs for individuals with disabilities.

Earnings

Median annual earnings of recreational therapists were $32,900 in May 2004. The middle 50 percent earned between $25,520 and $42,130. The lowest 10 percent earned less than $20,130, and the highest 10 percent earned more than $51,800. In May 2004, median annual earnings for recreational therapists were $28,130 in nursing care facilities.

Related Occupations

Recreational therapists primarily design activities to help people with disabilities lead more fulfilling and independent lives. Other workers who have similar jobs are occupational therapists, physical therapists, recreation workers, and rehabilitation counselors.

RECREATIONAL THERAPISTS RESOURCES

Don't forget! Refer to the general resources listed in Chapter Three. Look in the Occupational Therapists / Physical Therapists section of this chapter for other resources.

For a full explanation of these resources see the second page of Chapter 3.

American Alliance for Health, Physical Education, Recreation and Dance (AAHPERD) - 1900 Association Drive, Reston, VA 22091;

703/476-3400, 800/213-7193. (**http://www.aahperd.org,** info@aahperd.org) AAHPERD consists of 6 associations: American Association for Active Lifestyles and Fitness (AAALF), American Association for Health Education (AAHE), American Association for Leisure and Recreation (AALR), National Association for Girls and Women in Sport (NAGWS), National Association for Sport and Physical Education (NASPE), and National Dance Association (NDA). Career link oriented to the needs of senior and post graduate college students. Job fair at national convention.

American Art Therapy Association, Inc. (AATA) - 1202 Allanson Road, Mundelein, Illinois 60060; 888/290-0878, 847/949-6064. (**http://www.arttherapy.org,** info@arttherapy.org) Student section has listing of AATA approved graduate programs, educational requirements and scholarship information. Career center open only to members. Student membership $65.

American Dance Therapy Association (ADTA) - 2000 Century Plaza Suite 108, 10632 Little Patuxent Parkway, Columbia, MD 21044; 410/997-4040. (**http://www.adta.org,** info@adta.org) The Resource section of the web site has a directory of graduate and undergraduate programs, and a section on considering a career in dance therapy.

American Horticultural Therapy Association (AHTA) - 3570 E. 12th Avenue, Denver, CO 80206; 800/634-1603, 303/322-2482(AHTA). (**http://www.ahta.org,** info@ahta.org) Degree programs include associate, bachelor and advanced degrees. Work at approved colleges, botanical gardens, and other training facilities that are accredited by AHTA can lead to certification. Directory of programs in the US, internships, and certificate programs. Job opportunities section on web site for members only. Student membership $55.

American Therapeutic Recreation Association (ATRA) - 1414 Prince Street, Suite 204, Alexandria, VA 22314; 703/683-9420. (**http://www.atra-tr.org**) Directory by State of college programs from associate to doctoral, career information, and employment update in education tab.

Arts in Therapy Network - (**http://www.artsintherapy.com**) Online community for Creative Arts Therapists (CAT) Sign up for weekly Arts in Therapy Emailer offering up-to-date information on the CAT profession including job listings and searches, member requests, and announcements.

✺📄🗁⌒ **Canadian Art Therapy Association** - (www.catainfo.ca) Directory of Canadian programs. New employment listing currently has no jobs listed.

📄✎⌒ **Jobs in Therapy** - http://www.jobsintherapy.com/ Résumé posting is required before job searches and recruiting services offered.

✺🗁⌒ **National Association for Drama Therapy (NADT)** - 15 Post Side Lane, Pittsford, NY 14534; 585/381-5618. (**www.nadt.org/about.html**, answers@nadt.org) Directory of drama therapy programs and information on alternative training program for people with masters, or working on masters in a related field.

✺📄🗁⌒ **National Association for Music Therapy** - 8455 Colesville Road, Suite 1000, Silver Spring, MD 20910; 301/589-3300. Web site (**http://www.musictherapy.org**, info@musictherapy.org) offers information on career opportunities in music therapy as well as a directory of academic programs. Job and scholarship opportunities are on members only pages. Student membership $75.

✺🗁⌒ **National Association for Poetry Therapy** - 525 SW 5th St., Ste A, Des Moines, IA 50309; 866/844-NAPT. (**http://www.poetrytherapy.org**, info@poetrytherapy.org) Their Educational Resource list, organized alphabetically by state and country, lists educational programs, mentor-supervisors, classes, and workshops that support certification in poetry therapy. Education, training and background knowledge necessary for CPTs and RPTs to gain certification in poetry therapy are also given.

✺🗁⌒ **National Coalition of Creative Arts Therapies Associations (NCCATA)** - c/o AMTA, 8455 Colesville Rd., Suite 1000, Silver Spring MD 20910; 714/751-0103. (**http://www.nccata.org**) The council is an alliance of professional associations dedicated to the advancement of the arts as therapeutic modalities. Site provides links to six creative arts therapies organizations, with contact information: American Association for Music Therapy, American Art Therapy Association, American Dance Therapy Association, National Association for Drama Therapy, American Society for Group Psychotherapy & Psychodrama, and National Association for Poetry Therapy.

✺⌒ **National Council for Therapeutic Recreation Certification (NCTRC)** - 7 Elmwood Drive, New City, New York 10956; 845/639-1439.

(**http://www.nctrc.org,** ncrtc@nctrc.org) Certification standards and applications are available here.

✓ National Therapeutic Recreation Society (NTRS) - 22377
Belmont Ridge Rd., Ashburn, VA 20148; 703/858-0784. (**http://www.
nrpa.org**) A branch of the National Recreation and Park Association. Uses
the job service of the NRPA.

Therapeutic Recreation Directory - Address book listing
more than 600 users can be searched by locality. Job listings by state and
category. (**www.recreationtherapy.com**)

RESPIRATORY THERAPISTS

Significant Points
- Job opportunities will be very good, especially for therapists with
  cardiopulmonary care skills or experience working with infants.
- All States (except Alaska and Hawaii), the District of Columbia, and
  Puerto Rico require respiratory therapists to obtain a license.
- Hospitals will continue to employ the vast majority of respiratory
  therapists, but a growing number of therapists will work in other
  settings.

Nature of the Work
Respiratory therapists and respiratory therapy technicians—also
known as respiratory care practitioners—evaluate, treat, and care for
patients with breathing or other cardiopulmonary disorders. Practicing
under the direction of a physician, respiratory therapists assume primary
responsibility for all respiratory care therapeutic treatments and diagnostic procedures, including the supervision of respiratory therapy
technicians. Respiratory therapy technicians follow specific, well-defined
respiratory care procedures under the direction of respiratory therapists
and physicians. In clinical practice, many of the daily duties of therapists
and technicians overlap; furthermore, the two have the same education
and training requirements. However, therapists generally have greater
responsibility than technicians. For example, respiratory therapists will
consult with physicians and other health care staff to help develop and
modify individual patient care plans. Respiratory therapists also are more
likely to provide complex therapy requiring considerable independent
judgment, such as caring for patients on life support in intensive-care

units of hospitals. In this statement, the term respiratory therapists includes both respiratory therapists and respiratory therapy technicians.

Respiratory therapists evaluate and treat all types of patients, ranging from premature infants whose lungs are not fully developed to elderly people whose lungs are diseased. Respiratory therapists provide temporary relief to patients with chronic asthma or emphysema, as well as emergency care to patients who are victims of a heart attack, stroke, drowning, or shock.

To evaluate patients, respiratory therapists interview them, perform limited physical examinations, and conduct diagnostic tests. For example, respiratory therapists test patients' breathing capacity and determine the concentration of oxygen and other gases in patients' blood. They also measure patients' pH, which indicates the acidity or alkalinity of the blood. To evaluate a patient's lung capacity, respiratory therapists have the patient breathe into an instrument that measures the volume and flow of oxygen during inhalation and exhalation. By comparing the reading with the norm for the patient's age, height, weight, and sex, respiratory therapists can provide information that helps determine whether the patient has any lung deficiencies. To analyze oxygen, carbon dioxide, and pH levels, therapists draw an arterial blood sample, place it in a blood gas analyzer, and relay the results to a physician, who then may make treatment decisions.

To treat patients, respiratory therapists use oxygen or oxygen mixtures, chest physiotherapy, and aerosol medications. When a patient has difficulty getting enough oxygen into his or her blood, therapists increase the patient's concentration of oxygen by placing an oxygen mask or nasal cannula on the patient and set the oxygen flow at the level prescribed by a physician. Therapists also connect patients who cannot breathe on their own to ventilators that deliver pressurized oxygen to the lungs. The therapists insert a tube into the patient's trachea, or windpipe; connect the tube to the ventilator; and set the rate, volume, and oxygen concentration of the oxygen mixture entering the patient's lungs.

Therapists perform regular assessments of patients and equipment. If the patient appears to be having difficulty breathing or if the oxygen, carbon dioxide, or pH level of the blood is abnormal, therapists change the ventilator setting according to the doctor's orders or check the equipment for mechanical problems. In home care, therapists teach patients and their families to use ventilators and other life-support systems. In addition, therapists visit patients several times a month to inspect and clean equipment and to ensure its proper use. Therapists also make emergency visits if equipment problems arise.

Respiratory therapists perform chest physiotherapy on patients to remove mucus from their lungs and make it easier for them to breathe. For example, during surgery, anesthesia depresses respiration, so chest physiotherapy may be prescribed to help get the patient's lungs back to normal and to prevent congestion. Chest physiotherapy also helps patients suffering from lung diseases, such as cystic fibrosis, that cause mucus to collect in the lungs. Therapists place patients in positions that help drain mucus, and then vibrate the patients' rib cages and instruct the patients to cough.

Respiratory therapists also administer aerosols—liquid medications suspended in a gas that forms a mist which is inhaled—and teach patients how to inhale the aerosol properly to ensure its effectiveness.

In some hospitals, therapists perform tasks that fall outside their traditional role. Therapists' tasks are expanding into areas such as pulmonary rehabilitation, smoking cessation counseling, disease prevention, case management, and polysomnography—the diagnosis of breathing disorders during sleep, such as apnea. Respiratory therapists also increasingly treat critical care patients, either as part of surface and air transport teams or as part of rapid-response teams in hospitals.

Working Conditions

Respiratory therapists generally work between 35 and 40 hours a week. Because hospitals operate around the clock, therapists may work evenings, nights, or weekends. They spend long periods standing and walking between patients' rooms. In an emergency, therapists work under a great deal of stress. Respiratory therapists employed in home health care must travel frequently to the homes of patients.

Respiratory therapists are trained to work with hazardous gases stored under pressure. Adherence to safety precautions and regular maintenance and testing of equipment minimize the risk of injury. As in many other health occupations, respiratory therapists run the risk of catching an infectious disease, but carefully following proper procedures minimizes this risk.

Training, Other Qualifications, and Advancement

Formal training is necessary for entry into this field. Training is offered at the postsecondary level by colleges and universities, medical schools, vocational-technical institutes, and the Armed Forces. An associate's degree is required for entry into the field. Most programs award associate's or bachelor's degrees and prepare graduates for jobs as advanced respiratory therapists. A limited number of associate's degree programs lead to jobs as entry-level respiratory therapists. According to the Commission on Accreditation of Allied Health Education Programs (CAAHEP), 51 entry-level and 329 advanced respiratory therapy programs were accredited in the United States, including Puerto Rico, in 2005.

Among the areas of study in respiratory therapy are human anatomy and physiology, pathophysiology, chemistry, physics, microbiology, pharmacology, and mathematics. Other courses deal with therapeutic and diagnostic procedures and tests, equipment, patient assessment, cardiopulmonary resuscitation, the application of clinical practice guidelines, patient care outside of hospitals, cardiac and pulmonary rehabilitation, respiratory health promotion and disease prevention, and medical recordkeeping and reimbursement.

The National Board for Respiratory Care (NBRC) offers certification and registration to graduates of programs accredited by CAAHEP or the Committee on Accreditation for Respiratory Care (CoARC). Two credentials are awarded to respiratory therapists who satisfy the requirements: Registered Respiratory Therapist (RRT) and Certified Respiratory Therapist (CRT). Graduates from accredited entry-level or advanced-level programs in respiratory therapy may take the CRT examination. CRTs who were graduated from advanced-level programs and who meet additional experience requirements can take two separate examinations leading to the award of the RRT credential.

All states (except Alaska and Hawaii), the District of Columbia, and Puerto Rico require respiratory therapists to obtain a license. Passing the CRT exam qualifies respiratory therapists for state licenses. Also, most employers require respiratory therapists to maintain a cardiopulmonary resuscitation (CPR) certification. Supervisory positions and intensive-care specialties usually require the RRT or at least RRT eligibility.

Therapists should be sensitive to patients' physical and psychological needs. Respiratory care practitioners must pay attention to detail, follow instructions, and work as part of a team. In addition, operating advanced equipment requires proficiency with computers.

High school students interested in a career in respiratory care should take courses in health, biology, mathematics, chemistry, and physics. Respiratory care involves basic mathematical problem solving and an understanding of chemical and physical principles. For example, respiratory care workers must be able to compute dosages of medication and calculate gas concentrations.

Respiratory therapists advance in clinical practice by moving from general care to the care of critically ill patients who have significant problems in other organ systems, such as the heart or kidneys. Respiratory therapists, especially those with bachelor's or master's degrees, also may advance to supervisory or managerial positions in a respiratory therapy department. Respiratory therapists in home health care and equipment rental firms may become branch managers. Some respiratory therapists advance by moving into teaching positions.

Employment

Respiratory therapists held about 118,000 jobs in 2004. More than 4 out of 5 jobs were in hospital departments of respiratory care, anesthesiology, or pulmonary medicine. Most of the remaining jobs were in offices of physicians or other health practitioners, consumer-goods rental firms that supply respiratory equipment for home use, nursing care facilities, and home health care services. Holding a second job is relatively common for respiratory therapists. About 13 percent held another job, compared with 5 percent of workers in all occupations.

Job Outlook

Job opportunities are expected to be very good, especially for respiratory therapists with cardiopulmonary care skills or experience working with infants. Employment of respiratory therapists is expected to increase faster than average for all occupations through the year 2014, because of substantial growth in the numbers of the middle-aged and elderly population—a development that will heighten the incidence of cardiopulmonary disease—and because of the expanding role of respiratory therapists in the early detection of pulmonary disorders, case management, disease prevention, and emergency care.

Older Americans suffer most from respiratory ailments and cardiopulmonary diseases such as pneumonia, chronic bronchitis, emphysema, and heart disease. As their numbers increase, the need for respiratory therapists will increase as well. In addition, advances in inhalable medications and in the treatment of lung transplant patients, heart attack and accident victims, and premature infants (many of whom are dependent on a ventilator during part of their treatment) will increase the demand for the services of respiratory care practitioners.

Although hospitals will continue to employ the vast majority of therapists, a growing number can expect to work outside of hospitals in home health care services, offices of physicians or other health practitioners, or consumer-goods rental firms.

Earnings

Median annual earnings of respiratory therapists were $43,140 in May 2004. The middle 50 percent earned between $37,650 and $50,860. The lowest 10 percent earned less than $32,220, and the highest 10 percent earned more than $57,580. In general medical and surgical hospitals, median annual earnings of respiratory therapists were $43,140 in May 2004.

Median annual earnings of respiratory therapy technicians were $36,740 in May 2004. The middle 50 percent earned between $30,490 and $43,830. The lowest 10 percent earned less than $24,640, and the highest 10 percent earned more than $52,280. Median annual earnings of respiratory therapy technicians employed in general medical and surgical hospitals were $36,990 in May 2004.

Related Occupations

Under the supervision of a physician, respiratory therapists administer respiratory care and life support to patients with heart and lung difficulties. Other workers who care for, treat, or train people to improve their physical condition include registered nurses, occupational therapists, physical therapists, and radiation therapists.

RESPIRATORY THERAPISTS RESOURCES

Don't forget! Refer to the general resources listed in Chapter Three, the OT/PT section of this Chapter and Home Health Chapter, too.

♆Association   ▭Directory   🖊Resume Service   ⌖Web Site

▤Job Ads   🏃Job Alert E-mail/Hotline   ▷Job Fairs   📖Book

For a full explanation of these resources see the second page of Chapter 3.

♆▤▭⌖ **American Association for Respiratory Care (AARC)** - 9425 N. MacArthur Blvd. Suite 100, Irving, Texas 75063; 972/243-2272. (**http://www.aarc.org**, info@aarc.org) Take their "Be an RT" quiz in the Career tab, where there is also information on education for the career and an employment opportunities section. The Education tab has a listing of accredited 2-year and 4-year RT college programs searchable by state and a scholarships section.

♆▤▭⌖ **California Society for Respiratory Care (CSRC)** - 1961 Main Street, Suite #246, Watsonville, CA 95076; 888/730-CSRC (2772). (**http://www.csrc.org**). Web site has a member directory, a list of schools offering respiratory care programs in California, employment ads, and links to chapters in the state.

♆▤⌖ **Canadian Society of Respiratory Therapists (CSRT)** - 102-1785 Alta Vista Dr., Ottawa 0n K1G 3Y6. (**http://www.csrt.com**, csrt@csrt.com) Certification body as well as organization of Canadian RT's. The education tab has information on becoming an RT and a listing of accredited degree programs. The employment tab has a listing of jobs available.

▭⌖ **Committee on Accreditation for Respiratory Care (CoARC)** - 1248 Harwood Rd., Bedford, TX 76021; 817/283-2835. Web site located at (**http://www.coarc.com**). This accrediting agency for respiratory therapy educational programs has listings of both entry level and advanced practitioner educational programs by state.

▤🖊⌖ **Jobs in Therapy** - **http://www.jobsintherapy.com/** Résumé posting is required before job searches and recruiting services offered.

▭⌖ **National Board for Respiratory Care (NBRC)** - 8310 Nieman Road., Lenexa, Kansas 66214; 913/599-4200. (**http://www.nbrc.org**, nbrc-info@nbrc.org) Accrediting agency for respiratory therapists. Web site has exam schedules and application information.

♆🖊⌖ **The Respiratory Therapy Society of Ontario (RTSO)** - 6519-B Mississauga Road, Mississauga, Ontario, Canada L5N 1A6; 905/567-0020,

800/267-2687. (**http://www.rtso.org**) Ontario Canada RT's. Student corner under Resources has practice exam questions for the Canadian certification exam. They have a matching service for RT's and hospitals and other employers.

AUDIOLOGISTS

Significant Points
* Employment growth will be spurred by the expanding population in older age groups that are prone to medical conditions that result in hearing problems.
* More than half worked in health care facilities; many others were employed by educational services.
* A master's degree in audiology has been the standard credential; however, a clinical doctoral degree is becoming more common for new entrants and is expected to become the new standard for the profession.

Nature of the Work
Audiologists work with people who have hearing, balance, and related ear problems. They examine individuals of all ages and identify those with the symptoms of hearing loss and other auditory, balance, and related sensory and neural problems. They then assess the nature and extent of the problems and help the individuals manage them. Using audiometers, computers, and other testing devices, they measure the loudness at which a person begins to hear sounds, the ability to distinguish between sounds, and the impact of hearing loss on an individual's daily life. In addition, audiologists use computer equipment to evaluate and diagnose balance disorders. Audiologists interpret these results and may coordinate them with medical, educational, and psychological information to make a diagnosis and determine a course of treatment.

Hearing disorders can result from a variety of causes including trauma at birth, viral infections, genetic disorders, exposure to loud noise, certain medications, or aging. Treatment may include examining and cleaning the ear canal, fitting and dispensing hearing aids, and fitting and programming cochlear implants. Audiologic treatment also includes counseling on adjusting to hearing loss, training on the use of hearing instruments, and teaching communication strategies for use in a variety of environments. For example, they may provide instruction in listening strategies. Audiologists also may recommend, fit, and dispense personal or large area amplification systems and alerting devices.

In audiology (hearing) clinics, audiologists may independently develop and carry out treatment programs. They keep records on the initial evaluation, progress, and discharge of patients. In other settings, audiologists may work with other health and education providers as part of a team in planning and implementing services for children and adults, from birth to old age. Audiologists who diagnose and treat balance disorders often work in collaboration with physicians, and physical and occupational therapists.

Some audiologists specialize in work with the elderly, children, or hearing-impaired individuals who need special treatment programs. Others develop and implement ways to protect workers' hearing from on-the-job injuries. They measure noise levels in workplaces and conduct hearing protection programs in factories, as well as in schools and communities.

Audiologists who work in private practice also manage the business aspects of running an office, such as developing a patient base, hiring employees, keeping records, and ordering equipment and supplies.

A few audiologists conduct research on types of—and treatment for—hearing, balance, and related disorders. Others design and develop equipment or techniques for diagnosing and treating these disorders.

Working Conditions

Audiologists usually work at a desk or table in clean, comfortable surroundings. The job is not physically demanding but does require attention to detail and intense concentration. The emotional needs of patients and their families may be demanding. Most full-time audiologists work about 40 hours per week, which may include weekends and evenings to meet the needs of patients. Some work part time. Those who work on a contract basis may spend a substantial amount of time traveling between facilities.

Training, Other Qualifications, and Advancement

Audiologists are regulated in 49 States; all require that individuals have at least a master's degree in audiology. However, a clinical doctoral degree is expected to become the new standard, and several States are currently in the process of changing their regulations to require the Doctor of Audiology (Au.D.) degree or equivalent. A passing score on the national examination on audiology offered through the Praxis Series of the Educational Testing Service also is needed. Other requirements typically are 300 to 375 hours of supervised clinical experience and 9 months of postgraduate professional clinical experience. Forty-one states have continuing education requirements for licensure renewal. An additional examination and license is required in order to dispense hearing aids in some states. Medicaid, Medicare, and private health insurers generally require practitioners to be licensed to qualify for reimbursement.

In 2005, there were 24 master's degree programs and 62 clinical doctoral programs offered at accredited colleges and universities. Graduation from an accredited program may be required to obtain a license. Requirements for admission to programs in audiology include courses in English, mathematics, physics, chemistry, biology, psychology, and communication. Graduate course work in audiology includes physiology; anatomy; physics; genetics; normal and abnormal communication development; auditory, balance, and neural systems assessment and treatment; diagnosis and treatment; pharmacology; and ethics.

Audiologists can acquire the Certificate of Clinical Competence in Audiology (CCC-A) offered by the American Speech-Language-Hearing Association. To earn a CCC-A, a person must have a graduate degree and 375 hours of supervised clinical experience, complete a 36-week postgraduate clinical fellowship, and pass the Praxis Series examination in audiology, administered by the Educational Testing Service. According to the American Speech-Language-Hearing Association, as of 2007, audiologists will need to have a bachelor's degree and complete 75 hours of credit toward a doctoral degree in order to seek certification. As of 2012, audiologists will have to earn a doctoral degree in order to be certified.

Audiologists may also be certified through the American Board of Audiology. Applicants must earn a master's or doctoral degree in audiology from a regionally accredited college or university, achieve a passing score on a national examination in audiology, and demonstrate that they have completed a minimum of 2,000 hours of mentored professional practice in a two-year period with a qualified audiologist. Certificants must apply for renewal every three years. They must demonstrate that they have earned 45 hours of approved continuing education within the three-year period. Beginning in 2007, all applicants must earn a doctoral degree in audiology.

Audiologists should be able to effectively communicate diagnostic test results, diagnoses, and proposed treatments in a manner easily understood by their patients. They must be able to approach problems objectively and provide support to patients and their families. Because a patient's progress may be slow, patience, compassion, and good listening skills are necessary.

Employment

Audiologists held about 10,000 jobs in 2004. More than half of all jobs were in offices of physicians or other health practitioners, including audiologists; in hospitals; and in outpatient care centers. About 1 in 7 jobs was in educational services, including elementary and secondary schools. Other jobs for audiologists were in health and personal care stores, including hearing aid stores; scientific research and development services; and state and local governments.

A small number of audiologists were self-employed in private practice. They provided hearing health care services in their own offices or worked under contract for schools, health care facilities, or other establishments.

Job Outlook

Employment of audiologists is expected to grow about as fast as the average for all occupations through the year 2014. Because hearing loss is strongly associated with aging, rapid growth in older population groups will cause the number of persons with hearing and balance impairments to increase markedly. Medical advances are also improving the survival rate of premature infants and trauma victims, who then need assessment and possible treatment. Greater awareness of the importance of early identification and diagnosis of hearing disorders in infants also will increase employment. Most states now require that all newborns be screened for hearing loss and receive appropriate early intervention services.

Employment in educational services will increase along with growth in elementary and secondary school enrollments, including enrollment of special education students. The number of audiologists in private practice will rise due to the increasing demand for direct services to individuals as well as increasing use of contract services by hospitals, schools, and nursing care facilities.

Growth in employment of audiologists will be moderated by limitations on insurance reimbursements for the services they provide. Additionally, increased educational requirements may limit the pool of workers entering the profession and any resulting higher salaries may cause doctors to hire more lower paid ear technicians to perform the functions that audiologists held in doctor's offices. Only a few job openings for audiologists will arise from the need to replace those who leave the occupation, because the occupation is small.

Earnings

Median annual earnings of audiologists were $51,470 in May 2004. The middle 50 percent earned between $42,160 and $62,210. The lowest 10 percent earned less than $34,990, and the highest 10 percent earned more than $75,990.

According to a 2004 survey by the American Speech-Language-Hearing Association, the median annual salary for full-time certified audiologists who worked on a calendar-year basis, generally 11 or 12 months annually, was $56,000. For those who worked on an academic year basis, usually 9 or 10 months annually, the median annual salary was $53,000. The median starting salary for certified audiologists with one to three years of experience was $45,000 on a calendar-year basis.

RELATED OCCUPATIONS

Audiologists specialize in the prevention, diagnosis, and treatment of hearing problems. Workers in related occupations include occupational therapists, optometrists, physical therapists, psychologists, recreational therapists, rehabilitation counselors, and speech-language pathologists.

Speech-Language Pathologists

Speech-language pathologists, sometimes called speech therapists, assess, diagnose, treat, and help to prevent speech, language, cognitive communication, voice, swallowing, fluency, and other related disorders. Speech-language pathologists work with people who cannot produce speech sounds, or cannot produce them clearly; those with speech rhythm and fluency problems, such as stuttering; people with voice disorders, such as inappropriate pitch or harsh voice; those with problems understanding and producing language; those who wish to improve their communication skills by modifying an accent; and those with cognitive communication impairments, such as attention, memory, and problem solving disorders. They also work with people who have swallowing difficulties. Employment is expected to grow because the expanding population in older age groups is prone to medical conditions that result in speech, language, and swallowing problems. In 2005, 47 states required speech-language pathologists to be licensed if they worked in a health care setting, and all states required a master's degree or equivalent. A passing score on the national examination on speech-language pathology, offered through the Praxis Series of the Educational Testing Service, is needed as well. Other requirements typically are 300 to 375 hours of supervised clinical experience and 9 months of postgraduate professional clinical experience. Median annual earnings of speech-language pathologists were $52,410 in May 2004.

AUDIOLOGISTS and
SPEECH-LANGUAGE PATHOLOGISTS
RESOURCES

Don't forget! There are many good general resources listed in Chapter Three. Look in the Occupational Therapists / Physical Therapists section of this chapter for other resources.

♒ Association   📁 Directory   📧 Resume Service   🖱 Web Site

📋 Job Ads   ⚡ Job Alert E-mail/Hotline   🏷 Job Fairs   📖 Book

For a full explanation of these resources see the second page of Chapter 3.

♒ 📁 🖱 **Academy of Dispensing Audiologists (ADA)** - 401 N. Michigan Avenue, Suite 2200, Chicago, IL 60611; 866/493-5544. (**http://www.audiologist.org,** info@audiologist.org) Organization of dispensing audiologists. By 2012 a professional audiologist will be required to have an AuD degree (a 4-year postgraduate program) to be certified and to practice. They offer mentoring during the 3rd year. The 4th year consists of an internship.

📋 🏷 🖱 *ADVANCE for Speech-Language Pathologists and Audiologists* - 2900 Horizon Dr., Box 61556, King of Prussia, PA 19406; 610/278-1400. (**http://speech-language-pathology-audiology.advanceweb.com**) Web site has job listings and a schedule of job fairs. Subscriptions to magazine are free for qualified professionals.

♀⌐⊖ **The Alexander Graham Bell Association for the Deaf** - 3417 Volta Place N.W., Washington, DC 20007-2778; 202/337-5220.Scholarships for students who are hard of hearing. **(http://www.agbell.org)**

♀⌐⊖ **American Academy of Audiology (AAA)** - 11730 Plaza America Drive, Suite 300, Reston, VA 20190; 800-AAA-2336, 703-790-8466. **(http://www.audiology.org**) Student section has listing of contacts at all audiology programs in the US, "What Students Should Know and Look for when Seeking to Become an Audiologist" academic curriculum, and clinical training. Directory of audiologists available only to members; student membership $103.

♀⌐⊖ **American Academy of Private Practice in Speech Pathology and Audiology (AAPPSPA)** - 100 West Fairway Dr., Valdosta, GA 31605, **(http://www.aappspa.org**). This site has a listing of private practitioners by area.

⌐⊖ **American Board of Audiology** - 11730 Plaza America Dr., Suite 300, Reston, VA 20190; 800-AAA-2336. Find an audiologist with their search engine. **(http://www.americanboardofaudiology.org)**

♀⌐⌐⊖ **American Speech-Language-Hearing Association (ASHA)** - 10801 Rockville Pike, Rockville, MD 20852; 800/498-2071. Visit their web site at **(http://www.asha.org**). The audiologist profession is currently moving to PhD level of education for certification, with their standard being the AuD degree for dispensing audiologists and the PhD degree for researchers. Masters programs are still available at almost all institutions. The web site has a searchable database of currently accredited educational programs, which can most easily be found under the "Frequent Searches" tab. Under the Members and Professionals tab there is a listing of State contacts & licensure requirements with a searchable databaseby state.

♀⌐⌐⌐⊖ **California Speech Language and Hearing Association (CSHA)** - 825 University Avenue, Sacramento, CA 95825; 916/921-1568. **(http://www.csha.org**, csha@csha.org) Job fair at annual convention. Job listing and résumé posting on web site.

♀⌐⌐⊖ **Canadian Association of Speech Language Pathologists & Audiologists (CASLPA)** - 401- 200 Elgin Street, Ottawa, Ontario K2P 1L5; 800/259-8519. **(http://www.caslpa.ca**, caslpa@caslpa.ca) A well organized web site with information about the career, information for current and prospective students, directory of certified Canadian programs, and ads for jobs in Canada. Canadians have baccalaureate programs for Speech-Language Pathologist Assistant and Communicative Disorders Assistant as well as masters and doctoral programs similar to those in the US.

☤ ☐⁄🖱 Council of Academic Programs in Communication Sciences and Disorders (CGPCSD) - PO Box 26532, Minneapolis, MN 55426; 612/920-0966. (**http://www.capcsd.org**, cap@incnet.com) Lists of both member and non-member educational programs by name, or by state/province.

☤ 🖱 Educational Audiology Association (EAA) - 13153 N Dale Mabry Hwy, Suite 105, Tampa FL 33618; 800/460-7EAA (7322). (**http://edaud.org**, EAA@L-TGraye.com) An international organization of audiologists and related professionals who deliver hearing services to children, particularly in educational settings.

📱✍🖱 Jobs in Therapy - **http://www.jobsintherapy.com/** U.S. job openings for speech and other therapies. Résumé posting is required before job searches and recruiting services offered.

📱🖱 National Institute on Deafness and Other Communication Disorders (NIDCD) - 31 Center Drive, MSC 2320, Bethesda, MD USA 20892 (one of the National Institutes of Health) (**http://www.nidcd. nih.gov**, nidcdinfo@nidcd.nih.gov) Lists NIDCD student programs, graduate education and fellowship opportunities at NIDCD, and funding for independent research.

☤ 🖱 National Student Speech Language Hearing Association (NSSLHA) - 10801 Rockville Pike, Rockville, MD 20852; 800/498-2071 (**www.nsslha.org**, nsslha@asha.org) Sponsors job fair at the ASHA national convention for both masters and doctoral programs.

☐⁄🖱 University Programs in Speech-language Pathology and Audiology - (**http://facstaff.uww.edu/bradleys/cdprograms.html**) This site lists state programs and has certification organization information.

Chapter

7

NURSING CAREERS

Desiree Griffith

Desiree Griffith, a post-anesthesia care registered nurse at the Sewickley Hospital in Western Pennsylvania, was born in Guyana, South America on April 5, 1947. She came to America in 1968 just before turning 21. Desiree was a tax assessor in Guyana. Math and science were always her strong points and in New York she landed a job as a claims adjuster.

"I met a friend in New York that was in nursing school. She was having a great time and really loved what she was doing", said Desiree. "I wanted to deal more with people so I followed my friend's example and entered the Brooklyn Jewish Hospital's nursing program in 1969." Mrs. Griffith did very well in school and she said, "I loved it. I enjoyed working with people and it was always challenging."

Mrs. Griffith started working in a medical surgery unit and stayed there for six months. Then she went on maternity leave to have her first child. After returning from maternity leave she requested a recovery room assignment and has worked in this area since 1973. "Post-anesthesia Care is the section that you're taken to after surgery to recover patients from the effects of anesthesia," said Desiree, "This used to be called the recovery room."

In 1977 Desiree and her family moved to Charlotte, North Carolina and she landed a job in a cardiovascular recovery unit at the Charlotte Memorial Hospital. The last eighteen months at Charlotte Desiree worked in post-anesthesia care.

"One of the advantages of the nursing field is the ability to work diverse schedules depending on your personal circumstances," said Desiree. "In 1980 we moved to Pittsburgh where I worked casual (part-time) at the Sewickley Hospital due to my husband's work schedule. After my second child was born I opted to work on weekends only for a period of time. For several years I shared a job with another nurse; I worked Monday, Tuesday and a half day on Wednesday, my partner worked the remainder of the week."

"Nursing is a great field to work in - it's hard work without a doubt. The field is wide open with many career options. Also, as a registered nurse everyone in my unit is fully qualified to do the same function. Therefore, when I need a day off it isn't difficult to get someone to work for me."

"There are other things to consider," said Desiree, "You may be required to work rotating shifts, weekends, and holidays. The stress involved when you deal with life and death situations on a daily basis can get to you. If something is happening in recovery you don't have the option to just leave at the end of your shift. You must be willing to stay no matter what you have planned. Your patients depend on you entirely."

Desiree said, "You can always find a job in nursing if you really want to work. You may not find one with all daylight work and no weekends but you will find a job. Most of it is up to you."

This chapter features nursing. The major occupational groups are:

Licensed Practical Nurses   **Registered Nurses**
Nursing Aides and Psychiatric Aides

Each specialty is described below. Following all of the job descriptions is a job resource list: Associations, Books, Directories, Internet Sites, Job Ads, E-mail Job Notification/Job Hotlines, Job Fairs, and Résumé and Placement Services with icons guide you.

LICENSED PRACTICAL NURSES

Significant Points
*   Training lasting about 1 year is available in about 1,200 state approved programs, mostly in vocational or technical schools.
*   Applicants for jobs in hospitals may face competition as the number of hospital jobs for licensed practical nurses declines; however, rapid employment growth is projected in other health care industries, with the best job opportunities occurring in nursing care facilities and in home health care services.
*   Replacement needs will be a major source of job openings, as many workers leave the occupation permanently.

Nature of the Work
Licensed practical nurses (LPNs), or licensed vocational nurses (LVNs), care for the sick, injured, convalescent, and disabled under the direction of physicians and registered nurses. (The work of physicians and surgeons is described in Chapter 9 and that of registered nurses is described later in this chapter.)

Most LPNs provide basic bedside care, taking vital signs such as temperature, blood pressure, pulse, and respiration. They also prepare and give injections and enemas, monitor catheters, apply dressings, treat bedsores, and give alcohol rubs and massages. LPNs monitor their patients and report adverse reactions to medications or treatments. They collect samples for testing, perform routine laboratory tests, feed patients, and record food and fluid intake and output. To help keep patients comfortable, LPNs assist with bathing, dressing, and personal hygiene. In states where the law allows, they may administer prescribed medicines or start intravenous fluids. Some LPNs help to deliver, care for, and feed infants. Experienced LPNs may supervise nursing assistants and aides.

In addition to providing routine bedside care, LPNs in nursing care facilities help to evaluate residents' needs, develop care plans, and supervise the care provided by nursing aides. In doctors' offices and clinics, they also may make appointments, keep records, and perform other clerical duties.

Working Conditions

Most licensed practical nurses in hospitals and nursing care facilities work a 40-hour week, but because patients need round-the-clock care, some work nights, weekends, and holidays. They often stand for long periods and help patients move in bed, stand, or walk.

LPNs may face hazards from caustic chemicals, radiation, and infectious diseases such as hepatitis. They are subject to back injuries when moving patients and shock from electrical equipment. They often must deal with the stress of heavy workloads. In addition, the patients they care for may be confused, irrational, agitated, or uncooperative.

Training, Other Qualifications, and Advancement

All states and the District of Columbia require LPNs to pass a licensing examination, known as the NCLEX-PN, after completing a state approved practical nursing program. A high school diploma or its equivalent usually is required for entry, although some programs accept candidates without a diploma, and some are designed as part of a high school curriculum.

In 2004, approximately 1,200 state-approved programs provided training in practical nursing. Most training programs are available from technical and vocational schools, or from community and junior colleges. Other programs are available through high schools, hospitals, and colleges and universities.

Most practical nursing programs last about 1 year and include both classroom study and supervised clinical practice (patient care). Classroom study covers basic nursing concepts and patient care-related subjects, including anatomy, physiology, medical-surgical nursing, pediatrics, obstetrics, psychiatric nursing, the administration of drugs, nutrition, and first aid. Clinical practice usually is in a hospital, but sometimes includes other settings.

In some employment settings, such as nursing homes, LPNs can advance to become charge nurses who oversee the work of other LPNs and of nursing aides. Some LPNs also choose to become registered nurses through numerous LPN-to-RN training programs.

LPNs should have a caring, sympathetic nature. They should be emotionally stable because working with the sick and injured can be stressful. They also should have keen observational, decision-making, and communication skills. As part of a health care team, they must be able to follow orders and work under close supervision.

Employment

Licensed practical nurses held about 726,000 jobs in 2004. About 27 percent of LPNs worked in hospitals, 25 percent in nursing care facilities, and another 12 percent in offices of physicians. Others worked for home health care services; employment services; community care facilities for the elderly; public and private educational services; outpatient care centers; and federal, state, and local government agencies. About 1 in 5 worked part time.

Job Outlook

Employment of LPNs is expected to grow about as fast as average for all occupations through 2014 in response to the long-term care needs of an increasing elderly population and the general growth of health care services. Replacement needs will be a major source of job openings, as many workers leave the occupation permanently. Applicants for jobs in hospitals may face competition as the number of hospital jobs for LPNs declines; however, rapid employment growth is projected in other health care industries, with the best job opportunities occurring in nursing care facilities and in home health care services.

Employment of LPNs in hospitals is expected to continue to decline. Sophisticated procedures once performed only in hospitals are being performed in physicians' offices and in outpatient care centers such as ambulatory surgical and emergency medical centers, largely because of advances in technology. Consequently, employment of LPNs in most health care industries outside the traditional hospital setting is projected to grow faster than average.

Employment of LPNs is expected to grow much faster than average in home health care services. Home health care agencies also will offer the most new jobs for LPNs because of an increasing number of older persons with functional disabilities, consumer preference for care in the home, and technological advances that make it possible to bring increasingly complex treatments into the home.

Employment of LPNs in nursing care facilities is expected to grow about as fast as average because of the growing number of aged and disabled persons in need of long-term care. In addition, LPNs in nursing care facilities will be needed to care for the increasing number of patients who have been discharged from the hospital but who have not recovered enough to return home. However, changes in consumer preferences towards less restrictive and more cost-effective care from assisted living facilities and home health care agencies will limit employment growth.

Earnings

Median annual earnings of licensed practical nurses were $33,970 in May 2004. The middle 50 percent earned between $28,830 and $40,670. The lowest 10 percent earned less than $24,480, and the highest 10 percent earned more than $46,270. Median annual earnings in the industries employing the largest numbers of licensed practical nurses in May 2004 were: Employment services, $41,550; Nursing care facilities, $35,460; Home health care services, $35,180; General medical and surgical hospitals, $32,570; Offices of physicians $30,400.

Related Occupations

LPNs work closely with people while helping them. So do emergency medical technicians and paramedics; medical assistants; nursing, psychiatric, and home health aides; registered nurses; social and human service assistants; and surgical technologists.

NURSING, PSYCHIATRIC, and HOME HEALTH AIDES

OCCUPATIONAL TITLES:

Geriatric Aides	**Nursing Aides**
Home Health Aides	**Nursing Assistants**
Hospital Attendants	**Orderlies**
Mental Health Assistants	**Psychiatric Aides**

Significant Points

• Home health aides are projected to be the fastest growing occupation through 2014.

• Numerous job openings and excellent job opportunities are expected.

• Most jobs are in nursing and residential care facilities, hospitals, and home health care services.

• Modest entry requirements, low pay, high physical and emotional demands, and lack of advancement opportunities characterize this occupation.

Nature of the Work

Nursing and psychiatric aides help care for physically or mentally ill, injured, disabled, or infirm individuals confined to hospitals, nursing care facilities, and mental health settings. Home health aides have duties that are similar, but they work in patients' homes or residential care facilities.

Nursing aides—also known as nursing assistants, certified nursing assistants, geriatric aides, unlicenced assistive personnel, orderlies, or hospital attendants—perform routine tasks under the supervision of nursing and medical staff. They answer patients' call lights; deliver messages; serve meals; make beds; and help patients to eat, dress, and bathe. Aides also may provide skin care to patients; take their temperature, pulse rate, respiration rate, and blood pressure; and help them to get into and out of bed and walk. They also may escort patients to operating and examining rooms, keep patients' rooms neat, set up equipment, store and move supplies, and assist with some procedures. Aides observe patients' physical, mental, and emotional conditions and report any change to the nursing or medical staff.

Nursing aides employed in nursing care facilities often are the principal caregivers, having far more contact with residents than do other members of the staff. Because some residents may stay in a nursing care facility for months or even years, aides develop ongoing relationships with them and interact with them in a positive, caring way.

Home health aides help elderly, convalescent, or disabled persons live in their own homes instead of in a health care facility. Under the direction of nursing or medical staff, they provide health-related services, such as administering oral medications. (Personal and home care aides, who provide mainly housekeeping and routine personal care services, are discussed elsewhere in the Handbook.) Like nursing aides, home health aides may check patients' pulse rate, temperature, and respiration rate; help with simple prescribed exercises; keep patients' rooms neat; and help patients to move from bed, bathe, dress, and groom. Occasionally, they change non-sterile dressings, give massages and alcohol rubs, or assist with braces and artificial limbs. Experienced home health aides also may assist with medical equipment such as ventilators, which help patients breathe.

Most home health aides work with elderly or disabled persons who need more extensive care than family or friends can provide. Some help discharged hospital patients who have relatively short-term needs.

In home health agencies, a registered nurse, physical therapist, or social worker usually assigns specific duties to and supervises home health aides, who keep records of the services they perform and record each patient's condition and progress. The aides report changes in a patient's condition to the supervisor or case manager.

Psychiatric aides, also known as mental health assistants or psychiatric nursing assistants, care for mentally impaired or emotionally disturbed individuals. They work under a team that may include psychiatrists, psychologists, psychiatric nurses, social workers, and therapists. In addition to helping patients to dress, bathe, groom themselves, and eat, psychiatric aides socialize with them and lead them in educational and recreational activities. Psychiatric aides may play games such as cards with the patients, watch television with them, or participate in group activities, such as sports or field trips. They observe patients and report any physical or behavioral signs that might be important for the professional staff to know. They accompany patients to and from examinations and treatment. Because they have such close contact with patients, psychiatric aides can have a great deal of influence on their patients' outlook and treatment.

Working Conditions

Most full-time aides work about 40 hours a week, but, because patients need care 24 hours a day, some aides work evenings, nights, weekends, and holidays. Many work part time. In 2004, 25 percent of aides worked part time compared with 16 percent of all workers. Aides spend many hours standing and walking, and they often face heavy workloads. Aides must guard against back injury because they may have to move patients into and out of bed or help them to stand or walk. Aides also may face hazards from minor infections and major diseases, such as hepatitis, but can avoid infections by following proper procedures.

Aides often have unpleasant duties, such as emptying bedpans and changing soiled bed linens. The patients they care for may be disoriented, irritable, or uncooperative. Psychiatric aides must be prepared to care for patients whose illness may cause violent behavior. While their work can be emotionally demanding, many aides gain satisfaction from assisting those in need.

Home health aides may go to the same patient's home for months or even years. However, most aides work with a number of different patients, each job lasting a few hours, days, or weeks. Home health aides often visit multiple patients on the same day.

Home health aides generally work alone, with periodic visits from their supervisor. They receive detailed instructions explaining when to visit patients and what services to perform. Aides are individually responsible for getting to patients' homes, and they may spend a good portion of the working day traveling from one patient to another. Because mechanical lifting devices available in institutional settings are seldom available in patients' homes, home health aides are particularly susceptible to injuries resulting from overexertion when they assist patients.

Training, Other Qualifications, and Advancement

In many cases, a high school diploma or equivalent is necessary for a job as a nursing or psychiatric aide. However, a high school diploma generally is not required for jobs as home health aides. Hospitals may require previous experience as a nursing aide or home health aide. Nursing care facilities often hire inexperienced workers, who must complete a minimum of 75 hours of mandatory training and pass a competency evaluation as part of a state-approved training program within 4 months of their employment. Aides who complete the program are known as certified nurse assistants (CNAs) and are placed on the state registry of nursing aides. Some states also require psychiatric aides to complete a formal training program. However, most psychiatric aides learn their skills on the job from experienced workers.

Nursing and psychiatric aide training is offered in high schools, vocational-technical centers, some nursing care facilities, and some community colleges. Courses cover body mechanics, nutrition, anatomy and physiology, infection control, communication skills, and resident rights. Personal care skills, such as how to help patients to bathe, eat, and groom themselves, also are taught.

Some employers provide classroom instruction for newly hired aides, while others rely exclusively on informal on-the-job instruction by a licensed nurse or an experienced aide. Such training may last from several days to a few months. Aides also may attend lectures, workshops, and in-service training.

The federal government has guidelines for home health aides whose employers receive reimbursement from Medicare. Federal law requires home health aides to pass a competency test covering a wide range of areas: Communication; documentation of patient status and care provided; reading and recording of vital signs; basic infection-control procedures; basic bodily functions; maintenance of a healthy environment; emergency procedures; physical, emotional, and developmental characteristics of patients; personal hygiene and grooming; safe transfer techniques; normal range of motion and positioning; and basic nutrition.

A home health aide may receive training before taking the competency test. Federal law suggests at least 75 hours of classroom and practical training, supervised by a registered nurse. Training and testing programs may be offered by the employing agency but must meet the standards of the Center for Medicare and Medicaid Services. State regulations for training programs vary.

The National Association for Home Care offers national certification for home health aides. The certification is a voluntary demonstration that the individual has met industry standards. Some states also require aides to be licensed.

Aides must be in good health. A physical examination, including state-regulated tests such as those for tuberculosis, may be required. A criminal background check also is usually required for employment.

Applicants should be tactful, patient, understanding, emotionally stable, and dependable and should have a desire to help people. They also should be able to work as part of a team, have good communication skills, and be willing to perform repetitive, routine tasks. Home health aides should be honest and discreet, because they work in private homes. They also will need access to their own car or public transportation to reach patients' homes.

For some individuals, these occupations serve as entry-level jobs, as in the case of high school and college students who may work while also attending school. In addition, experience as an aide can help individuals decide whether to pursue a career in health care. Opportunities for advancement within these occupations are limited. Aides generally need additional formal training or education in order to enter other health occupations. The most common health care occupations for former aides are licensed practical nurse, registered nurse, and medical assistant.

Employment

Nursing, psychiatric, and home health aides held about 2.1 million jobs in 2004. Nursing aides held the most jobs—approximately 1.5 million. Home health aides held roughly 624,000 jobs and psychiatric aides held about 59,000 jobs. Around 42 percent of nursing aides worked in nursing care facilities, and another 27 percent worked in hospitals. Most home health aides—about 34 percent—were employed by home health care services. Others were employed in nursing and residential care facilities and social assistance agencies. Around 54 percent of all psychiatric aides worked in hospitals, primarily in psychiatric and substance abuse hospitals, although some also worked in the psychiatric units of general medical and surgical hospitals. Others were employed in State government agencies; residential mental retardation, mental health, and substance abuse facilities; outpatient care centers; and nursing care facilities.

Job Outlook

Numerous job openings for nursing, psychiatric, and home health aides will arise from a combination of fast employment growth and high replacement needs. High replacement needs in this large occupation reflect modest entry requirements, low pay, high physical and emotional demands, and lack of opportunities for advancement. For these same reasons, many people are unwilling to perform the kind of work required by the occupation, limiting the number of entrants. Many aides also leave the occupation to attend training programs for other health care occupations. Therefore, persons who are interested in, and suited for, this work should have excellent job opportunities.

Overall employment of nursing, psychiatric, and home health aides is projected to grow much faster than average for all occupations through the year 2014, although individual occupational growth rates will vary. Home health aides is expected to be the fastest growing occupation, as a result of both growing demand for home services from an aging population and efforts to contain costs by moving patients out of hospitals and nursing care facilities as quickly as possible. Consumer preference for care in the home and improvements in medical technologies for in-home treatment also will contribute to much-faster-than-average employment growth for home health aides.

Nursing aide employment will not grow as fast as home health aide employment, largely because nursing aides are concentrated in slower growing nursing care facilities and hospitals. Employment of nursing aides is expected to grow faster than average for all occupations through 2014, in response to the long-term care needs of an increasing elderly population. Financial pressures on hospitals to discharge patients as soon as possible should boost admissions to nursing care facilities. As a result, job opportunities will be more numerous in nursing and residential care facilities than in hospitals. Modern medical technology also will drive demand for nursing aides because, as the technology saves and extends more lives, it increases the need for long-term care provided by aides.

Employment of psychiatric aides—the smallest of the three occupations—is expected to grow more slowly than average for all occupations. Most psychiatric aides currently work in hospitals, but most job growth will be in residential mental health facilities and in home health care agencies. There is a long-term trend toward treating mental health patients outside of hospitals because it is more cost effective and allows patients to live more normal lives. Demand for psychiatric aides in residential facilities will rise in response to growth in the number of older persons—many of whom will require mental health services—but also as an increasing number of mentally disabled adults, who were formerly cared for by their elderly parents, seek care. Job growth also could be affected by changes in government funding of programs for the mentally ill.

Earnings
Median hourly earnings of nursing aides, orderlies, and attendants were $10.09 in May 2004. The middle 50 percent earned between $8.59

and $12.09 an hour. The lowest 10 percent earned less than $7.31, and the highest 10 percent earned more than $14.02 an hour. Median hourly earnings in the industries employing the largest numbers of nursing aides, orderlies, and attendants in May 2004 were: Employment services, $11.29; Local government, $11.10; General medical and surgical hospitals, $10.44; Nursing care facilities, $9.86; Community care facilities for the elderly, $9.56.

Nursing and psychiatric aides in hospitals generally receive at least 1 week of paid vacation after 1 year of service. Paid holidays and sick leave, hospital and medical benefits, extra pay for late-shift work, and pension plans also are available to many hospital employees and to some nursing care facility employees.

Median hourly earnings of home health aides were $8.81 in May 2004. The middle 50 percent earned between $7.52 and $10.38 an hour. The lowest 10 percent earned less than $6.52, and the highest 10 percent earned more than $12.32 an hour. Median hourly earnings in the industries employing the largest numbers of home health aides in May 2004 were as follows: Nursing care facilities, $9.11; Residential mental retardation, mental health and substance abuse facilities, $8.97; Home health care services, $8.57; Community care facilities for the elderly, $8.57; Individual and family services, $8.47.

Home health aides receive slight pay increases with experience and added responsibility. Usually, they are paid only for the time worked in the home, not for travel time between jobs. Most employers hire only on-call hourly workers and provide no benefits.

Median hourly earnings of psychiatric aides were $11.19 in May 2004. The middle 50 percent earned between $9.09 and $14.09 an hour. The lowest 10 percent earned less than $7.63, and the highest 10 percent earned more than $16.74 an hour. Median hourly earnings in the industries employing the largest numbers of psychiatric aides in May 2004 were as follows: General medical and surgical hospitals, $11.31; Psychiatric and substance abuse hospitals, $11.06; Residential mental retardation, mental health and substance abuse facilities, $9.37.

Related Occupations
Nursing, psychiatric, and home health aides help people who need routine care or treatment. So do childcare workers, licensed practical and licensed vocational nurses, medical assistants, occupational therapist

assistants and aides, personal and home care aides, physical therapist assistants and aides, and registered nurses.

REGISTERED NURSES

Significant Points

* Registered nurses constitute the largest health care occupation, with 2.4 million jobs.
* About 3 out of 5 jobs are in hospitals.
* The three major educational paths to registered nursing are a bachelor's degree, an associate degree, and a diploma from an approved nursing program.
* Registered nurses are projected to create the second largest number of new jobs among all occupations; job opportunities in most specialties and employment settings are expected to be excellent, with some employers reporting difficulty in attracting and retaining enough RNs.

Nature of the Work

Registered nurses (RNs), regardless of specialty or work setting, perform basic duties that include treating patients, educating patients and the public about various medical conditions, and providing advice and emotional support to patients' family members. RNs record patients' medical histories and symptoms, help to perform diagnostic tests and analyze results, operate medical machinery, administer treatment and medications, and help with patient follow-up and rehabilitation.

RNs teach patients and their families how to manage their illness or injury, including post-treatment home care needs, diet and exercise programs, and self-administration of medication and physical therapy. Some RNs also are trained to provide grief counseling to family members of critically ill patients. RNs work to promote general health by educating the public on various warning signs and symptoms of disease and where to go for help. RNs also might run general health screening or immunization clinics, blood drives, and public seminars on various conditions.

RNs can specialize in one or more patient care specialties. The most common specialties can be divided into roughly four categories—by work setting or type of treatment; disease, ailment, or condition; organ or body system type; or population. RNs may combine specialties from more than one area—for example, pediatric oncology or cardiac emergency—depending on personal interest and employer needs.

RNs may specialize by work setting or by type of care provided. For example, ambulatory care nurses treat patients with a variety of illnesses and injuries on an outpatient basis, either in physicians' offices or in clinics. Some ambulatory care nurses are involved in telehealth, providing care and advice through electronic communications media such as video-conferencing or the Internet. Critical care nurses work in critical or intensive care hospital units and provide care to patients with cardiovascular, respiratory, or pulmonary failure. Emergency, or trauma, nurses work in hospital emergency departments and treat patients with life-threatening conditions caused by accidents, heart attacks, and strokes. Some emergency nurses are flight nurses, who provide medical care to patients who must be flown by helicopter to the nearest medical facility. Holistic nurses provide care such as acupuncture, massage and aroma therapy, and biofeedback, which are meant to treat patients' mental and spiritual health in addition to their physical health. Home health care nurses provide at-home care for patients who are recovering from surgery, accidents, and childbirth. Hospice and palliative care nurses provide care for, and help ease the pain of, terminally ill patients outside of hospitals. Infusion nurses administer medications, fluids, and blood to patients through injections into patients' veins. Long- term care nurses provide medical services on a recurring basis to patients with chronic physical or mental disorders. Medical-surgical nurses provide basic medical care to a variety of patients in all health settings. Occupational health nurses provide treatment for job-related injuries and illnesses and help employers to detect workplace hazards and implement health and safety standards. Perianesthesia nurses provide preoperative and postoperative care to patients undergoing anesthesia during surgery. Perioperative nurses assist surgeons by selecting and handling instruments, controlling bleeding, and suturing incisions. Some of these nurses also can specialize in plastic and reconstructive surgery. Psychiatric nurses treat patients with personality and mood disorders. Radiologic nurses provide care to patients undergoing diagnostic radiation procedures such as ultrasounds and magnetic resonance imaging. Rehabilitation nurses care for patients with temporary and permanent disabilities. Transplant nurses care for both transplant recipients and living donors and monitor signs of organ rejection.

RNs specializing in a particular disease, ailment, or condition are employed in virtually all work settings, including physicians' offices, outpatient treatment facilities, home health care agencies, and hospitals. For instance, addictions nurses treat patients seeking help with alcohol, drug, and tobacco addictions. Developmental disabilities nurses provide care for patients with physical, mental, or behavioral disabilities; care may include help with feeding, controlling bodily functions, and sitting or standing independently. Diabetes management nurses help diabetics to manage their disease by teaching them proper nutrition and showing them how to test blood sugar levels and administer insulin injections. Genetics nurses provide early detection screenings and treatment of patients with genetic disorders, including cystic fibrosis and Huntington's disease. HIV/AIDS nurses care for patients diagnosed with HIV and AIDS. Oncology nurses care for patients with various types of cancer and may administer radiation and chemotherapies. Finally, wound, ostomy, and continence nurses treat patients with wounds caused by traumatic injury, ulcers, or arterial disease; provide postoperative care for patients with openings that allow for alternative methods of bodily waste elimination; and treat patients with urinary and fecal incontinence.

RNs specializing in treatment of a particular organ or body system usually are employed in specialty physicians' offices or outpatient care facilities, although some are employed in hospital specialty or critical care units. For example, cardiac and vascular nurses treat patients with coronary disease and those who have had heart surgery, providing services such as postoperative rehabilitation. Dermatology nurses treat patients with disorders of the skin, such as skin cancer and psoriasis. Gastroenterology nurses treat patients with digestive and intestinal disorders, including ulcers, acid reflux disease, and abdominal bleeding. Some nurses in this field also specialize in endoscopic procedures, which look inside the gastrointestinal tract using a tube equipped with a light and a camera that can capture images of diseased tissue. Gynecology nurses provide care to women with disorders of the reproductive system, including endometriosis, cancer, and sexually transmitted diseases. Nephrology nurses care for patients with kidney disease caused by diabetes, hypertension, or substance abuse. Neuroscience nurses care for patients with dysfunctions of the nervous system, including brain and spinal cord injuries and seizures. Ophthalmic nurses provide care to patients with disorders of the eyes, including blindness and glaucoma, and to patients undergoing eye surgery. Orthopedic nurses care for patients with muscular and skeletal problems, including arthritis, bone fractures, and muscular dystrophy. Otorhinolaryngology nurses care for patients with ear, nose, and throat disorders, such as cleft palates, allergies, and sinus disorders. Respiratory nurses provide care to patients with respiratory disorders such as asthma, tuberculosis, and cystic fibrosis. Urology nurses care for patients with disorders of the kidneys, urinary tract, and male reproductive organs, including infections, kidney and bladder stones, and cancers.

Finally, RNs may specialize by providing preventive and acute care in all health care settings to various segments of the population, including newborns (neonatology), children and adolescents (pediatrics), adults, and the elderly (gerontology or geriatrics). RNs also may provide basic health care to patients outside of health care settings in such venues as including correctional facilities, schools, summer camps, and the military. Some RNs travel around the United States and abroad providing care to patients in areas with shortages of medical professionals.

Most RNs work as staff nurses, providing critical health care services along with physicians, surgeons, and other health care practitioners. However, some RNs choose to become advanced practice nurses, who often are considered primary health care practitioners and work independently or in collaboration with physicians. For example, clinical nurse specialists provide direct patient care and expert consultations in one of many of the nursing specialties listed above. Nurse anesthetists administer anesthesia, monitor patient's vital signs during surgery, and provide post-anesthesia care. Nurse midwives provide primary care to women, including gynecological exams, family planning advice, prenatal care, assistance in labor and delivery, and neonatal care. Nurse practitioners provide basic preventive health care to patients, and increasingly serve as primary and specialty care providers in mainly medically underserved areas. The most common areas of specialty for nurse practitioners are family practice, adult practice, women's health, pediatrics, acute care, and gerontology; however, there are many other specialties. In most states, advanced practice nurses can prescribe medications.

Some nurses have jobs that require little or no direct patient contact. Most of these positions still require an active RN license. Case managers ensure that all of the medical needs of patients with severe injuries and illnesses are met, including the type, location, and duration of treatment. Forensics nurses combine nursing with law enforcement by treating and investigating victims of sexual assault, child abuse, or accidental death. Infection control nurses identify, track, and control infectious outbreaks in health care facilities; develop methods of outbreak prevention and biological terrorism responses; and staff immunization clinics. Legal nurse consultants assist lawyers in medical cases by interviewing patients and witnesses, organizing medical records, determining damages and costs, locating evidence, and educating lawyers about medical issues. Nurse administrators supervise nursing staff, establish work schedules and budgets, and maintain medical supply inventories. Nurse educators teach student nurses and also provide continuing education for RNs. Nurse informaticists collect, store, and analyze nursing data in order to improve efficiency, reduce risk, and improve patient care. RNs also may work as health care consultants, public policy advisors, pharmaceutical and medical supply researchers and sales persons, and medical writers and editors.

Working Conditions

Most RNs work in well-lighted, comfortable health care facilities. Home health and public health nurses travel to patients' homes, schools, community centers, and other sites. RNs may spend considerable time walking and standing. Patients in hospitals and nursing care facilities require 24-hour care; consequently, nurses in these institutions may work nights, weekends, and holidays. RNs also may be on call— available to work on short notice. Nurses who work in office settings are more likely to work regular business hours. About 23 percent of RNs worked part time in 2004, and 7 percent held more than one job.

Nursing has its hazards, especially in hospitals, nursing care facilities, and clinics, where nurses may care for individuals with infectious diseases. RNs must observe rigid, standardized guidelines to guard against disease and other dangers, such as those posed by radiation, accidental needle sticks, chemicals used to sterilize instruments, and anesthetics. In addition, they are vulnerable to back injury when moving patients, shocks from electrical equipment, and hazards posed by compressed gases. RNs who work with critically ill patients also may suffer emotional strain from observing patient suffering and from close personal contact with patients' families.

Training, Other Qualifications, and Advancement

In all states and the District of Columbia, students must graduate from an approved nursing program and pass a national licensing examination, known as the NCLEX-RN, in order to obtain a nursing license. Nurses may be licensed in more than one state, either by examination or by the endorsement of a license issued by another state. Currently 18 states participate in the Nurse Licensure Compact Agreement, which allows nurses to practice in member states without recertifying. All states require periodic renewal of licenses, which may involve continuing education.

There are three major educational paths to registered nursing: A bachelor's of science degree in nursing (BSN), an associate degree in nursing (AND), and a diploma. BSN programs, offered by colleges and universities, take about 4 years to complete. In 2004, 674 nursing programs offered degrees at the bachelor's level. AND programs, offered by community and junior colleges, take about 2 to 3 years to complete. About 846 RN programs in 2004 granted associate degrees. Diploma programs, administered in hospitals, last about 3 years. Only 69 programs offered diplomas in 2004. Generally, licensed graduates of any of the three types of educational programs qualify for entry-level positions as staff nurses.

Many RNs with an AND or diploma later enter bachelor's programs to prepare for a broader scope of nursing practice. Often, they can find a staff nurse position and then take advantage of tuition reimbursement benefits to work toward a BSN by completing an RN-to-BSN program. In 2004, there were 600 RN-to-BSN programs in the United States. Accelerated master's degree programs in nursing also are available.

These programs combine 1 year of an accelerated BSN program with 2 years of graduate study. In 2004, there were 137 RN-to-MSN programs.

Accelerated BSN programs also are available for individuals who have a bachelor's or higher degree in another field and who are interested in moving into nursing. In 2004, more than 165 of these programs were available. Accelerated BSN programs last 12 to 18 months and provide the fastest route to a BSN for individuals who already hold a degree.

Individuals considering nursing should carefully weigh the advantages and disadvantages of enrolling in a BSN program, because, if they do, their advancement opportunities usually are broader. In fact, some career paths are open only to nurses with a bachelor's or master's degree. A bachelor's degree often is necessary for administrative positions and is a prerequisite for admission to graduate nursing programs in research, consulting, and teaching, and all four advanced practice nursing specialties—clinical nurse specialists, nurse anesthetists, nurse midwives, and nurse practitioners. Individuals who complete a bachelor's receive more training in areas such as communication, leadership, and critical thinking, all of which are becoming more important as nursing care becomes more complex. Additionally, bachelor's degree programs offer more clinical experience in nonhospital settings. In 2004, 417 nursing schools offered master's degrees, 93 offered doctoral degrees, and 46 offered accelerated BSN-to-doctoral programs.

All four advanced practice nursing specialties require at least a master's degree. Most programs last about 2 years and require a BSN degree and some programs require at least 1 to 2 years of clinical experience as an RN for admission. In 2004, there were 329 master's and post-master's programs offered for nurse practitioners, 218 master's and post-master's programs for clinical nurse specialists, 92 programs for nurse anesthetists, and 45 programs for nurse midwives. Upon completion of a program, most advanced practice nurses become nationally certified in their area of specialty. In some States, certification in a specialty is required in order to practice that specialty.

All nursing education programs include classroom instruction and supervised clinical experience in hospitals and other health care facilities. Students take courses in anatomy, physiology, microbiology, chemistry, nutrition, psychology and other behavioral sciences, and nursing. Course work also includes the liberal arts for AND and BSN students.

Supervised clinical experience is provided in hospital departments such as pediatrics, psychiatry, maternity, and surgery. A growing number of programs include clinical experience in nursing care facilities, public health departments, home health agencies, and ambulatory clinics.

Nurses should be caring, sympathetic, responsible, and detail oriented. They must be able to direct or supervise others, correctly assess patients' conditions, and determine when consultation is required. They need emotional stability to cope with human suffering, emergencies, and other stresses.

Some RNs start their careers as licensed practical nurses or nursing aides, and then go back to school to receive their RN degree. Most RNs begin as staff nurses, and with experience and good performance often are promoted to more responsible positions. In management, nurses can advance to assistant head nurse or head nurse and, from there, to assistant director, director, and vice president. Increasingly, management-level nursing positions require a graduate or an advanced degree in nursing or health services administration. They also require leader-ship, negotiation skills, and good judgment.

Some nurses move into the business side of health care. Their nursing expertise and experience on a health care team equip them to manage ambulatory, acute, home-based, and chronic care. Employers—including hospitals, insurance companies, pharmaceutical manufacturers, and managed care organizations, among others—need RNs for health planning and development, marketing, consulting, policy development, and quality assurance. Other nurses work as college and university faculty or conduct research.

Foreign-educated nurses wishing to work in the United States must obtain a work visa. Applicants are required to undergo a review of their education and licensing credentials and pass a nursing certification and English proficiency exam, both conducted by the Commission on Graduates of Foreign Nursing Schools. (The commission is an immigration-neutral, nonprofit organization that is recognized internationally as an authority on credentials evaluation in the health care field.) Applicants from Australia, Canada (except Quebec), Ireland, New Zealand, and the United Kingdom are exempt from the language proficiency exam. In addition to these national requirements, most states have their own requirements.

Employment

As the largest health care occupation, registered nurses held about 2.4 million jobs in 2004. About 3 out of 5 jobs were in hospitals, in inpatient and outpatient departments. Others worked in offices of physicians, nursing care facilities, home health care services, employment services, government agencies, and outpatient care centers. The remainder worked mostly in social assistance agencies and educational services, public and private. About 1 in 4 RNs worked part time.

Job Outlook

Job opportunities for RNs in all specialties are expected to be excellent. Employment of registered nurses is expected to grow much faster than average for all occupations through 2014, and, because the occupation is very large, many new jobs will result. In fact, registered nurses are projected to create the second largest number of new jobs among all occupations. Thousands of job openings also will result from the need to replace experienced nurses who leave the occupation, especially as the median age of the registered nurse population continues to rise.

Much faster-than-average growth will be driven by technological advances in patient care, which permit a greater number of medical problems to be treated, and by an increasing emphasis on preventive care. In addition, the number of older people, who are much more likely than younger people to need nursing care, is projected to grow rapidly.

Employers in some parts of the country and in certain employment settings are reporting difficulty in attracting and retaining an adequate number of RNs, primarily because of an aging RN workforce and a lack of younger workers to fill positions. Enrollments in nursing programs at all levels have increased more rapidly in the past couple of years as students seek jobs with stable employment. However, many qualified applicants are being turned away because of a shortage of nursing faculty to teach classes. The need for nursing faculty will only increase as a large number of instructors nears retirement. Many employers also are relying on foreign-educated nurses to fill open positions.

Even though employment opportunities for all nursing specialties are expected to be excellent, they can vary by employment setting. For example, employment is expected to grow more slowly in hospitals—which comprise health care's largest industry—than in most other health care industries. While the intensity of nursing care is likely to increase, requiring more nurses per patient, the number of inpatients (those who remain in the hospital for more than 24 hours) is not likely to grow by much. Patients are being discharged earlier, and more procedures are being done on an outpatient basis, both inside and outside hospitals. Rapid growth is expected in hospital outpatient facilities, such as those providing same-day surgery, rehabilitation, and chemotherapy.

Despite the slower employment growth in hospitals, job opportunities should still be excellent because of the relatively high turnover of hospital nurses. RNs working in hospitals frequently work overtime and night and weekend shifts and also treat seriously ill and injured patients, all of which can contribute to stress and burnout. Hospital departments in which these working conditions occur most frequently—critical care units, emergency departments, and operating rooms—generally will have more job openings than other departments.

To attract and retain qualified nurses, hospitals may offer signing bonuses, family-friendly work schedules, or subsidized training. A growing number of hospitals also are experimenting with online bidding to fill open shifts, in which nurses can volunteer to fill open shifts at premium wages. This can decrease the amount of mandatory overtime that nurses are required to work.

More and more sophisticated procedures, once performed only in hospitals, are being performed in physicians' offices and in outpatient care centers, such as freestanding ambulatory surgical and emergency centers. Accordingly, employment is expected to grow much faster than average in these places as health care in general expands. However, RNs may face greater competition for these positions because they generally offer regular working hours and more comfortable working environments.

Employment in nursing care facilities is expected to grow faster than average because of increases in the number of elderly, many of whom require long-term care. In addition, the financial pressure on hospitals to discharge patients as soon as possible should produce more admissions to nursing care facilities. Job growth also is expected in units that provide specialized long-term rehabilitation for stroke and head injury patients, as well as units that treat Alzheimer's victims.

Employment in home health care is expected to increase rapidly in response to the growing number of older persons with functional disabilities, consumer preference for care in the home, and technological advances that make it possible to bring increasingly complex treatments into the home. The type of care demanded will require nurses who are able to perform complex procedures.

Generally, RNs with at least a bachelor's degree will have better job prospects than those without a bachelor's. In addition, all four advanced practice specialties—clinical nurse specialists, nurse practitioners, midwives, and anesthetists—will be in high demand, particularly in medically underserved areas such as inner cities and rural areas. Relative to physicians, these RNs increasingly serve as lower-cost primary care providers.

Earnings

Median annual earnings of registered nurses were $52,330 in May 2004. The middle 50 percent earned between $43,370 and $63,360. The lowest 10 percent earned less than $37,300, and the highest 10 percent earned more than $74,760. Median annual earnings in the industries employing the largest numbers of registered nurses in May 2004 were as follows: Employment services, $63,170; General medical and surgical hospitals, $53,450; Home health care services, $48,990; Offices of physicians, $48,250; Nursing care facilities, $48,220.

Many employers offer flexible work schedules, child care, educational benefits, and bonuses.

Related Occupations

Workers in other health care occupations with responsibilities and duties related to those of registered nurses are cardiovascular technologists and technicians; diagnostic medical sonographers; dietitians and nutritionists; emergency medical technicians and paramedics; licensed practical and licensed vocational nurses; massage therapists; medical and health services managers; nursing, psychiatric, and home health aides; occupational therapists; physical therapists; physician assistants; physicians and surgeons; radiologic technologists and technicians; respiratory therapists; and surgical technologists.

NURSING CAREER RESOURCES

Don't forget! Refer to the general resources listed in Chapter Three and the Home Health Care Chapter (Chapter Ten).

☤Association 📁Directory 🖉Resume Service 🖰Web Site

📰Job Ads ⚡Job Alert E-mail/Hotline 🏷Job Fairs 📖Book

For a full explanation of these resources see the second page of Chapter 3.

📖 **101 Careers in Nursing** - by Jeanne M. Novotny, Doris T. Lippman, Nicole K. Sanders, Joyce J. Fitzpatrick; Springer Publishing Company, 2003, $33.95, ISBN: 0826120148. Profiles of careers, educational requirements, resources, and personal stories from practicing nurses.

📰🏷🖰 **ADVANCE Newsmagazines** -650 Park Avenue West, Box 61556, King of Prussia, PA 19406-0956; 800/355-1088. Publishes *ADVANCE* *for Nurses, ADVANCE for LPNs* and *ADVANCE for Nurse Practitioners* are free to qualified professionals and have extensive classified ads. (**http://www.advanceweb.com**) Web site has job fair information.

📖 **Advancing Your Career : Concepts of Professional Nursing** - by Rose Kearney, $44.95. Publisher: FA Davis, 2004. ISBN: 0803608071

⚕ 📱🖰 **Air and Surface Transport Nurses Association (ASTNA)** - 7995 East Prentice Avenue, Suite 100, Greenwood Village, CO 80111, 800/897-NFNA. (**http://www.astna.org/**, astna@gwami.com) Also known as the National Flight Nurses Association, job ads on web site.

📁🖰 **All Nursing Schools** - **http://www.allnursingschools.com/** Online directory of nursing schools. Their "Find a School" section allows you to search for nursing programs by state, degree type, specialty or school name. Address, phone numbers and degrees offered are given for all schools and NLNAC accreditation is indicated. Schools who advertise on the site have basic information about their institution and allow you to fill in a form to receive additional information,

⚕🖰 **American Academy of Nurse Practitioners (AANP)** - P.O. Box 12846, Austin, TX 78711; 512/442-4262. (**http://www.aanp.org**) Provides certification and scholarship information. Their CareerLink will connect members with recruiters and employers online. You can also get a brochure or video about nurse practitioner as a career.

⚕📱📁🖰 **American Association of Colleges of Nursing (AACN)** - One Dupont Circle, NW, Suite 530, Washington, DC 20036; 202/463-6930. (**http://www.aacn.nche.edu**) Publishes *Journal of the American Colleges of Nursing*. The Web site has a directory of hospitals and to search for jobs by country, state or specialty. Student Center has information on nursing education programs, financial aid and nursing careers.

⚕📱🖰 **American Association of Neuroscience Nurses (AANN)** - 4700 W. Lake Ave. Glenview, IL 60025; 847/375-4733 or 888/557-2266. (**http://www.aann.org**, info@aann.org). Use the web site to find jobs through the AANN Job Mart or find information on scholarships and certification. Network on the Listservs or by joining local chapters.

⚕📱📁🖰 **American Association of Nurse Anesthetists (AANA)** - 222 South Prospect, Park Ridge, IL 60068-4001; 847/692-7050. (**http://www.aana.com**, info@aana.com) Their web site has information about the career, scholarships, and a directory of accredited education programs. Post your résumé or search job ads online. The *AANA Journal* has about several employment ads per issue and these are not posted on the web site.

♀🖳📧⌐⊙ **American Association of Occupational Health Nurses (AAOHN)** - 2920 Brandywine Road, Suite 100 Atlanta, GA 30341; 707/455-7757, fax: 707/455-7271. (**http://www.aaohn.org**) Organization consists of nurses employed by businesses. Employment Information Service is free to members, (nonmember rate is $150 for two months) and will publish brief résumés (100 words). The Web site contains links to information on employment and certification.

♀⌐⊙ **American College of Nurse Midwives (ACNW)** - 8403 Colesville Rd, Ste 1550, Silver Spring MD 20910; 240-485-1800. ACWN's web site (**http://www.acnm.org/**) provides information on careers, scholarships, credentialing and more. The career section links to another web site: **midwifejobs.com**.

♀⌐⊙ **American College of Nurse Practitioners (ACNP)** - 1111 19th Street, NW Suite 404, Washington, DC 20036; 202-659-2190. Web site has facts about NPs and extensive links to specialty nursing organizations. (**http://www.nurse.org/acnp/**, acnp@acnpweb.org)

♀⌐⊙ **American Forensic Nurses (AFN)** - 255 N. El Cielo Road, Suite 195, Palm Springs, CA 92262; 760/322-9925. (**http://www.amrn.com/**, info@amrn.com) AFN provides medical forensic services to law enforcement agencies and develops forensic services, procedures and education. Information about certificate programs.

♀🖳⌐⊙ **American Holistic Nurses Association (AHNA)** - P. O. Box 2130, Flagstaff, AZ 86003; 800/278-AHNA. (**http://ahna.org**) Provides a directory of practitioners in the holistic field, and information on schools and scholarships. Job ads are posted on the web site.

♀🖳⌐⊙ **American Nephrology Nurses Association (ANNA)** - East Holly Avenue, Box 56, Pitman, NJ 08071-0056; 888/600-2662. (**http://anna.inurse.com**, anna@ajj.com) Membership includes registered nurses. Publishes newsletters and several journals with job ads. Visit their web site to see job ads or download a brochure about the specialty.

♀🖳📁⌐⊙ **American Nurses Association (ANA)** - 8515 Georgia Avenue, Suite 400, Silver Spring, MD 20910; 301/628-5000 or 800/274-4ANA. (**http://www.nursingworld.org**, memberinfo@ana.org)

The ANA, established in 1896, is a full-service professional organization. Career center on web site has a job agent and allows members to post résumé. Financial aid information, links to specialty nursing associations and much more can be viewed on the web site. Students may subscribe to access more extensive web information for $10. *Planning A Career In Nursing* booklet can be downloaded from the web. Online catalog lists dozens of publications, including books on taking certification tests. *The American Nurse* is $10/yr for students, $20 for practicing nurses (800/637-0323).

Anatomy of a Job Search - A Nurse's Guide to Finding and Landing the Job You Want - by Jeanna Bozell, Paperback, 146 pages, $25.95, Lippincott Williams & Wilkins, 1999, ISBN: 0874349508. The author, a nurse recruiter gives advice on résumés & marketing yourself.

Association of Operating Room Nurses, Inc. (AORN) - 2170 S. Parker Rd., Suite 300, Denver, CO 80231-5711; 303/755-6304 , 800/755-2676. **(http://www.aorn.org)** Search their very informative web site for perioperative job opportunities. Online bookstore, videos, nursing links and information on scholarships, certification and discussion groups.

Association of Rehabilitation Nurses (ARN) - 4700 W. Lake Avenue, Glenview, IL 60025; 800/229-7530 or 847/375-4710. Membership consists of RNs, LPNs and LVNs. Web site has job ads and a directory of local chapters, with membership directory for members only. **(http://www.rehabnurse.org**, info@rehabnurse.org)

Association of Women's Health, Obstetric and Neonatal Nurses 2000 L Street NW, Suite 740, Washington, DC 20036; 800/673-8499 or 202/261-2400. **(http://www.awhonn.org)** Local chapter and networking information is online, as is the Career Center with job ads.

Discover Nursing - http://www.discovernursing.com/ This site is provided by Johnson & Johnson, and has a wealth of information including free brochures on nursing as a career, articles about many specialties, profiles of nurses, information on preparing for nursing school and scholarship searching.

Emergency Nurses Association (ENA) -P.O. Box 1005, Bedford Park, IL 60499-1005; 800/243-8362. **(https://www.ena.org/**, enainfo@ena.org) Web site has scholarship information, membership directory (members only), state chapters. Student membership is $36.

📁⁀🖰 **Forensic Nurse Magazine** - http://www.forensicnursemag.com/ The web site has a directory of forensic science and forensic nursing programs.

📖 **How to Survive and Maybe Even Love Nursing School!: A Guide for Students by Students** - by Kelli S. Dunham, F. A. Davis Company, 2004, $22.95, ISBN: 0803611579. Informative, with lots of resources.

⚕📱⁀🖰 **Minority Nurse** - http://www.minoritynurse.com This site has links to minority nursing associations and minority health associations. It provides a discussion forum, scholarship information and job postings. Featured stories section is loaded with information for students and nurses. Minority Nurse magazine has information on education, career development and minority health.

📱🐁⁀🖰 **NurseWeek** - 1156 Aster Ave., Suite C, Sunnyvale, CA 94086; 800/859-2091. (**http://www.nurseweek.com**) Newsletter with classified ads for registered nurses is $45, but can be read free online. The web site has information on dozens of specialty nursing careers, career fairs, a list of schools. Search job ads online by state or specialty.

⚕📁⁀🖰 **National Association of Pediatric Nurse Practitioners (NAPNAP)** - 20 Brace Road, Suite 200, Cherry Hill, NJ 08034-2634; 856/857-9700. (**http://www.napnap.org/,**) Publishes *Nurse Practitioner Career Resource Guide* ($18 for students, member $22, non-member $30). Online student section to locate NP schools and a member directory.

⚕📁⁀🖰 **National Association for Practical Nurse Education and Service (NAPNES)** - P O Box 25647, Alexandria, VA 22313; 703/933-1003. (http://www.napnes.org/schools/index.htm) World's oldest organization for licensed practical nurses and licensed vocational nurses, it has networking opportunities, a directory of schools and information on certification. Student membership is $25/yr.

⚕⁀🖰 **National Black Nurses Association (NBNA)** - 8630 Fenton Street, Ste. 330, Silver Springs, MD 20910, 301/589-3200. (**http://www.nbna.org,** NBNA@erols.com) Online Career Center, List of local chapters and scholarship program information. Student membership is $35. Members receive the *Journal of NBNA, NBNA News* and *Minority Nurse* magazine.

📁⁀🖰 **National Council of State Boards of Nursing (NCSBN)** - http://www.ncsbn.org/ Directory of state boards of nursing.

National Federation of Licensed Practical Nurses (NFLPN) - 605 Poole Drive, Garner, North Carolina 27529; 919/779-0046. (**http://www.nflpn.org**) Information on careers and scholarships for vocational and licensed practical nurses. Online directory of state organizations and local events/meetings. Career Center lets you view job ads, post résumé and receive job alerts by email.

National League for Nursing (NLN) - 61 Broadway, New York, New York 10006, 212/363-5555, 800/669-1656. (**http://www.nln.org**, generalinfo@nln.org) Members are nurse educators, but the online job postings are for all nurses. Post a profile and receive job alerts by email. Publishes lists of schools of nursing for RNs, LPNs and LVNs.

National Student Nurses' Association (NSNA) - 45 Main Street, Ste. 606, Brooklyn, NY 11201; 718/210-0705. (**http://www.nsna.org**, nsna@nsna.org) Online Career Center has information about nursing, career planning, internships and a directory of health care facilities. Web site networking opportunities include Live Chat and links to local chapters and state nursing associations. NSNA holds Career Planning Conferences, offers courses to prepare for the NCLEX exam, offers member discounts on nursing books, such as *Career Planning for Nurses* by Bette Case and *Mosby's Tour Guide to Nursing School, A Students' Road Survival Kit*. Members can get scholarship information. Download a list of professional organizations for nurses; there are dozens of specialties.

NP Central - 10024 S.E. 240th St., Suite #102, Kent, WA 98031; 253/852-9042.(**http://www.npcentral.net/**, npss@nurse.net) Online job search by specialty and state. Provides résumé advice. Post your résumé. Provides directories of NP practices and specialty nursing associations.

Nurse.org - **http://www.nurse.org** Online directory of specialty nursing organizations and state nursing organizations.

Nurse Options USA - **http://www.nurseoptions.com**; 800/828-0665. Registered Nurse and Nurse Management permanent, temporary, and travel positions throughout the USA. Part of Med Options USA. Free job listing information by phone or email.

NurseWeek Magazine - 6860 Santa Teresa Blvd, San Jose, CA 95119; 800/859-2091. (**http://www.nurseweek.com**) Free subscriptions for registered nurses. Web site has a directory of nursing schools, link to career fairs, résumé writing help, and job search by state and specialty.

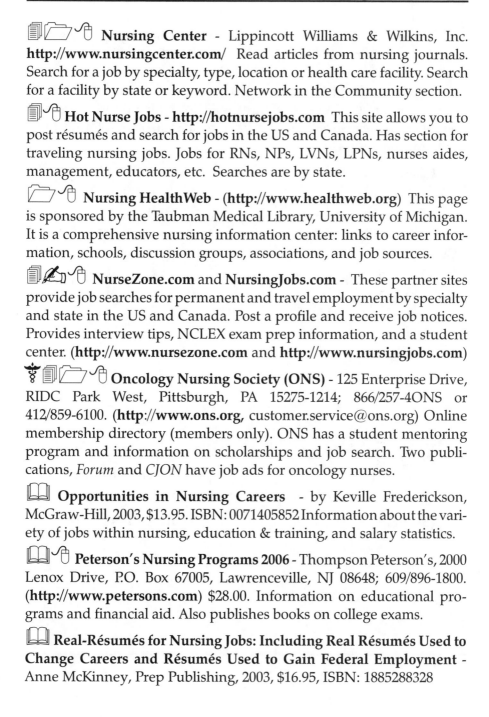

Nursing Center - Lippincott Williams & Wilkins, Inc. http://www.nursingcenter.com/ Read articles from nursing journals. Search for a job by specialty, type, location or health care facility. Search for a facility by state or keyword. Network in the Community section.

Hot Nurse Jobs - http://hotnursejobs.com This site allows you to post résumés and search for jobs in the US and Canada. Has section for traveling nursing jobs. Jobs for RNs, NPs, LVNs, LPNs, nurses aides, management, educators, etc. Searches are by state.

Nursing HealthWeb - (http://www.healthweb.org) This page is sponsored by the Taubman Medical Library, University of Michigan. It is a comprehensive nursing information center: links to career information, schools, discussion groups, associations, and job sources.

NurseZone.com and NursingJobs.com - These partner sites provide job searches for permanent and travel employment by specialty and state in the US and Canada. Post a profile and receive job notices. Provides interview tips, NCLEX exam prep information, and a student center. (http://www.nursezone.com and http://www.nursingjobs.com)

Oncology Nursing Society (ONS) - 125 Enterprise Drive, RIDC Park West, Pittsburgh, PA 15275-1214; 866/257-4ONS or 412/859-6100. (http://www.ons.org, customer.service@ons.org) Online membership directory (members only). ONS has a student mentoring program and information on scholarships and job search. Two publications, *Forum* and *CJON* have job ads for oncology nurses.

Opportunities in Nursing Careers - by Keville Frederickson, McGraw-Hill, 2003, $13.95. ISBN: 0071405852 Information about the variety of jobs within nursing, education & training, and salary statistics.

Peterson's Nursing Programs 2006 - Thompson Peterson's, 2000 Lenox Drive, P.O. Box 67005, Lawrenceville, NJ 08648; 609/896-1800. (http://www.petersons.com) $28.00. Information on educational programs and financial aid. Also publishes books on college exams.

Real-Résumés for Nursing Jobs: Including Real Résumés Used to Change Careers and Résumés Used to Gain Federal Employment - Anne McKinney, Prep Publishing, 2003, $16.95, ISBN: 1885288328

 **Sigma Theta Tau International Honor Society of Nursing -** http://www.nursingsociety.org/ An honor society for nurses, this group's web site has information for those considering a nursing career and for nurses seeking to expand their careers. Resources section contains links to local chapters, state boards of nursing, scholarship opportunities and specialty nursing associations. Site has information on mentoring and a student resources page.

Résumés for Nursing Careers - by Editors of VGM, McGraw-Hill, 2001, $10.95, ISBN: 0658017721. Includes sample résumé s & cover letters.

Stressed Out About Nursing School! An Insider's Guide to Success by Stephanie Thibeault, Bandido Books, 2001, $22.95, ISBN: 1929693168

Your Career In Nursing: Manage Your Future in the Changing World of Healthcare - by Annette Vallano, Published by Kaplan, 2002, $18.00, ISBN: 0743235215. Career guide and how to market your skills.

"If you wish to succeed in life, make perserverance your bosom friend, experience your wise counselor, caution your elder brother, and hope your guardian genius."   — Joseph Addison

Chapter

8

HEALTH & SOCIAL SERVICES OCCUPATIONS

Sabrina Damp

Sabrina Damp started out as a Medical Assistant with the High-Mark Blue Cross Blue Shield Primary Care Center in Pittsburgh's North Hills. In 1999 she transferred within the same company to the practice of Dr. Paul Zubritzky and Associates in Robinson Township, PA. Sabrina graduated with honors from North Hills School of Health Occupations in October of 1997. "I became interested in the medical field while I was hospitalized during my first semester of college. Shortly thereafter, I decided not to return to college for the second semester. Instead, I enrolled in the Medical Assisting program at the North Hills School of Health Occupations in April of 1997," said Sabrina. She is currently enrolled in a Respiratory Therapy program at the Community College of Allegheny County.

I asked Sabrina if she had difficulty finding employment as a MA after graduation. She said, "Opportunities were plentiful. I had four or five interviews the first month and two job offers. I selected Blue Cross Blue Shield because the job they offered was interesting with prospects for advancement as I gained job experience and successfully completed various training programs."

Sabrina completed her business degree program at Robert Morris University through their Saturday and evening program in 2004. Last September Sabrina decided to go back to school full time for respiratory therapy and her employer kept her on part time while attending school. Her goal is to complete the two year course at the Community College of Allegheny County and become a registered respiratory therapist (RRT).

"The course work is considerable," said Sabrina. "You must make a personal commitment to get through this program and there is much to learn. I'm now in my second semester and study at least 30 hours or more a week to not only make the grade but comprehend the complexities of the occupation." Her goal is to work in the area after graduation.

Sabrina stated that her MA work has been rewarding and she works both front office administrative duties and back office patient care as needed. She said, "I enjoy the diversity of working both front and back office. The day goes very fast and I enjoy helping patients, doctors and physician assistants."

She recommends that to be successful you must be yourself and reflect a positive attitude toward coworkers and patients. "It's important to deal professionally with everyone at all levels and you must be sensitive to patients' needs at all times," Ms. Damp said. She is looking forward to entering the respiratory therapy field when she graduates.

This chapter presents occupations that are in the health services group. The occupations are:

Medical Assistants
Social and Human Service Assistants
Social Workers

See chapter 10 for health service careers involving home health care, including **Personal and Home Care Aides.**

Following each job description is a list of job resources: Associations, Books, Directories, Internet Sites, Job Ads, E-mail Job Notification/Job Hotlines, Job Fairs, and Résumé/Placement Services with icons to guide you.

MEDICAL ASSISTANTS

Significant Points
- About 6 out of 10 medical assistants work in offices of physicians.
- Some medical assistants are trained on the job, but many complete 1- or 2-year programs in vocational-technical high schools, post-secondary vocational schools, and community and junior colleges.
- Medical assistant positions are projected to be one of the fastest growing occupations over the 2004-14 period.
- Job prospects should be best for medical assistants with formal training or experience, particularly those with certification.

Nature of the Work
Medical assistants perform administrative and clinical tasks to keep the offices of physicians, podiatrists, chiropractors, and other health practitioners running smoothly. They should not be confused with physician assistants, who examine, diagnose, and treat patients under the direct supervision of a physician. (Physician assistants are discussed in Chapter 10.)

The duties of medical assistants vary from office to office, depending on the location and size of the practice and the practitioner's specialty. In small practices, medical assistants usually are generalists, handling both administrative and clinical duties and reporting directly to an office manager, physician, or other health practitioner. Those in large practices tend to specialize in a particular area, under the supervision of department administrators.

Medical assistants perform many administrative duties, including answering telephones, greeting patients, updating and filing patients' medical records, filling out insurance forms, handling correspondence, scheduling appointments, arranging for hospital admission and laboratory services, and handling billing and bookkeeping.

Clinical duties vary according to state law and include taking medical histories and recording vital signs, explaining treatment procedures to patients, preparing patients for examination, and assisting the physician during the examination. Medical assistants collect and prepare laboratory specimens or perform basic laboratory tests on the premises, dispose of contaminated supplies, and sterilize medical instruments. They instruct patients about medications and special diets, prepare and administer medications as directed by a physician, authorize drug refills as directed, telephone prescriptions to a pharmacy, draw blood, prepare patients for x rays, take electrocardiograms, remove sutures, and change dressings.

Medical assistants also may arrange examining room instruments and equipment, purchase and maintain supplies and equipment, and keep waiting and examining rooms neat and clean.

Ophthalmic medical assistants and podiatric medical assistants are examples of specialized assistants who have additional duties. Ophthalmic medical assistants help ophthalmologists provide eye care. They conduct diagnostic tests, measure and record vision, and test eye muscle function. They also show patients how to insert, remove, and care for contact lenses, and they apply eye dressings. Under the direction of the physician, ophthalmic medical assistants may administer eye medications. They also maintain optical and surgical instruments and may assist the ophthalmologist in surgery. Podiatric medical assistants make castings of feet, expose and develop x-rays, and assist podiatrists in surgery.

Working Conditions
Medical assistants work in well-lighted, clean environments. They constantly interact with other people and may have to handle several responsibilities at once.

Most full-time medical assistants work a regular 40-hour week. Many work part time, evenings, or weekends.

Training, Other Qualifications, and Advancement

Most employers prefer graduates of formal programs in medical assisting. Such programs are offered in vocational-technical high schools, post-secondary vocational schools, and community and junior colleges. Post-secondary programs usually last either 1 year, resulting in a certificate or diploma, or 2 years, resulting in an associate degree. Courses cover anatomy, physiology, and medical terminology, as well as typing, transcription, recordkeeping, accounting, and insurance processing. Students learn laboratory techniques, clinical and diagnostic procedures, pharmaceutical principles, the administration of medications, and first aid. They study office practices, patient relations, medical law, and ethics. Accredited programs include an internship that provides practical experience in physicians' offices, hospitals, or other health care facilities.

Both the Commission on Accreditation of Allied Health Education Programs (CAAHEP) and the Accrediting Bureau of Health Education Schools (ABHES) accredit programs in medical assisting. In 2005, there were over 500 medical assisting programs accredited by CAAHEP and about 170 accredited by ABHES. The Committee on Accreditation for Ophthalmic Medical Personnel approved 17 programs in ophthalmic medical assisting and 2 programs in ophthalmic clinical assisting.

Formal training in medical assisting, while generally preferred, is not always required. Some medical assistants are trained on the job, although this practice is less common than in the past. Applicants usually need a high school diploma or the equivalent. Recommended high school courses include mathematics, health, biology, typing, bookkeeping, computers, and office skills. Volunteer experience in the health care field also is helpful.

Although medical assistants are not licensed, some states require them to take a test or a course before they can perform certain tasks, such as taking x rays or giving injections.

Employers prefer to hire experienced workers or certified applicants who have passed a national examination, indicating that the medical assistant meets certain standards of competence. The American Association of Medical Assistants awards the Certified Medical Assistant credential; American Medical Technologists awards the Registered Medical Assistant credential; the American Society of Podiatric Medical Assistants awards the Podiatric Medical Assistant, Certified credential; and the Joint Commission on Allied Health Personnel in Ophthalmology awards credentials at three levels: Certified Ophthalmic Assistant; Certified Ophthalmic Technician; and Certified Ophthalmic Medical Technologist.

Medical assistants deal with the public; therefore, they must be neat and well groomed and have a courteous, pleasant manner. Medical assistants must be able to put patients at ease and explain physicians' instructions. They must respect the confidential nature of medical information. Clinical duties require a reasonable level of manual dexterity and visual acuity.

Medical assistants may be able to advance to office manager. They may qualify for a variety of administrative support occupations or may teach medical assisting. With additional education, some enter other health occupations, such as nursing and medical technology.

Employment

Medical assistants held about 387,000 jobs in 2004. About 6 out of 10 worked in offices of physicians; about 14 percent worked in public and private hospitals, including inpatient and outpatient facilities; and 11 percent worked in offices of other health practitioners, such as chiropractors, optometrists, and podiatrists. The rest worked mostly in outpatient care centers, public and private educational services, other ambulatory health care services, state and local government agencies, employment services, medical and diagnostic laboratories, and nursing care facilities.

Job Outlook

Employment of medical assistants is expected to grow much faster than average for all occupations through the year 2014 as the health care industry expands because of technological advances in medicine and the growth and aging of the population. Increasing utilization of medical assistants in the rapidly growing health care industry will further stimulate job growth. In fact, medical assistants are projected to be one of the fastest growing occupations over the 2004–14 period.

Employment growth will be driven by the increase in the number of group practices, clinics, and other health care facilities that need a high proportion of support personnel, particularly the flexible medical assistant who can handle both administrative and clinical duties. Medical assistants work primarily in outpatient settings, a rapidly growing sector of the health care industry.

In view of the preference of many health care employers for trained personnel, job prospects should be best for medical assistants with formal training or experience, particularly for those with certification.

Earnings

The earnings of medical assistants vary, depending on their experience, skill level, and location. Median annual earnings of medical assistants were $24,610 in May 2004. The middle 50 percent earned between $20,650 and $28,930. The lowest 10 percent earned less than $18,010, and the highest 10 percent earned more than $34,650. Median annual earnings in the industries employing the largest numbers of medical assistants in May 2004 were: Colleges, universities, and professional schools,$27,490; Outpatient care centers, $25,360; General medical and surgical hospitals, $25,160; Offices of physicians, $24,930, Offices of other health practitioners, $21,930.

Related Occupations

Workers in other medical support occupations include dental assistants, medical records and health information technicians, medical secretaries, occupational therapist assistants and aides, pharmacy aides, and physical therapist assistants and aides.

MEDICAL ASSISTANTS RESOURCES

Don't forget! Refer to the general resources listed in Chapter Three.

---

§Association 📁Directory 📧Resume Service 🖥Web Site

📄Job Ads 📋Job Alert E-mail/Hotline 📂Job Fairs 📖Book

For a full explanation of these resources see the second page of Chapter 3.

---

§📁🖥 **Accrediting Bureau of Health Education Schools (ABHES)** - 7777 Leesburg Pike, Suite 314 North Falls Church, Virginia 22043; 703/917-9503. (**http://www.abhes.org**, info@abhes.org) One of two accrediting agencies for medical assistant educational programs. Provides a list of accredited educational programs in medical assisting.

§📄📁📧🖥 **The American Association of Medical Assistants (AAMA)** 20 North Wacker Drive, Suite 1575, Chicago, IL 60606-2963; 312/899-1500. (**http://www.aama-ntl.org**) The AAMA offers a national examination leading to the Certified Medical Assistant (CMA) credential. Web site has a quiz and information on the field, links to the two accrediting agencies of educational programs for their lists of schools, and information on studying for and taking the certification exam. They also have a mentoring program for members.

§📄📁🖥 **American Medical Technologists (AMT)** - 710 Higgins Road, Park Ridge, IL 60068; 800/275-1268. (**http://www.amt1.com**) The AMT administers the Registered Medical Assistant (RMA) certification exam as well as exams for Medical Technologist, Medical Laboratory Technician, Registered Phlebotomy Technician (RPT), Registered Dental Assistant (RDA), Certified Office Laboratory Technician (COLT), Allied Health Instructor (AHI) and Certified Laboratory Consultant (CLC). Student membership $5. Link to job and scholarship information.

§📄🖥 **American Society of Podiatric Medical Assistants** - 2124 S. Austin Blvd., Cicero, IL 60804; 708/863-6303, 888-88ASPMA (27762). (**http://aspma.org/aboutus.html**, aspmaex@aol.com) Web site has job ads for members and career and certification information.

§📄🖥 **Association of Technical Personnel in Ophthalmology (ATPO)** - 2025 Woodlane Drive, St. Paul, MN 55125; 800/284-3937, 651/731-7233.

(**http://www.atpo.org**, ATPOpresident@yahoo.com) Offers CE credits for ophthalmic staff and has job bank on web.

📁✎ **Commission on Accreditation of Allied Health Education Programs (CAAHEP)** - 1361 Park Street, Clearwater, Florida 33756; 727/210-2350. (**http://www.caahep.org**, mail@caahep.org) Accredits 22 allied health programs from anesthesiologist assistant to surgical technologist, including medical assistant. Search for a program by state and/or by specialty.

⚕📁✎ **Joint Commission on Allied Health Personnel in Ophthalmology (JCAHPO)** - 2025 Woodlane Dr., St. Paul, MN 55125; 800/284-3937. (**http://www.jcahpo.org**, jcahpo@jcahpo.org) Certifies assistants, technicians and technologists. Assistant programs include only an educational component, whereas the technician, and medical technologist level programs include educational and supervised clinical components. Career brochures are online. The web site has "What is Ophthalmic Medical Assisting?" and offers several audio tape classes for credit , an online course for assistants and a directory of schools.

📖 **Medical Technicians** - Ferguson Publishing Company, 1998, $13.95, ISBN: 0894342460 Careers covered include biomedical equipment technicians, dialysis technicians, medical assistants, psychiatric technicians and surgical technologists.

SOCIAL AND HUMAN SERVICE ASSISTANTS

OCCUPATIONAL TITLES:

Social Service Technician   Mental Health Technician
Case Management Aide   Child Abuse Worker
Social Work Assistant   Community Outreach Worker
Residential Counselor   Gerontology Aide
Alcohol or Drug Abuse Counselor

Significant Points
- While a bachelor's degree usually is not required, employers increasingly seek individuals with relevant work experience or education beyond high school.
- Employment is projected to grow much faster than average.
- Job opportunities should be excellent, particularly for applicants with appropriate post-secondary education, but pay is low.

Nature of the Work

Social and human service assistant is a generic term for people with a wide array of job titles, including human service worker, case management aide, social work assistant, community support worker, mental health aide, community outreach worker, life skill counselor, or gerontology aide. They usually work under the direction of workers from a variety of fields, such as nursing, psychiatry, psychology, rehabilitative or physical therapy, or social work. The amount of responsibility and supervision they are given varies a great deal. Some have little direct supervision; others work under close direction.

Social and human service assistants provide direct and indirect client services to ensure that individuals in their care reach their maximum level of functioning. They assess clients' needs, establish their eligibility for benefits and services such as food stamps, Medicaid, or welfare, and help to obtain them. They also arrange for transportation and escorts, if necessary, and provide emotional support. Social and human service assistants monitor and keep case records on clients and report progress to supervisors and case managers.

Social and human service assistants play a variety of roles in a community. They may organize and lead group activities, assist clients in need of counseling or crisis intervention, or administer a food bank or emergency fuel program. In halfway houses, group homes, and government-supported housing programs, they assist adults who need supervision with personal hygiene and daily living skills. They review clients' records, ensure that they take correct doses of medication, talk with family members, and confer with medical personnel and other caregivers to gain better insight into clients' backgrounds and needs. Social and human service assistants also provide emotional support and help clients become involved in their own well-being, in community recreation programs, and in other activities.

In psychiatric hospitals, rehabilitation programs, and outpatient clinics, social and human service assistants work with professional care providers, such as psychiatrists, psychologists, and social workers, to help clients master everyday living skills, communicate more effectively, and get along better with others. They support the client's participation in a treatment plan, such as individual or group counseling or occupational therapy.

Working Conditions

Working conditions of social and human service assistants vary. Some work in offices, clinics, and hospitals, while others work in group homes, shelters, sheltered workshops, and day programs. Many work under close supervision, while others work much of the time on their own, such as those who spend their time in the field visiting clients. Sometimes visiting clients can be dangerous even though most agencies do everything they can to ensure their workers' safety. Most work a 40-hour week, although some work in the evening and on weekends.

The work, while satisfying, can be emotionally draining. Understaffing and relatively low pay may add to the pressure. Turnover is reported to be high, especially among workers without academic preparation for this field.

Training, Other Qualifications, and Advancement

While a bachelor's degree usually is not required for entry into this occupation, employers increasingly seek individuals with relevant work experience or education beyond high school. Certificates or associate degrees in subjects such as social work, human services, gerontology, or one of the social or behavioral sciences meet most employers' requirements. Some jobs may require a bachelor's or master's degree in human services or a related field such as counseling, rehabilitation, or social work.

Human services degree programs have a core curriculum that trains students to observe patients and record information, conduct patient interviews, implement treatment plans, employ problem-solving techniques, handle crisis intervention matters, and use proper case management and referral procedures. General education courses in liberal arts, sciences, and the humanities also are part of the curriculum. Most programs offer the opportunity to take specialized courses related to addictions, gerontology, child protection, and other areas. Many degree programs require completion of a supervised internship.

Educational attainment often influences the kind of work employees may be assigned and the degree of responsibility that may be entrusted to them. For example, workers with no more than a high school education are likely to receive extensive on-the-job training to work in direct-care services, while employees with a college degree might be assigned to do supportive counseling, coordinate program activities, or manage a group home. Social and human service assistants with proven leadership ability, either from previous experience or as a volunteer in the field, often have greater autonomy in their work. Regardless of the academic or work background of employees, most employers provide some form of in service training, such as seminars and workshops, to their employees.

There may be additional hiring requirements in group homes. For example, employers may require employees to have a valid driver's license or to submit to a criminal background investigation.

Employers try to select applicants who have a strong desire to help others, have effective communication skills, a strong sense of responsibility, and the ability to manage time effectively. Many human services jobs involve direct contact with people who are vulnerable to exploitation or mistreatment; therefore, patience, understanding, and a strong desire to help others are highly valued characteristics.

Formal education almost always is necessary for advancement. In general, advancement requires a bachelor's or master's degree in human services, counseling, rehabilitation, social work, or a related field. Typically, advancement brings case management, supervision, and administration roles.

Employment
Social and human service assistants held about 352,000 jobs in 2004. More than half worked in the health care and social assistance industries. One in three were employed by state and local governments, primarily in public welfare agencies and facilities for mentally disabled and developmentally challenged individuals.

Job Outlook
Job opportunities for social and human service assistants are expected to be excellent, particularly for applicants with appropriate postsecondary education. The number of social and human service assistants is projected to grow much faster than the average for all occupations

between 2004 and 2014—ranking the occupation among the most rapidly growing. Many additional job opportunities will arise from the need to replace workers who advance into new positions, retire, or leave the workforce for other reasons. There will be more competition for jobs in urban areas than in rural areas, but qualified applicants should have little difficulty finding employment. Faced with rapid growth in the demand for social and human services, many employers increasingly rely on social and human service assistants to undertake greater responsibility for delivering services to clients.

Opportunities are expected to be good in private social service agencies, which provide such services as adult day care and meal delivery programs. Employment in private agencies will grow as state and local governments continue to contract out services to the private sector in an effort to cut costs. Demand for social services will expand with the growing elderly population, who are more likely to need these services. In addition, more social and human service assistants will be needed to provide services to pregnant teenagers, the homeless, the mentally disabled and developmentally challenged, and substance abusers. Some private agencies have been employing more social and human service assistants in place of social workers, who are more educated and, thus, more highly paid.

Job training programs also are expected to require additional social and human service assistants. As social welfare policies shift focus from benefit-based programs to work-based initiatives there will be more demand for people to teach job skills to the people who are new to, or returning to, the workforce.

Residential care establishments should face increased pressures to respond to the needs of the mentally and physically disabled. Many of these patients have been deinstitutionalized and lack the knowledge or the ability to care for themselves. Also, more community-based programs and supportive independent-living sites are expected to be established to house and assist the homeless and the mentally and physically disabled. As substance abusers are increasingly being sent to treatment programs instead of prison, employment of social and human service assistants in substance abuse treatment programs also will grow.

The number of jobs for social and human service assistants in local governments will grow but not as fast as employment for social and human service assistants in other industries. Employment in the public sector may fluctuate with the level of funding provided by state and local governments. Also, some state and local governments are contracting out selected social services to private agencies in order to save money.

Earnings

Median annual earnings of social and human service assistants were $24,270 in May 2004. The middle 50 percent earned between $19,220 and $30,900. The top 10 percent earned more than $39,620, while the lowest 10 percent earned less than $15,480.

Median annual earnings in the industries employing the largest numbers of social and human service assistants in May 2004 were: State government, $29,270; Local government, $28,230; Individual and family services, $23,400; Vocational rehabilitation services, $21,770; Residential mental retardation, mental health and substance abuse facilities, $20,410.

Related Occupations

Workers in other occupations that require skills similar to those of social and human service assistants include social workers; counselors; childcare workers; occupational therapist assistants and aides; physical therapist assistants and aides; and nursing, psychiatric, and home health aides.

SOCIAL AND HUMAN SERVICE ASSISTANTS

Resources for social and human service assistants are combined with social workers, as many resources serve both professions. See the end of the social workers section.

SOCIAL WORKER

Significant Points

- About 9 out of 10 jobs were in health care and social assistance industries, as well as state and local government agencies.
- While a bachelor's degree is the minimum requirement, a master's degree in social work or a related field has become the standard for many positions.
- Employment is projected to grow faster than average.
- Competition for jobs is expected in cities, but opportunities should be good in rural areas.

Nature of the Work

Social work is a profession for those with a strong desire to help improve people's lives. Social workers help people function the best way they can in their environment, deal with their relationships, and solve personal and family problems. Social workers often see clients who face a life-threatening disease or a social problem, such as inadequate housing, unemployment, a serious illness, a disability, or substance abuse. Social workers also assist families that have serious domestic conflicts, sometimes involving child or spousal abuse.

Social workers often provide social services in health-related settings that now are governed by managed care organizations. To contain costs, these organizations emphasize short-term intervention, ambulatory and community-based care, and greater decentralization of services.

Most social workers specialize. Although some conduct research or are involved in planning or policy development, most social workers prefer an area of practice in which they interact with clients.

Child, family, and school social workers provide social services and assistance to improve the social and psychological functioning of children and their families and to maximize the family well-being and academic functioning of children. Some social workers assist single parents, arrange adoptions, or help find foster homes for neglected, abandoned, or abused children. In schools, they address such problems as teenage pregnancy, misbehavior, and truancy and advise teachers on how to cope with problem students. Increasingly, school social workers are teaching workshops to an entire class. Some social workers specialize in services for senior citizens, running support groups for family caregivers or for the adult children of aging parents, advising elderly people or family members about choices in areas such as housing, transportation, and long-term care, and coordinating and monitoring these services. Through employee assistance programs, they may help workers cope with job-related pressures or with personal problems that affect the quality of their work. Child, family, and school social workers typically work for individual and family services agencies, schools, or state or local governments. These social workers may be known as child welfare social workers, family services social workers, child protective services social workers, occupational social workers, or gerontology social workers.

Medical and public health social workers provide persons, families, or vulnerable populations with the psychosocial support needed to cope with chronic, acute, or terminal illnesses, such as Alzheimer's disease, cancer, or AIDS. They also advise family caregivers, counsel patients, and help plan for patients' needs after discharge by arranging for at-home services, from meals-on-wheels to oxygen equipment. Some work on interdisciplinary teams that evaluate certain kinds of patients—geriatric or organ transplant patients, for example. Medical and public health social workers may work for hospitals, nursing and personal care facilities, individual and family services agencies, or local governments.

Mental health and substance abuse social workers assess and treat individuals with mental illness or substance abuse problems, including abuse of alcohol, tobacco, or other drugs. Such services include individual and group therapy, outreach, crisis intervention, social rehabilitation, and training in skills of everyday living. They also may help plan for supportive services to ease patients' return to the community. Mental health and substance abuse social workers are likely to work in hospitals, substance abuse treatment centers, individual and family services agencies, or local governments. These social workers may be known as clinical social workers.

Other types of social workers include social work planners and policymakers, who develop programs to address such issues as child abuse, homelessness, substance abuse, poverty, and violence. These workers research and analyze policies, programs, and regulations. They identify social problems and suggest legislative and other solutions. They may help raise funds or write grants to support these programs.

Working Conditions
Full-time social workers usually work a standard 40-hour week; however, some occasionally work evenings and weekends to meet with clients, attend community meetings, and handle emergencies. Some, particularly in voluntary nonprofit agencies, work part time. Social workers usually spend most of their time in an office or residential facility, but also may travel locally to visit clients, meet with service providers, or attend meetings. Some may use one of several offices within a local area in which to meet with clients. The work, while satisfying, can be emotionally draining. Understaffing and large caseloads add to the pressure in some agencies. To tend to patient care or client needs, many hospitals and long-term care facilities are employing social workers on teams with a broad mix of occupations, including clinical specialists, registered nurses, and health aides.

Training, Other Qualifications, and Advancement

A bachelor's degree in social work (BSW) degree is the most common minimum requirement to qualify for a job as a social worker; however, majors in psychology, sociology, and related fields may qualify for some entry-level jobs, especially in small community agencies. Although a bachelor's degree is sufficient for entry into the field, an advanced degree has become the standard for many positions. A master's degree in social work (MSW) is typically required for positions in health settings and is required for clinical work as well. Some jobs in public and private agencies also may require an advanced degree, such as a master's degree in social services policy or administration. Supervisory, administrative, and staff training positions usually require an advanced degree. College and university teaching positions and most research appointments normally require a doctorate in social work (DSW or Ph.D.).

As of 2004, the Council on Social Work Education (CSWE) accredited 442 BSW programs and 168 MSW programs. The Group for the Advancement of Doctoral Education (GADE) listed 80 doctoral programs in social work (DSW or Ph.D.). BSW programs prepare graduates for direct service positions, such as caseworker, and include courses in social work values and ethics, dealing with a culturally diverse clientele, at-risk populations, promotion of social and economic justice, human behavior and the social environment, social welfare policy and services, social work practice, social research methods, and field education. Accredited BSW programs require a minimum of 400 hours of supervised field experience.

Master's degree programs prepare graduates for work in their chosen field of concentration and continue to develop the skills required to perform clinical assessments, manage large caseloads, take on supervisory roles, and explore new ways of drawing upon social services to meet the needs of clients. Master's programs last 2 years and include a minimum of 900 hours of supervised field instruction, or internship. A part-time program may take 4 years. Entry into a master's program does not require a bachelor's degree in social work, but courses in psychology, biology, sociology, economics, political science, and social work are recommended. In addition, a second language can be very helpful. Most master's programs offer advanced standing for those with a bachelor's degree from an accredited social work program.

All states and the District of Columbia have licensing, certification, or registration requirements regarding social work practice and the use of professional titles. Although standards for licensing vary by State, a growing number of states are placing greater emphasis on communications skills, professional ethics, and sensitivity to cultural diversity issues. Most states require two years (3,000 hours) of supervised clinical experience for licensure of clinical social workers. In addition, the National Association of Social Workers (NASW) offers voluntary credentials. Social workers with an MSW may be eligible for the Academy of Certified Social Workers (ACSW), the Qualified Clinical Social Worker (QCSW), or the Diplomate in Clinical Social Work (DCSW) credential, based on their professional experience. Credentials are particularly important for those in private practice; some health insurance providers require social workers to have them in order to be reimbursed for services.

Social workers should be emotionally mature, objective, and sensitive to people and their problems. They must be able to handle responsibility, work independently, and maintain good working relationships with clients and coworkers. Volunteer or paid jobs as a social work aide offer ways of testing one's interest in this field.

Advancement to supervisor, program manager, assistant director, or executive director of a social service agency or department is possible, but usually requires an advanced degree and related work experience. Other career options for social workers include teaching, research, and consulting. Some of these workers also help formulate government policies by analyzing and advocating policy positions in government agencies, in research institutions, and on legislators' staffs.

Some social workers go into private practice. Most private practitioners are clinical social workers who provide psychotherapy, usually paid for through health insurance or by the client themselves. Private practitioners must have at least a master's degree and a period of supervised work experience. A network of contacts for referrals also is essential. Many private practitioners split their time between working for an agency or hospital and working in their private practice. They may continue to hold a position at a hospital or agency in order to receive health and life insurance.

Employment

Social workers held about 562,000 jobs in 2004. About 9 out of 10 jobs were in health care and social assistance industries, as well as state and local government agencies, primarily in departments of health and human services. Although most social workers are employed in cities or suburbs, some work in rural areas. The following tabulation shows 2004 employment by type of social worker: Child, family, and school social workers, 272,000; Mental health and substance abuse social workers, 116,000; Medical and public health social workers, 110,000; Social workers, all other, 64,000.

Job Outlook

Competition for social worker jobs is expected in cities, where demand for services often is highest and training programs for social workers are prevalent. However, opportunities should be good in rural areas, which often find it difficult to attract and retain qualified staff. By specialty, job prospects may be best for those social workers with a background in gerontology and substance abuse treatment.

Employment of social workers is expected to increase faster than the average for all occupations through 2014. The rapidly growing elderly population and the aging baby boom generation will create greater demand for health and social services, resulting in particularly rapid job growth among gerontology social workers. Many job openings also will stem from the need to replace social workers who leave the occupation.

As hospitals continue to limit the length of patient stays, the demand for social workers in hospitals will grow more slowly than in other areas. Because hospitals are releasing patients earlier than in the past, social worker employment in home health care services is growing. However, the expanding senior population is an even larger factor. Employment opportunities for social workers with backgrounds in gerontology should be good in the growing numbers of assisted-living and senior-living communities. The expanding senior population also will spur demand for social workers in nursing homes, long-term care facilities, and hospices.

Strong demand is expected for substance abuse social workers over the 2004–14 projection period. Substance abusers are increasingly being placed into treatment programs instead of being sentenced to prison. Because of the increasing numbers of individuals sentenced to prison or probation who are substance abusers, correctional systems are increasingly requiring substance abuse treatment as a condition added to their sentencing or probation. As this trend grows, demand will increase for treatment programs and social workers to assist abusers on the road to recovery.

Employment of social workers in private social service agencies also will increase. However, agencies increasingly will restructure services and hire more lower paid social and human service assistants instead of social workers. Employment in state and local government agencies may grow somewhat in response to increasing needs for public welfare, family services, and child protection services; however, many of these services will be contracted out to private agencies. Employment levels in public and private social services agencies may fluctuate, depending on need and government funding levels.

Employment of school social workers also is expected to grow as expanded efforts to respond to rising student enrollments and continued emphasis on integrating disabled children into the general school population lead to more jobs. There could be competition for school social work jobs in some areas because of the limited number of openings. The availability of federal, state and local funding will be a major factor in determining the actual job growth in schools.

Opportunities for social workers in private practice will expand, but growth may be somewhat hindered by restrictions that managed care organizations put on mental health services. The growing popularity of employee assistance programs is expected to spur demand for private practitioners, some of whom provide social work services to corporations on a contractual basis. However, the popularity of employee assistance programs will fluctuate with the business cycle, because businesses are not likely to offer these services during recessions.

Earnings

Median annual earnings of child, family, and school social workers were $34,820 in May 2004. The middle 50 percent earned between $27,840 and $45,140. The lowest 10 percent earned less than $23,130, and the top 10 percent earned more than $57,860. Median annual earnings in the industries employing the largest numbers of child, family, and school social workers in May 2004 were: Elementary and secondary schools, $44,300; Local government, $40,620; State government, $35,070; Individual and family services, $30,680; Other residential care facilities, $30,550.

Median annual earnings of medical and public health social workers were $40,080 in May 2004. The middle 50 percent earned between $31,620 and $50,080. The lowest 10 percent earned less than $25,390, and the top 10 percent earned more than $58,740. Median annual earnings in the industries employing the largest numbers of medical and public health social workers in May 2004 were: General medical and surgical hospitals, $44,920; Home health care services, $42,710; Local government, $39,390; Nursing care facilities, $35,680; Individual and family services, $32,100.

Median annual earnings of mental health and substance abuse social workers were $33,920 in May 2004. The middle 50 percent earned between $26,730 and $43,430. The lowest 10 percent earned less than $21,590, and the top 10 percent earned more than $54,180. Median annual earnings in the industries employing the largest numbers of mental health and substance abuse social workers in May 2004 were: Psychiatric and substance abuse hospitals, $36,170; Local government, $35,720; Outpatient care centers, $33,220; Individual and family services, $32,810; Residential mental retardation, mental health and substance abuse facilities, $29,110.

Median annual earnings of social workers, all other were $39,440 in May 2004. The middle 50 percent earned between $30,350 and $51,530. The lowest 10 percent earned less than $24,080, and the top 10 percent earned more than $62,720. Median annual earnings in the industries employing the largest numbers of social workers, all other in May 2004 were: Local government, $42,570; State government, $40,940; Individual and family services, $32,280.

About 1 out of 5 social workers is a member of a union. Many belong to the union associated with their place of employment.

Related Occupations

Through direct counseling or referral to other services, social workers help people solve a range of personal problems. Workers in occupations with similar duties include counselors, probation officers and correctional treatment specialists, psychologists, and social and human services assistants.

Resources for social and human service assistants are combined with social workers, as many resources serve both professions.

Information on job openings may be available from state employment service offices or directly from city, county, or state departments of health, mental health and mental retardation, and human resources.

SOCIAL WORKERS and SOCIAL AND
HUMAN SERVICE ASSISTANTS RESOURCES

Don't forget! Refer to the general resources listed in Chapter Three.

For a full explanation of these resources see the second page of Chapter 3.

American Association of State Social Work Boards - 400 South Ridge Parkway, Suite B, Culpeper, Virginia 22701; 800/225-6880. (**http://www.aswb.org**, info@aswb.org) Grants licenses in four categories; Bachelors, Masters, Advanced Generalist, and Clinical. Has listing of which licenses are appropriate for each state. Maintains an official registry of licensed social workers, with their educational and licensing data, available to prospective employers at the social worker's request.

American Counseling Association (ACA) - 5999 Stevenson Ave., Alexandria, VA 22304; 800/347-6647. (**http://www.counseling.org**) Web site has career center with listings of jobs available, most of which are in educational institutions, information on scholarships, and information about state licensing requirements.

American Public Human Services Association (APHSA) - 810 First Street, Northeast, Washington, DC 20002; 202/682-0100. (**http://www.aphsa.org**) The APWA publishes an annual *Public Human Services Directory*, $95 for members, $115 to nonmembers, with free updates on the web to members, which includes human service agency contacts in all 50 states plus territories. Online job ads do not require membership.

American Society on Aging - 833 Market Street, Suite 511, San Francisco, California 94103; 800/537-9728. (**http://www.asaging.org**, info@asaging.org) Members are nurses, doctors, social workers and anyone providing services to the aging. Job ads online are open to public.

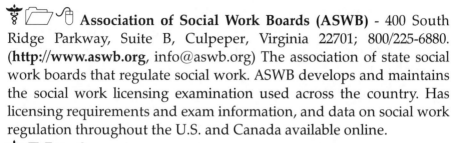 **Association of Social Work Boards (ASWB)** - 400 South Ridge Parkway, Suite B, Culpeper, Virginia 22701; 800/225-6880. (**http://www.aswb.org**, info@aswb.org) The association of state social work boards that regulate social work. ASWB develops and maintains the social work licensing examination used across the country. Has licensing requirements and exam information, and data on social work regulation throughout the U.S. and Canada available online.

Child Welfare League of America (CWLA) - 440 First Street Northwest, Third Floor, Washington, DC 20001; 202/638-2952. (**http://www.cwla.org**) Association of over 900 public and private non-profit agencies that serve and advocate for abused, neglected, and otherwise vulnerable children. Listing of member agencies by region or state, as well as listing of national agencies. The League offers a place-ment service on the web under the membership tab, searchable by region. They also have an internship program.

Clinical Social Work Federation (CSWF) - 800/270-9739. (**http://www.cswf.org**, nfscswlo@aol.com) As of early 2006, transitioning to an Association. Online job search tends toward college teaching positions. You can upload an anonymous résumé, and be notified when jobs with your criteria come up.

Council for Accreditation of Counseling and Related Educational Programs (CACREP) - 5999 Stevenson Avenue, 4th Floor, Alexandria, Virginia 22304; 703/823-9800 ext. 301. (**http://www.cacrep.org**, cacrep@cacrep.org) CACREP accredits counseling programs and has a downloadable directory of accredited programs in the various specialties of counseling on the web site.

Council for Standards in Human Service Education (CSHSE) - Harrisburg Area Community College, Human Services Program, 1 HACC Dr., Harrisburg, PA 17110. (**http://www.cshse.org**) Accrediting agency for human service education programs. Has directory of ac-credited programs.

Council on Social Work Education - 1725 Duke St., Suite 500, Alexandria, VA 22314; 703/683-8080. (**http://www.cswe.org**) Directory of accredited social work programs on web.

Catholic Charities - 1731 King Street, Alexandria, Virginia 22314; 703/549-1390. (**http://www.catholiccharitiesinfo.org**) Catholic Charities is the largest private network of social service organizations in the United States. The Jobs/Volunteer Opportunities has a few listings, and a search tool for finding local Catholic Charities offices which can be checked for jobs.

Employee Assistance Professional Association (EAPA) - 4350 North Fairfax Drive, Suite 410, Arlington, Virginia 22203; 783/387-1000. (**http://www.eap-association.com**) Members are individuals world wide working in the employee assistance field, in such specialties as workplace and family wellness, employee benefits, and organizational development. The EAPA credentials individuals who work in employee assistance/counseling services. The web site has a job bank and information on credentialing.

Gerontological Society of America - 1030 15th Street North West, Suite 250, Washington, DC 20005; 202/842-1275. (**http://www.geron.org**, geron@geron.org) The Age Work Career Center is free to all job seekers. It has , in addition to listing of jobs, provision for uploading your résumé, and being notified by email if a job with your specifications is posted. The student section, called the Emerging Scholar and Professional Organization accessed from the Become a Member tab has information on scholarships. To search their database for educational programs you fill out a 2 page PDF form and fax or mail it to them. There is a charge for this service.

Good Works: A Guide to Social Change Careers - Essential Information, P.O. Box 19405, Washington, DC 20036. *Good Works* is a national directory of social change organizations, listing over 1000 organizations, with information on contacts, staff openings, internships, etc. ($24.00) (**http://goodworksfirst.org**)

The Helping Professions : A Careers Sourcebook - by William R. Burger et al, Wadsworth Publishing, 1999; ISBN: 0534364756. All about helping professions jobs by a retired Professor of Social Work. A good resource for those who are trying to decide on a career path.

Latino Social Workers Organization (LSWO) - Student Summit gives student a chance to network. Job bank on internet. (**http://www.lswo.org** and **http://www.lswocontinuingeducation.org**, LSWO@aol.com)

📮🖱 **Mental Health Net** - (http://www.mentalhelp.net) The web site has a job posting page and links to State regulatory agencies both for counselors and social workers to find local licensing requirements.

⚕📮🖱 **National Association of Alcoholism and Drug Abuse Counselors (NAADAC)** - 901 N. Washington St. Suite 600, Alexandria, VA 22314; 800-548-0497. (http://www.naadac.org, naadac@naadac.org) Certifies addiction counselors at three levels and qualifies substance abuse professionals (SAP). Has employment listings on web

⚕📮📁🏃📧🖱 **National Association of Social Workers (NASW)** 750 First Street NE, Suite. 700, Washington DC, 20002; 202/408-8600. (http://www.naswdc.org, membership@naswdc.org) Links to state organizations, information on certification, and job link, available to all, but with résumé upload and email job alerts only for members.

⚕📁🖱 **National Board for Certified Counselors (NBCC)** - 3 Terrace Way, Suite D, Greensboro, North Carolina 27403; 336/547-0607. (http://www.nbcc.org, nbcc@nbcc.org) Sign up for their new free student e-news. Get information on national and state credentialing.

⚕🖱 **National Organization for Human Service Education (NOHSE)** - 5601 Brodie Lane, Suite 620-215, Austin, Texas 78745; 512/692-9361. (http://www.nohse.com, anne@nationalhumanservices.org) An organization serving job categories from aide to case worker and counselor. They have a new certification program for graduates of academic programs that are accredited by the Council for Standards in Human Service Education; Certified Human Services Professional (CHSP). As of the date of publication, states have not regulated this certification.

📖📮🏃📧🖱 **New Social Worker** - White Hat Communications, P.O. Box 5390, Harrisburg, Pennsylvania 17110; 717/238-3787. Print edition $15/yr, new digital edition $9.99/yr. They sponsor the Social Work Job Bank online, a well organized job site, which is free to job seekers. (http://www.socialworker.com, linda.grobman@ paonline.com) Most jobs listed are for case workers and supervisors. Look at job listings, post an anonymous résumé, and get an e-mail when any employer who meets your criteria posts a job. They also have a book store and discussion forum for networking.

School Social Work Association of America (SSWAA) - P.O. Box 2072, Northlake, IL 60164; 847/288-4527 (voice message system). (http://sswaa.org, sswaa@aol.com) Links to the 50 state departments of education to inquire about job opportunities, certification requirements and other job related questions as well as links to state social work organizations and state job banks.

socialservice.com (http://socialservice.com) Employment ads for social work or social service jobs. Search for jobs based on your education, starting with no college degree. High volume of jobs listed. Register and create a Job Agent which will e-mail you notices of new job postings that match the geographic, educational and keyword criteria you select.

Social Work and Social Services Jobs Online - George Warren Brown School of Social Work, (http://gwbweb.wustl.edu/jobs). A resource listing jobs in diverse areas of social work. Search by state or keyword.

Chapter

9

HEALTH DIAGNOSING OCCUPATIONS & ASSISTANTS

Paul M. Zubritzky, M.D.

Paul M. Zubritzky, M.D. graduated Cum Laude from the University of Pittsburgh in May of 1973. He graduated from Temple University School of Medicine in May of 1977 and served his residency at Western Pennsylvania Hospital from June 1, 1977 through June 30, 1981. He was certified in 1984 by the American Board of Obstetrics and Gynecology.

Doctor Zubritzky has been in private practice specializing in Obstetrics, Gynecology and Infertility for the past 25 years with offices in the suburbs of Pittsburgh. He is also the Chief of Obstetrics and Gynecology at the Ohio Valley General Hospital.

I asked Dr. Zubritzky why he entered the field, he stated, "I was highly influenced by my father who was a physician. I never contemplated any other career." Kiddingly, he followed up with several exceptions. "At age five I thought about being an auto mechanic. Then at ten a cartoonist and like most 16 year olds I wanted to be a rock star."

Doctor Zubritzky is a member of a number of prestigious professional organizations including the American Medical Association, Pennsylvania Medical Society, American College of Obstetricians and Gynecologists, Diplomat of the American Board of Obstetricians and Gynecologists to name a few. I asked him if he was aware of any unique publications or resources for those seeking career information or placement services. He suggested a number of publications and journals including OB GYN News. This publication offers a number of job classified ads for the field. Many of these resources are listed in this chapter.

The Bureau of Labor Statistics projects that employment of physicians will grow faster than the average for all occupations through the year 2008 due to continued expansion of the health care industries. I asked Dr. Zubritzky what advice he would give to others who want to enter this field. He stated, "It takes lots of work and a total commitment. This is a profession and not a nine to five job. It requires personal integrity, a considerable amount of your time, and you must realize that up front before entering the field." He further stated that, "your personal time and life will be sacrificed, however, there is a balance of both good and bad days." One other point he stressed was that you must have good people skills to be successful and be cognizant of the fact that medicine is in evolution and constantly changing. He said, "you must keep up—more today than when I first started out—with these changes, especially now with the advances that are being made in all fields."

This chapter features occupations that are in the Health Diagnosing and Assistants group. The major occupational groups are:

Chiropractors   **Physicians**
Dentists   **Physician Assistants**
Optometrists   **Veterinarians**

Following each job description are job resource lists: Associations, Books, Directories, Internet Sites, Job Ads, Job Alerts/Hotlines, Job Fairs, and Placement Services. Job sources are listed alphabetically with the larger sources underlined.

CHIROPRACTORS

Significant Points
- Job prospects should be good; employment is expected to increase faster than average as demand for alternative health care grows.
- Chiropractors must be licensed, requiring 2 to 4 years of undergraduate education, the completion of a 4-year chiropractic college course, and passing national and state examinations.
- About 58 percent of chiropractors are self-employed.
- Earnings are relatively low in the beginning, but increase as the practice grows.

Nature of the Work
Chiropractors, also known as doctors of chiropractic or chiropractic physicians, diagnose and treat patients whose health problems are associated with the body's muscular, nervous, and skeletal systems, especially the spine. Chiropractors believe that interference with these systems impairs the body's normal functions and lowers its resistance to disease. They also hold that spinal or vertebral dysfunction alters many important body functions by affecting the nervous system and that skeletal imbalance through joint or articular dysfunction, especially in the spine, can cause pain.

The chiropractic approach to health care is holistic, stressing the patient's overall health and wellness. It recognizes that many factors affect health, including exercise, diet, rest, environment, and heredity. Chiropractors provide natural, drugless, nonsurgical health treatments and rely on the body's inherent recuperative abilities. They also recommend changes in lifestyle—in eating, exercise, and sleeping habits, for example—to their patients. When appropriate, chiropractors consult with and refer patients to other health practitioners.

Like other health practitioners, chiropractors follow a standard routine to secure the information they need for diagnosis and treatment. They take the patient's medical history; conduct physical, neurological, and orthopedic examinations; and may order laboratory tests. X-rays and other diagnostic images are important tools because of the chiropractor's emphasis on the spine and its proper function. Chiropractors also employ a postural and spinal analysis common to chiropractic diagnosis.

In cases in which difficulties can be traced to the involvement of musculoskeletal structures, chiropractors manually adjust the spinal column. Some chiropractors use water, light, massage, ultrasound, electric stimulation, acupuncture, and heat therapy. They also may apply supports such as straps, tapes, and braces. Chiropractors counsel patients about wellness concepts such as nutrition, exercise, changes in lifestyle, and stress management, but do not prescribe drugs or perform surgery.

Some chiropractors specialize in sports injuries, neurology, orthopedics, pediatrics, nutrition, internal disorders, or diagnostic imaging.

Many chiropractors are solo or group practitioners who also have the administrative responsibilities of running a practice. In larger offices, chiropractors delegate these tasks to office managers and chiropractic assistants. Chiropractors in private practice are responsible for developing a patient base, hiring employees, and keeping records.

Working Conditions

Chiropractors work in clean, comfortable offices. Their average workweek is about 40 hours, although longer hours are not uncommon. Solo practitioners set their own hours, but may work evenings or weekends to accommodate patients.

Like other health practitioners, chiropractors are sometimes on their feet for long periods. Chiropractors who take x-rays must take appropriate precautions against repeated exposure to radiation.

Training, Other Qualifications, and Advancement

All states and the District of Columbia regulate the practice of chiropractic and grant licenses to chiropractors who meet the educational and examination requirements established by the state. Chiropractors can practice only in states where they are licensed. Some states have agreements permitting chiropractors licensed in one state to obtain a license in another without further examination, provided their educational, examination, and practice credentials meet state specifications.

Most state boards require at least 2 years of undergraduate education; an increasing number are requiring a 4-year bachelor's degree. All boards require the completion of a 4-year program at an accredited chiropractic college leading to the Doctor of Chiropractic degree.

For licensure, most state boards recognize either all or part of the four-part test administered by the National Board of Chiropractic Examiners. State examinations may supplement the National Board tests, depending on state requirements. All states except New Jersey require the completion of a specified number of hours of continuing education each year in order to maintain licensure. Chiropractic associations and accredited chiropractic programs and institutions offer continuing education programs.

In 2005, 15 chiropractic programs and 2 chiropractic institutions in the United states were accredited by the Council on Chiropractic Education. Applicants are required to have at least 90 semester hours of undergraduate study leading toward a bachelor's degree, including courses in English, the social sciences or humanities, organic and inorganic chemistry, biology, physics, and psychology. Many applicants have a bachelor's degree, which may eventually become the minimum entry requirement. Several chiropractic colleges offer pre-chiropractic study, as well as a bachelor's degree program. Recognition of prechiropractic education offered by chiropractic colleges varies among the state boards.

Chiropractic programs require a minimum of 4,200 hours of combined classroom, laboratory, and clinical experience. During the first 2 years, most chiropractic programs emphasize classroom and laboratory work in basic science subjects such as anatomy, physiology, public health, microbiology, pathology, and biochemistry. The last 2 years stress courses in manipulation and spinal adjustment and provide clinical experience in physical and laboratory diagnosis, neurology, orthopedics, geriatrics, physiotherapy, and nutrition. Chiropractic programs and institutions grant the degree of Doctor of Chiropractic.

Chiropractic colleges also offer postdoctoral training in orthopedics, neurology, sports injuries, nutrition, rehabilitation, radiology, industrial consulting, family practice, pediatrics, and applied chiropractic sciences. Once such training is complete, chiropractors may take specialty exams leading to "diplomate" status in a given specialty. Exams are administered by specialty chiropractic associations.

Chiropractic requires keen observation to detect physical abnormalities. It also takes considerable manual dexterity, but not unusual strength or endurance, to perform adjustments. Chiropractors should be able to work independently and handle responsibility. As in other health-related occupations, empathy, understanding, and the desire to help others are good qualities for dealing effectively with patients.

Newly licensed chiropractors can set up a new practice, purchase an established one, or enter into partnership with an established practitioner. They also may take a salaried position with an established chiropractor, a group practice, or a health care facility.

Employment
Chiropractors held about 53,000 jobs in 2004. Approximately 58 percent of chiropractors are self-employed. Most chiropractors are in solo practice, although some are in group practice or work for other chiropractors. A small number teach, conduct research at chiropractic institutions, or work in hospitals and clinics.

Many chiropractors are located in small communities. However, there still often are geographic imbalances in the distribution of chiropractors, in part because many establish practices close to one of the few chiropractic institutions.

Job Outlook
Job prospects are expected to be good for persons who enter the practice of chiropractic. Employment of chiropractors is expected to grow faster than average for all occupations through the year 2014 as consumer demand for alternative health care grows. Because chiropractors emphasize the importance of healthy lifestyles and do not prescribe drugs or perform surgery, chiropractic care is appealing to many health-conscious Americans. Chiropractic treatment of the back,

neck, extremities, and joints has become more accepted as a result of research and changing attitudes about alternative, noninvasive health care practices. The rapidly expanding older population, with its increased likelihood of mechanical and structural problems, also will increase demand for chiropractors.

Demand for chiropractic treatment, however, is related as well to the ability of patients to pay, either directly or through health insurance. Although more insurance plans now cover chiropractic services, the extent of such coverage varies among plans. Increasingly, chiropractors must educate communities about the benefits of chiropractic care in order to establish a successful practice.

In this occupation, replacement needs arise almost entirely from retirements. Chiropractors usually remain in the occupation until they retire; few transfer to other occupations. Establishing a new practice will be easiest in areas with a low concentration of chiropractors.

Earnings

Median annual earnings of salaried chiropractors were $69,910 in May 2004. The middle 50 percent earned between $46,710 and $118,280 a year. In 2005, the mean salary for chiropractors was $104,363, according to a survey conducted by *Chiropractic Economics* magazine.

In chiropractic, as in other types of independent practice, earnings are relatively low in the beginning and increase as the practice grows. Geographic location and the characteristics and qualifications of the practitioner also may influence earnings. Self-employed chiropractors must provide their own health insurance and retirement.

Related Occupations

Chiropractors treat patients and work to prevent bodily disorders and injuries. So do athletic trainers, massage therapists, occupational therapists, physical therapists, physicians and surgeons, podiatrists, and veterinarians.

CHIROPRACTORS RESOURCES

Don't forget! Refer to the general resources listed in Chapter Three.

⚕Association   ☐Directory   ✍Resume Service   Web Site

▤Job Ads   ⚡Job Alert E-mail/Hotline   Job Fairs   📖Book

For a full explanation of these resources see the second page of Chapter 3.

⚕▤☐ **American Chiropractic Association (ACA)** - 1701 Clarendon Blvd., Arlington, VA 22209; 800/986-4636. (**www.amerchiro.org**, memberinfo@acatoday.org) The ACA has about 20,000 members who are doctors or chiropractic assistants. The Education and Training section of the web site, accessible in the patient information tab, has information about education requirements and includes lists of colleges and state licensing boards. The membership tab includes job ads and practices for sale.

⚕ **Canadian Chiropractic Association** - 1396 Eglinton Avenue West, Toronto, Ontario M6R 2H2, Canada; 416/781-5656. Information on education, certification and the Student Canadian Chiropractic Association is located on this site. To access information about becoming a chiropractor in Canada go to their web site at (**http://www.ccachiro.org**, ccachiro@ccachiro.org).

☐ **Council on Chiropractic Education** - 8049 North 85th Way, Scottsdale, Arizona 85258-4321; 480/443-8877. Accreditation agency for chiropractic education. Has list of accredited chiropractic programs and institutions in the US. (**http://cce-usa.org**, cce@cce-usa.org)

▤☐ **Dynamic Chiropractic**, P.O. Box 4109, Huntington, CA 92605; 714/230-3150. (**http://www.chiroweb.com**) Has print magazine for chiropractors as well as web site with pages for consumers and students. Student pages include discussion forums and free positions wanted postings. Consumer pages include a chiropractor directory.

⚕☐ **Federation of Chiropractic Licensing Boards**, 5401 W. 10th Street, Suite 101, Greeley, CO 80634; 970/356-3500. (**http://www.fclb.org**, info@fclb.org) Organization of state boards in the US, Canadian provinces and Australia. Contact for information on state education and licensing requirements. Also has directory of educational programs.

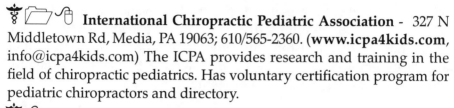 **International Chiropractic Pediatric Association** - 327 N Middletown Rd, Media, PA 19063; 610/565-2360. (**www.icpa4kids.com**, info@icpa4kids.com) The ICPA provides research and training in the field of chiropractic pediatrics. Has voluntary certification program for pediatric chiropractors and directory.

International Chiropractic Association (ICA) - 1110 N Glebe Rd., Suite 650, Arlington, VA 22201; 800/423-4690. Association of chiropractors. (**http://www.chiropractic.org**, chiro@chiropractic.org) Student section has scholarships, health insurance, and seminars.

National Association for Chiropractic Medicine (NACM) - 15427 Baybrook Drive, Houston, Texas 77062. (**http://www.chiromed.org**, ronlslaughter@hotmail.com) Association of conservative chiropractors.

National Directory of Chiropractic - 406 East 300 South, Box 305, Salt Lake City, Utah 84111; 1-800-888-7914. Printed directory and web search engine with database of over 65,000 chiropractors in the US. (**http://www.chirodirectory.com**, info@chirodirectory.com)

Opportunities in Chiropractic Health-Care Careers - by Bart Green, Claire Johnson, and Louis Sportelli, McGraw-Hill, 2004. ISBN: 007141164X. Provides essential information for a career in the chiropractic field, including advice on selecting a college and financing education.

DENTISTS

Significant Points
- Most dentists are solo practitioners.
- Dentists usually complete at least 8 years of education beyond high school.
- Employment is projected to grow about as fast as average, and most job openings will result from the need to replace the large number of dentists expected to retire.
- Job prospects should be good.

Nature of the Work
Dentists diagnose, prevent, and treat problems with teeth or mouth tissue. They remove decay, fill cavities, examine x-rays, place protective plastic sealants on children's teeth, straighten teeth, and repair fractured teeth. They also perform corrective surgery on gums and supporting

bones to treat gum diseases. Dentists extract teeth and make models and measurements for dentures to replace missing teeth. They provide instruction on diet, brushing, flossing, the use of fluorides, and other aspects of dental care. They also administer anesthetics and write prescriptions for antibiotics and other medications.

Dentists use a variety of equipment, including x-ray machines; drills; and instruments such as mouth mirrors, probes, forceps, brushes, and scalpels. They wear masks, gloves, and safety glasses to protect themselves and their patients from infectious diseases.

Dentists in private practice oversee a variety of administrative tasks, including bookkeeping and buying equipment and supplies. They may employ and supervise dental hygienists, dental assistants, dental laboratory technicians, and receptionists.

Most dentists are general practitioners, handling a variety of dental needs. Other dentists practice in any of nine specialty areas. Orthodontists, the largest group of specialists, straighten teeth by applying pressure to the teeth with braces or retainers. The next largest group, oral and maxillofacial surgeons, operates on the mouth and jaws. The remainder may specialize as pediatric dentists (focusing on dentistry for children); periodontists (treating gums and bone supporting the teeth); prosthodontists (replacing missing teeth with permanent fixtures, such as crowns and bridges, or with removable fixtures such as dentures); endodontists (performing root canal therapy); public health dentists (promoting good dental health and preventing dental diseases within the community); oral pathologists (studying oral diseases); or oral and maxillofacial radiologists (diagnosing diseases in the head and neck through the use of imaging technologies).

Working Conditions

Most dentists work 4 or 5 days a week. Some work evenings and weekends to meet their patients' needs. Most full-time dentists work between 35 and 40 hours a week, but others work more. Initially, dentists may work more hours as they establish their practice. Experienced dentists often work fewer hours. Many continue in part-time practice well beyond the usual retirement age.

Most dentists are solo practitioners, meaning that they own their own businesses and work alone or with a small staff. Some dentists have partners, and a few work for other dentists as associate dentists.

Training, Other Qualifications, and Advancement

All 50 states and the District of Columbia require dentists to be licensed. To qualify for a license in most states, candidates must graduate from 1 of the 56 dental schools accredited by the American Dental Association's (ADA's) Commission on Dental Accreditation in 2004, and then must pass written and practical examinations. Candidates may fulfill the written part of the state licensing requirements by passing the National Board Dental Examinations. Individual states or regional testing agencies administer the written or practical examinations.

Dental schools require a minimum of 2 years of college-level predental education, regardless of the major chosen. However, most dental students have at least a bachelor's degree. Predental education emphasizes coursework in science, and many applicants to dental school major in a science such as biology or chemistry, while other applicants major in another subject and take many science courses as well. A few applicants are accepted to dental school after 2 or 3 years of college and complete their bachelor's degree while attending dental school.

All dental schools require applicants to take the Dental Admissions Test (DAT). When selecting students, schools consider scores earned on the DAT, applicants' grade point averages, and information gathered through recommendations and interviews. Competition for admission to dental school is keen.

Dental school usually lasts 4 academic years. Studies begin with classroom instruction and laboratory work in basic sciences, including anatomy, microbiology, biochemistry, and physiology. Beginning courses in clinical sciences, including laboratory techniques, also are provided at this time. During the last 2 years, students treat patients, usually in dental clinics, under the supervision of licensed dentists. Most dental schools award the degree of Doctor of Dental Surgery (DDS). The rest award an equivalent degree, Doctor of Dental Medicine (DMD).

Some dental school graduates work for established dentists as associates for 1 to 2 years to gain experience and save money to equip an office of their own. Most dental school graduates, however, purchase an established practice or open a new one immediately after graduation.

In 2004, 17 states licensed or certified dentists who intended to practice in a specialty area. Requirements include 2 to 4 years of postgraduate education and, in some cases, the completion of a special state examination. Most state licenses permit dentists to engage in both general and specialized practice. Dentists who want to teach or conduct research usually spend an additional 2 to 5 years in advanced dental training, in programs operated by dental schools or hospitals. According to the ADA, each year about 12 percent of new graduates enroll in postgraduate training programs to prepare for a dental specialty.

Dentistry requires diagnostic ability and manual skills. Dentists should have good visual memory, excellent judgment regarding space and shape, a high degree of manual dexterity, and scientific ability. Good business sense, self-discipline, and good communication skills are helpful for success in private practice. High school and college students who want to become dentists should take courses in biology, chemistry, physics, health, and mathematics.

Employment

Dentists held about 150,000 jobs in 2004. Employment was distributed among general practitioners and specialists as follows: Dentists, general, 128,000; Orthodontists, 10,000; Oral and maxillofacial surgeons, 6,000; Prosthodontists, 1,000; and Dentists, all other specialists, 5,000.

About one third of dentists were self-employed and not incorporated. Almost all dentists work in private practice. According to ADA, 78 percent of dentists in private practice are sole proprietors, and 14 percent belong to a partnership. A few salaried dentists work in hospitals and offices of physicians.

Job Outlook

Employment of dentists is projected to grow about as fast as average for all occupations through 2014. Although employment growth will provide some job opportunities, most jobs will result from the need to replace the large number of dentists expected to retire. Job prospects should be good as new dentists take over established practices or start their own.

Demand for dental care should grow substantially through 2014. As members of the baby-boom generation advance into middle age, a large number will need complicated dental work, such as bridges. In addition, elderly people are more likely to retain their teeth than were their predecessors, so they will require much more care than in the past. The younger generation will continue to need preventive checkups despite treatments such as fluoridation of the water supply, which decreases the incidence of tooth decay. However, employment of dentists is not expected to grow as rapidly as the demand for dental services. As their practices expand, dentists are likely to hire more dental hygienists and dental assistants to handle routine services.

Dentists will increasingly provide care and instruction aimed at preventing the loss of teeth, rather than simply providing treatments such as fillings. Improvements in dental technology also will allow dentists to offer more effective and less painful treatment to their patients.

Earnings

Median annual earnings of salaried dentists were $129,920 in May 2004. Earnings vary according to number of years in practice, location, hours worked, and specialty.

Self-employed dentists in private practice tend to earn more than do salaried dentists, and a relatively large proportion of dentists is self-employed. Like other business owners, these dentists must provide their own health insurance, life insurance, and retirement benefits.

Related Occupations

Dentists examine, diagnose, prevent, and treat diseases and abnormalities. Chiropractors, optometrists, physicians and surgeons, podiatrists, psychologists, and veterinarians do related work.

DENTISTS RESOURCES

Don't forget! Refer to the general resources listed in Chapter Three.

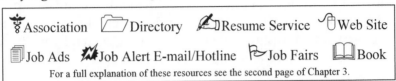

For a full explanation of these resources see the second page of Chapter 3.

🦷📁🖲 **Academy of General Dentistry (AGD)** - 211 East Chicago Ave., Ste 900, Chicago, IL 60611; 888/243-3368. (**http://www.agd.org**) Their "Smile Line" allows anyone to ask a dentist a question, either by phone, or by web message. The members-only area offers a membership directory.

🦷📁🖲 **American Academy of Pediatric Dentistry (AAPD)** - 211 E. Chicago Ave., Suite 700, Chicago, IL 60611; 312/337-2169. The AAPD web site has AT (http://aapd.org) lists pediatric dental residence programs and a directory to find a pediatric dentist.

🦷📁🖲 **American Association of Orthodontists** - 401 North Lindbergh Boulevard, St., Louis, Missouri 63141; 1-800-STRAIGHT. (**www.aaortho.org/**, info@aaortho.org) After dental school, at least two or three academic years of advanced specialty education in an ADA-accredited orthodontic residency program is required to be an orthodontist. Only 6 percent of dentists are orthodontists. Web site has listing of programs in the U.S. and Canada, and information about becoming an orthodontist.

🦷📁🖲 **American Association of Public Health Dentistry (AAPHD)** - P.O. Box 7536, Springfield, IL 62791-7536; 217/ 391-0218. Web site (**http://www.aaphd.org,** natoff@aaphd.org) has directory of residencies in public health dentistry. Sponsors the American Board of Dental Public Health, which certifies dentists in public health.

🦷📁🖲 **American Dental Association (ADA)** - 211 E. Chicago Ave., Chicago, IL 60611; 312/440-2500 (**http://www.ada.org**) As a part of their mentoring program, the ADA has a job shadow program that lets high school students shadow a dentist for a day to see if they are interested in a dental career. Includes abundant information on becoming a dentist, including listing of contacts for the mentoring program.

American Dental Education Association - 1400 K Street, NW, Suite 1100, Washington, DC 20005; 202/289-7201. Association of dental schools with a directory of United States and Canadian schools. (**http://www.adea.org**)

American Student Dental Association (ASDA) - 211 E. Chicago Ave., Ste 1160 Chicago, IL 60611-2687; 312/440-2795. The organization represents dental students on issues with the dental profession and government. Over 85% of all dental students are members of the ASDA. (**http://www.asdanet.org**, ASDA@ASDAnet.org)

California Dental Association (CDA) - 1201 K St. Sacramento, CA 95814; 916/443-3382. (**http://www.cda.org**) The CDA web site has extensive job listings and information for people interested in a career in dentistry.

Canadian Dental Association - 1815 Alta Vista Dr., Ottawa, Ontario, Canada K1G 3Y6; 613/523-1770. (**http://www.cda-adc.ca**, reception@cda-adc.ca) Under the Dental Profession tab on the web site you can find extensive information on the profession and how to navigate the educational and licensing process as well as grant and scholarship information. Take their online Dental Aptitude test.

The Dental Site - (**http://www.dentalsite.com**) This web site provides lots of directories and links. The "For Dentists" area lists links to dental web sites by area of specialty.

DentalGiant.com - (**http://www.dentalgiant.com**) Dentists are able to search for jobs, practices for sale, practice transitions, and partnerships. Sign in, search by state, and post your résumé.

Dental Watch - (**http://www.dentalwatch.org/**) This site has links to accredited schools. The State Board of Dental Examiners in each state can supply information on licensing requirements: links at **http://www.dentalwatch.org/org/boards.html**

National Dental Association (NDA) - 3517 16th Street, N.W. Washington, DC 20010; 202/588-1697. Represents minority oral health professionals. Provides scholarship information and mentoring. The Internet web site has extensive links to dental schools and local chapters. (**http://www.ndaonline.org**, admin@ndaonline.org)

♆ 📋🖱 **New York State Dental Association** - 121 State St., Albany, NY 12207; 518/465-0044, (**http://www.dssny.org,** info@nysdental.org) Information on licensing in the state of New York and job listings.

♆ 📁🖱 **Student National Dental Association (SNDA)** - A division of the NDA, the SNDA aids in the advancement of minority students in dentistry. (**www.sndaonline.com**) Provides scholarships and networking, with an online directory of local chapters. Information on how dental schools work. Membership is $15 for undergraduates and $40 for those enrolled in dental school.

OPTOMETRISTS

Significant Points
- Admission to optometry school is competitive.
- To be licensed, optometrists must earn a Doctor of Optometry degree from an accredited optometry school and pass a written National Board exam and a clinical examination.
- Employment is expected to grow faster than average in response to the vision care needs of a growing and aging population.

Nature of the Work

Optometrists, also known as doctors of optometry, or ODs, provide most primary vision care. They examine people's eyes to diagnose vision problems and eye diseases, and they test patients' visual acuity, depth and color perception, and ability to focus and coordinate the eyes. Optometrists prescribe eyeglasses and contact lenses and provide vision therapy and low-vision rehabilitation. Optometrists analyze test results and develop a treatment plan. They administer drugs to patients to aid in the diagnosis of vision problems and prescribe drugs to treat some eye diseases. Optometrists often provide preoperative and postoperative care to cataract patients, as well as to patients who have had laser vision correction or other eye surgery. They also diagnose conditions caused by systemic diseases such as diabetes and high blood pressure, referring patients to other health practitioners as needed.

Optometrists should not be confused with ophthalmologists or dispensing opticians. Ophthalmologists are physicians who perform eye surgery, as well as diagnose and treat eye diseases and injuries. Like optometrists, they also examine eyes and prescribe eyeglasses and contact lenses. Dispensing opticians fit and adjust eyeglasses and, in some states, may fit contact lenses according to prescriptions written by ophthalmologists or optometrists.

Most optometrists are in general practice. Some specialize in work with the elderly, children, or partially sighted persons who need specialized visual devices. Others develop and implement ways to protect workers' eyes from on-the-job strain or injury. Some specialize in contact lenses, sports vision, or vision therapy. A few teach optometry, perform research, or consult.

Most optometrists are private practitioners who also handle the business aspects of running an office, such as developing a patient base, hiring employees, keeping paper and electronic records, and ordering equipment and supplies. Optometrists who operate franchise optical stores also may have some of these duties.

Working Conditions

Optometrists work in places—usually their own offices—that are clean, well lighted, and comfortable. Most full-time optometrists work about 40 hours a week. Many work weekends and evenings to suit the needs of patients. Emergency calls, once uncommon, have increased with the passage of therapeutic drug laws expanding optometrists' ability to prescribe medications.

Training, Other Qualifications, and Advancement

All states and the District of Columbia require that optometrists be licensed. Applicants for a license must have a Doctor of Optometry degree from an accredited optometry school and must pass both a written National Board examination and a national, regional, or state clinical board examination. The written and clinical examinations of the National Board of Examiners in Optometry usually are taken during the student's academic career. Many states also require applicants to pass an examination on relevant state laws. Licenses are renewed every 1 to 3 years and, in all states, continuing education credits are needed for renewal.

The Doctor of Optometry degree requires the completion of a 4-year program at an accredited optometry school, preceded by at least 3 years of preoptometric study at an accredited college or university. Most optometry students hold a bachelor's or higher degree. In 2004, 17 U.S. schools and colleges of optometry offered programs accredited by the

Accreditation Council on Optometric Education of the American Optometric Association.

Requirements for admission to schools of optometry include courses in English, mathematics, physics, chemistry, and biology. A few schools also require or recommend courses in psychology, history, sociology, speech, or business. Because a strong background in science is important, many applicants to optometry school major in a science such as biology or chemistry, while other applicants major in another subject and take many science courses offering laboratory experience. Applicants must take the Optometry Admissions Test, which measures academic ability and scientific comprehension. Admission to optometry school is competitive. As a result, most applicants take the test after their sophomore or junior year, allowing them an opportunity to take the test again and raise their score. A few applicants are accepted to optometry school after 3 years of college and complete their bachelor's degree while attending optometry school.

Optometry programs include classroom and laboratory study of health and visual sciences, as well as clinical training in the diagnosis and treatment of eye disorders. Courses in pharmacology, optics, vision science, biochemistry, and systemic disease are included.

Business ability, self-discipline, and the ability to deal tactfully with patients are important for success. The work of optometrists requires attention to detail and manual dexterity.

Optometrists wishing to teach or conduct research may study for a master's or Ph.D. degree in visual science, physiological optics, neurophysiology, public health, health administration, health information and communication, or health education. One-year postgraduate clinical residency programs are available for optometrists who wish to obtain advanced clinical competence. Specialty areas for residency programs include family practice optometry, pediatric optometry, geriatric optometry, vision therapy and rehabilitation, low-vision rehabilitation, cornea and contact lenses, refractive and ocular surgery, primary eye care optometry, and ocular disease.

Employment

Optometrists held about 34,000 jobs in 2004. The number of jobs is greater than the number of practicing optometrists because some optometrists hold two or more jobs. For example, an optometrist may have a private practice but also work in another practice, in a clinic, or in a vision care center. According to the American Optometric Association, about three-fourths of practicing optometrists are in private practice. Although many practice alone, optometrists increasingly are in a partnership or group practice.

Salaried jobs for optometrists were primarily in offices of optometrists; offices of physicians, including ophthalmologists; and health and personal care stores, including optical goods stores. A few salaried jobs for optometrists were in hospitals, the Federal government, or outpatient care centers including health maintenance organizations. Almost one third of optometrists were self-employed and not incorporated.

Job Outlook

Employment of optometrists is expected to grow faster than average for all occupations through 2014, in response to the vision care needs of a growing and aging population. As baby boomers age, they will be more likely to visit optometrists and ophthalmologists because of the onset of vision problems in middle age, including those resulting from the extensive use of computers. The demand for optometric services also will increase because of growth in the oldest age group, with its increased likelihood of cataracts, glaucoma, diabetes, and hypertension. Greater recognition of the importance of vision care, along with rising personal incomes and growth in employee vision care plans, also will spur job growth.

Employment of optometrists would grow more rapidly were it not for anticipated productivity gains that will allow each optometrist to see more patients. These expected gains stem from greater use of optometric assistants and other support personnel, who will reduce the amount of time optometrists need with each patient. Also, laser surgery that can correct some vision problems is available, and although optometrists still will be needed to provide preoperative and postoperative care for laser surgery patients, patients who successfully undergo this surgery may not require optometrists to prescribe glasses or contacts for several years.

In addition to growth, the need to replace optometrists who retire or leave the occupation for another reason will create employment opportunities.

Earnings

Median annual earnings of salaried optometrists were $88,410 in May 2004. The middle 50 percent earned between $63,840 and $118,320. Median annual earnings of salaried optometrists in May 2004 were $87,430 in offices of optometrists. Salaried optometrists tend to earn more initially than do optometrists who set up their own practices. In the long run, however, those in private practice usually earn more.

According to the American Optometric Association, median net annual income for all optometrists, including the self-employed, was $114,000 in 2004. The middle 50 percent earned between $84,000 and $166,000.

Related Occupations

Other workers who apply scientific knowledge to prevent, diagnose, and treat disorders and injuries are chiropractors, dentists, physicians and surgeons, psychologists, podiatrists, and veterinarians.

OPTOMETRISTS RESOURCES

Don't forget! Refer to the general resources listed in Chapter Three.

✉ Association   📁 Directory   📇 Resume Service   🖰 Web Site

🗐 Job Ads   🏃 Job Alert E-mail/Hotline   🏳 Job Fairs   📖 Book

For a full explanation of these resources see the second page of Chapter 3.

✉ 📁 🖰 **American Academy of Optometry (AAO)** - 6110 Executive Blvd, Ste. 506, Rockville, MD 20852; 301/984-1441. (**www.aaopt.org**/, aaoptom@aol.com) The Student page on the web site has directory of student and faculty liaisons at schools of optometry in the U.S., as well as some international schools.

✉ 🗐 📁 🏳 📇 🖰 **American Optometric Association (AOA)** - 243 N. Lindberg Boulevard., First Floor, St. Louis, MO 63141; 800/365-2219. (**http://www.aoanet.org**/) Provides a job fair at the annual AOA Congress. Publishes a journal, newsletter, and educational materials. The Educational Center of the web site has career guidance with a list of schools. There is a financial aid page for members. Online career center has opportunities for employment, associates, partnerships independent contractors and practice sales. Upload your résumé.

♆ ☐◞ **Association of Schools and Colleges of Optometry (ASCO)** -
6110 Executive Boulevard, Suite 510, Rockville, MD 20852; 301/231-5944.
(http://www.opted.org) Student and Advisor section of web site has
admission requirements, online registration for Optometry Admission
Test (OAT), a career guide, and a directory of schools.

♆◞ **The Canadian Association of Optometrists** - 234 Argyle Avenue,
Ottawa, Ontario K2P 1B9, Canada; 888/263-4676. Information on becoming an optometrist or an optometrist assistant, including costs.
(www.opto.ca/en/public, info@opto.ca)

▤✍◞ **Eye Hunter** - **(http://www.eyehunter.com)** Classified ads for
jobs, equipment and practices. Major job site. Seek employment or relief
work.

♆ ☐◞ **National Optometric Association (NOA)** - Contact Dr.
Charles Comer, director, 3723 Main St., or P.O. Box F, East Chicago, IN
46312; 877/394-2020. **(http:/natoptassoc.org**, ccomer2@aol.com) Organization of minority optometrists. Student association has listing of student
contacts at schools of optometry.

▤✍◞ **OphthalJobs** - 2354 Hassell Road, Suite D, Hoffman
Estates, IL-60195; 877/885-7655. Ophthalmology job board with résumé
and job posting. Tips on résumé and classified advertisement writing.
(www.ophthaljobs.com, jobs@ophthaljobs.com)

▤✍◞ **Optometry.com** - Job service for the eye care industry
including opticians, optometrists, ophthalmologists and office staff. Listings by category and state. **(www.optometry.com/jobs/index.php)**

▤ **Opportunities in Eye Care Careers** by Kathleen M. Belikoff.
McGraw-Hill, 2003, $11.95. ISBN: 007141150X. Presents advice and
up-to-date information on career opportunities in eye care. It covers
what life is like on the job, training requirements, and places to go for
more information.

PHYSICIAN ASSISTANTS

Significant Points

- Physician assistant programs usually last at least 2 years; admission requirements vary by program, but many require at least 2 years of college and some health care experience.
- All states require physician assistants to complete an accredited education program and to pass a national exam in order to obtain a license.
- Physician assistants rank among the fastest growing occupations, as physicians and health care institutions increasingly utilize physician assistants in order to contain costs.
- Job opportunities should be good, particularly in rural and inner city clinics.

Nature of the Work

Physician assistants (PAs) practice medicine under the supervision of physicians and surgeons. They should not be confused with medical assistants, who perform routine clinical and clerical tasks. (Medical assistants are discussed elsewhere in the this book.) PAs are formally trained to provide diagnostic, therapeutic, and preventive health care services, as delegated by a physician. Working as members of the health care team, they take medical histories, examine and treat patients, order and interpret laboratory tests and x-rays, and make diagnoses. They also treat minor injuries, by suturing, splinting, and casting. PAs record progress notes, instruct and counsel patients, and order or carry out therapy. In 48 states and the District of Columbia, physician assistants may prescribe medications. PAs also may have managerial duties. Some order medical supplies or equipment and supervise technicians and assistants.

Physician assistants work under the supervision of a physician. However, PAs may be the principal care providers in rural or inner city clinics, where a physician is present for only 1 or 2 days each week. In such cases, the PA confers with the supervising physician and other medical professionals as needed and as required by law. PAs also may make house calls or go to hospitals and nursing care facilities to check on patients, after which they report back to the physician.

The duties of physician assistants are determined by the supervising physician and by state law. Aspiring PAs should investigate the laws and regulations in the states in which they wish to practice.

Many PAs work in primary care specialties, such as general internal medicine, pediatrics, and family medicine. Other specialty areas include general and thoracic surgery, emergency medicine, orthopedics, and geriatrics. PAs specializing in surgery provide preoperative and post-operative care and may work as first or second assistants during major surgery.

Working Conditions

Although PAs usually work in a comfortable, well-lighted environment, those in surgery often stand for long periods, and others do considerable walking. Schedules vary according to the practice setting, and often depend on the hours of the supervising physician. The work week of hospital-based PAs may include weekends, nights, or early morning hospital rounds to visit patients. These workers also may be on call. PAs in clinics usually work a 40-hour week.

Training, Other Qualifications, and Advancement

All states require that PAs complete an accredited, formal education program and pass a National exam to obtain a license. PA programs usually last at least 2 years and are full time. Most programs are in schools of allied health, academic health centers, medical schools, or 4-year colleges; a few are in community colleges, the military, or hospitals. Many accredited PA programs have clinical teaching affiliations with medical schools.

In 2005, more than 135 education programs for physician assistants were accredited or provisionally accredited by the American Academy of Physician Assistants. More than 90 of these programs offered the option of a master's degree, and the rest offered either a bachelor's degree or an associate degree. Most applicants to PA educational programs already have a bachelor's degree.

Admission requirements vary, but many programs require 2 years of college and some work experience in the health care field. Students should take courses in biology, English, chemistry, mathematics, psychology, and the social sciences. Many PAs have prior experience as registered nurses, while others come from varied backgrounds, including military corpsman/medics and allied health occupations such as respiratory therapists, physical therapists, and emergency medical technicians and paramedics.

PA education includes classroom instruction in biochemistry, pathology, human anatomy, physiology, microbiology, clinical pharmacology, clinical medicine, geriatric and home health care, disease prevention, and medical ethics. Students obtain supervised clinical training in several areas, including family medicine, internal medicine, surgery, prenatal care and gynecology, geriatrics, emergency medicine, psychiatry, and pediatrics. Sometimes, PA students serve one or more of these "rotations" under the supervision of a physician who is seeking to hire a PA. The rotations often lead to permanent employment.

All states and the District of Columbia have legislation governing the qualifications or practice of physician assistants. All jurisdictions require physician assistants to pass the Physician Assistant National Certifying Examination, administered by the National Commission on Certification of Physician Assistants (NCCPA) and open only to graduates of accredited PA education programs. Only those successfully completing the examination may use the credential "Physician Assistant Certified." In order to remain certified, PAs must complete 100 hours of continuing medical education every 2 years. Every 6 years, they must pass a recertification examination or complete an alternative program combining learning experiences and a take-home examination.

Some PAs pursue additional education in a specialty such as surgery, neonatology, or emergency medicine. PA postgraduate educational programs are available in areas such as internal medicine, rural primary care, emergency medicine, surgery, pediatrics, neonatology, and occupational medicine. Candidates must be graduates of an accredited program and be certified by the NCCPA.

Physician assistants need leadership skills, self-confidence, and emotional stability. They must be willing to continue studying throughout their career to keep up with medical advances.

As they attain greater clinical knowledge and experience, PAs can advance to added responsibilities and higher earnings. However, by the very nature of the profession, clinically practicing PAs always are supervised by physicians.

Employment

Physician assistants held about 62,000 jobs in 2004. The number of jobs is greater than the number of practicing PAs because some hold two or more jobs. For example, some PAs work with a supervising physician, but also work in another practice, clinic, or hospital. According to the American Academy of Physician Assistants, about 15 percent of actively practicing PAs worked in more than one clinical job concurrently in 2004.

More than half of jobs for PAs were in the offices of physicians. About a quarter were in hospitals, public or private. The rest were mostly in outpatient care centers, including health maintenance organizations; the federal government; and public or private colleges, universities, and professional schools. A few were self-employed.

Job Outlook

Employment of PAs is expected to grow much faster than average for all occupations through the year 2014, ranking among the fastest growing occupations, due to anticipated expansion of the health care industry and an emphasis on cost containment, resulting in increasing utilization of PAs by physicians and health care institutions.

Physicians and institutions are expected to employ more PAs to provide primary care and to assist with medical and surgical procedures because PAs are cost-effective and productive members of the health care team. Physician assistants can relieve physicians of routine duties and procedures. Telemedicine—using technology to facilitate interactive consultations between physicians and physician assistants—also will expand the use of physician assistants. Job opportunities for PAs should be good, particularly in rural and inner city clinics, because those settings have difficulty attracting physicians.

Besides the traditional office-based setting, PAs should find a growing number of jobs in institutional settings such as hospitals, academic medical centers, public clinics, and prisons. Additional PAs may be needed to augment medical staffing in inpatient teaching hospital settings as the number of hours physician residents are permitted to work is reduced, encouraging hospitals to use PAs to supply some physician resident services. Opportunities will be best in states that allow PAs a wider scope of practice.

Earnings

Median annual earnings of physician assistants were $69,410 in May 2004. The middle 50 percent earned between $57,110 and $83,560. The lowest 10 percent earned less than $37,320, and the highest 10 percent earned more than $94,880. Median annual earnings of physician assistants in 2004 were $70,310 in general medical and surgical hospitals and $69,210 in offices of physicians.

According to the American Academy of Physician Assistants, median income for physician assistants in full-time clinical practice in 2004 was $74,264; median income for first-year graduates was $64,536. Income varies by specialty, practice setting, geographical location, and years of experience. Employers often pay for their employees' liability insurance, registration fees with the Drug Enforcement Administration, state licensing fees, and credentialing fees.

Related Occupations

Other health care workers who provide direct patient care that requires a similar level of skill and training include audiologists, occupational therapists, physical therapists, registered nurses, and speech language pathologists.

PHYSICIAN ASSISTANTS

Don't forget! Refer to the general resources listed in Chapter Three.

☤ Association	🗁 Directory	✍ Resume Service	☋ Web Site
📑 Job Ads	💥 Job Alert E-mail/Hotline	☞ Job Fairs	📖 Book

For a full explanation of these resources see the second page of Chapter 3.

📑☞☋ **ADVANCE Newsmagazines** -2900 Horizon Drive, King of Prussia, PA 19406-0956; 800/355-5627. (**http://www.advanceweb.com/**) Publishes *ADVANCE for Physician Assistants*, free for professionals, numerous job ads. Web site has a well-designed section to find job ads by state, city or employer and a section on job fairs. Online access to "Talking to Talent" surveys of allied health professionals.

📑💥✍☋ Advancedpracticejobs - (**www.advancedpracticejobs.com**, info@avancedpracticejobs.com) Jobs for physician assistants and advanced practice nurses. Search by region or state, by specialty, or by employment status. Register free to receive emails about jobs that fit your classification.

☤📱📂🔨🖌️🖱️ **American Academy of Physician Assistants (AAPA)** - 950 North Washington St., Alexandria, VA 22314; 703/836-2272. (**http://www.aapa.org/**, aapa@aapa.org) Offers an extensive array of member services. The web site "Employment Opportunities" section is a part of healthecareers network. Log on to post your résumé and get notices of jobs fitting your qualifications. View a list of all PA specialties at **http://members.aapa.org/extra/constituents/special-menu.cfm**.

☤📱📂🖱️ **American Association of Pathologists' Assistants** - Rosewood Office Plaza, Suite 300N, 1711 W. County Road B, Roseville, MN 55113; 1-800-532-AAPA. (**http://www.pathologistsassistants.org**) The web site has a section describing the profession and training with a job area for members.

☤📱📂🖱️ **American Association of Surgical Physician Assistants (AASPA)** - PMB 201, 4267 NW Federal Highway, Jensen Beach, FL 34957; 888/882-2772. (**http://www.aaspa.com**, aaspa@aaspa.com). The web site posts job opportunities and has a section for pre-PA students. Student membership benefits include a résumé review service, mentoring or networking opportunities, and scholarship opportunities.

☤🖱️ **Association of Physician Assistants in Cardiovascular Surgery (APACVS)** P. O. Box 4834, Engelwood, CO 80155; 877/221-5651. Online description of work and training of Cardiovascular Physician Assistants. (**http://www.apacvs.org**)

☤📱🖱️ **Association of Physician Assistants in Obstetrics and Gynecology (APAOG)** - PO Box 1109, Madison, WI 53701-1109; 800/545-0636. (**http://www.paobgyn.org**, apaog@paobgyn.org) Web site has tips for looking for a job, and information on scholarships and grants. Link to the PA Job Link for job ads.

📱🔨🖱️ **ER 365** - **http://www.er365.com** Emergency medicine jobs for nurses, physicians and physician assistants. Search by state or locality, or get on their email notification list.

📖 **Getting Into the Physician Assistant School of Your Choice** - by Andrew J. Rodican, McGraw-Hill Medical, 2003, ISBN: 0071421858. This book addresses every step of the application process, including what schools look for in an applicant, financial aid, Internet resources, and information on PA programs.

MED OPTIONS USA - 6617 W Boynton Beach Blvd., #202, Boynton Beach, Florida 33437; Phone: 800/817-4903, fax: 800/357-8684, (http://www.medoptions.com). Free nurse practitioner and physician assistant job service. They give your profile to prospective employers and have unadvertised as well as advertised job listings.

National Commission on Certification of Physician Assistants, Inc. - 12000 Findley Road, Suite 200, Duluth, GA 30097; 678/417-8100. (Http://www.nccpa.net, nccpa@nccpa.net). Administers the Physician Assistant National Certifying Examination (PANCE) that is a prerequisite for licensure in all U.S. states. Contact for eligibility requirements and a description of the examination.

Opportunities in Physician Assistant Careers - by Terence J. Sacks and Ann L. Elderkin, McGraw-Hill, 2002, ISBN: 0071387269. Offers essential information about a variety of careers available assisting medical personnel and includes training and education requirements, salary statistics, and professional and internet resources.

Physician Assistant Education Association (PAEA) - 950 North Washington Street, Alexandria, Virginia 22314: 703/548-5538. (www.apap.org, techsupport@apap.org).

Physician Assistants in American Medicine by Roderick S. Hooker & James F. Cawley. Churchill Livingstone Pub., 2002. ISBN: 0443065977. Traces the origins of physician assisting, examines education, career opportunities, and future trends.

Physician Assistants in Orthopedic Surgery (PAOS) - PO Box 10871, Glendale, Arizona 85318; 800/804-7267. (http://www.paos.org, info@paos.org) Description of duties and responsibilities, and job opportunities listed on web site.

Society of Emergency Medicine Physician Assistants (SEMPA) - 222 S. Westmonte Drive, #101, Altamonte Springs, FL 32714; 407/774-7880. (http://www.sempa.org, info@sempa.org) Web site has listing of surgical PA programs, and describes scholarship program for members.

PHYSICIANS and SURGEONS

Significant Points

- Many physicians and surgeons work long, irregular hours; over one-third of full-time physicians worked 60 or more hours a week in 2004.
- Formal education and training requirements are among the most demanding of any occupation, but earnings are among the highest.
- Job opportunities should be very good, particularly in rural and low-income areas.
- New physicians are much less likely to enter solo practice and more likely to work as salaried employees of group medical practices, clinics, hospitals, or health networks.

Nature of the Work

Physicians and surgeons serve a fundamental role in our society and have an effect upon all our lives. They diagnose illnesses and prescribe and administer treatment for people suffering from injury or disease. Physicians examine patients, obtain medical histories, and order, perform, and interpret diagnostic tests. They counsel patients on diet, hygiene, and preventive health care.

There are two types of physicians: M.D.—Doctor of Medicine—and D.O.—Doctor of Osteopathic Medicine. M.D.s also are known as allopathic physicians. While both M.D.s and D.O.s may use all accepted methods of treatment, including drugs and surgery, D.O.s place special emphasis on the body's musculoskeletal system, preventive medicine, and holistic patient care. D.O.s are more likely than M.D.s to be primary care specialists although they can be found in all specialties. About half of D.O.s practice general or family medicine, general internal medicine, or general pediatrics.

Physicians work in one or more of several specialties, including, but not limited to, anesthesiology, family and general medicine, general internal medicine, general pediatrics, obstetrics and gynecology, psychiatry, and surgery.

Anesthesiologists. Anesthesiologists focus on the care of surgical patients and pain relief. Like other physicians, they evaluate and treat patients and direct the efforts of those on their staffs. Anesthesiologists confer with other physicians and surgeons about appropriate treatments and procedures before, during, and after operations. These critical care specialists are responsible for maintenance of the patient's vital life functions—heart rate, body temperature, blood pressure, breathing—through continual monitoring and assessment during surgery. They often work outside of the operating room, providing pain relief in the intensive care unit, during labor and delivery, and for those who suffer from chronic pain.

Family and general practitioners. Family and general practitioners are often the first point of contact for people seeking health care, acting as the traditional family doctor. They assess and treat a wide range of conditions, ailments, and injuries, from sinus and respiratory infections to broken bones and scrapes. Family and general practitioners typically have a patient base of regular, long-term visitors. Patients with more serious conditions are referred to specialists or other health care facilities for more intensive care.

General internists. General internists diagnose and provide nonsurgical treatment for diseases and injuries of internal organ systems. They provide care mainly for adults who have a wide range of problems associated with the internal organs, such as the stomach, kidneys, liver, and digestive tract. Internists use a variety of diagnostic techniques to treat patients through medication or hospitalization. Like general practitioners, general internists are commonly looked upon as primary care specialists. They have patients referred to them by other specialists, in turn referring patients to those and yet other specialists when more complex care is required.

General pediatricians. Providing care from birth to early adulthood, pediatricians are concerned with the health of infants, children, and teenagers. They specialize in the diagnosis and treatment of a variety of ailments specific to young people and track their patients' growth to adulthood. Like most physicians, pediatricians work with different health care workers, such as nurses and other physicians, to assess and treat children with various ailments, such as muscular dystrophy. Most of the work of pediatricians, however, involves treating day-to-day illnesses that are common to children—minor injuries, infectious diseases, and immunizations—much as a general practitioner treats adults. Some pediatricians specialize in serious medical conditions and pediatric surgery, treating autoimmune disorders or serious chronic ailments.

Obstetricians and gynecologists. Obstetricians and gynecologists (ob/gyns) are specialists whose focus is women's health. They are responsible for general medical care for women, but also provide care related to pregnancy and the reproductive system. Like general practitioners, ob/gyns are concerned with the prevention, diagnosis, and treatment of general health problems, but they focus on ailments specific to the female anatomy, such as breast and cervical cancer, urinary tract and pelvic disorders, and hormonal disorders. Ob/gyns also specialize in childbirth, treating and counseling women throughout their pregnancy, from giving prenatal diagnoses to delivery and postpartum care. Ob/gyns track the health of, and treat, both mother and fetus as the pregnancy progresses.

Psychiatrists. Psychiatrists are the primary caregivers in the area of mental health. They assess and treat mental illnesses through a combination of psychotherapy, psychoanalysis, hospitalization, and medication. Psychotherapy involves regular discussions with patients about their problems; the psychiatrist helps them find solutions through changes in their behavioral patterns, the exploration of their past experiences, and group and family therapy sessions. Psychoanalysis involves long-term psychotherapy and counseling for patients. In many cases, medications are administered to correct chemical imbalances that may be causing emotional problems. Psychiatrists may also administer electroconvulsive therapy to those of their patients who do not respond to, or who cannot take, medications.

Surgeons. Surgeons are physicians who specialize in the treatment of injury, disease, and deformity through operations. Using a variety of instruments, and with patients under general or local anesthesia, a surgeon corrects physical deformities, repairs bone and tissue after injuries, or performs preventive surgeries on patients with debilitating diseases or disorders. Although a large number perform general surgery, many surgeons choose to specialize in a specific area. One of the most prevalent specialties is orthopedic surgery: the treatment of the musculoskeletal system. Others include neurological surgery (treatment of the brain and nervous system), cardiovascular surgery, otolaryngology (treatment of the ear, nose, and throat), and plastic or reconstructive surgery. Like primary care and other specialist physicians, surgeons also examine patients, perform and interpret diagnostic tests, and counsel patients on preventive health care.

A number of other medical specialists, including allergists, cardiologists, dermatologists, emergency physicians, gastroenterologists, ophthalmologists, pathologists, and radiologists, also work in clinics, hospitals, and private offices.

Working Conditions

Many physicians—primarily general and family practitioners, general internists, pediatricians, ob/gyns, and psychiatrists—work in small private offices or clinics, often assisted by a small staff of nurses and other administrative personnel. Increasingly, physicians are practicing in groups or health care organizations that provide backup coverage and allow for more time off. These physicians often work as part of a team coordinating care for a population of patients; they are less independent than solo practitioners of the past.

Surgeons and anesthesiologists typically work in well-lighted, sterile environments while performing surgery and often stand for long periods. Most work in hospitals or in surgical outpatient centers. Many physicians and surgeons work long, irregular hours. Over one-third of full-time physicians and surgeons worked 60 hours or more a week in 2004. Only 8 percent of all physicians and surgeons worked part-time, compared with 16 percent for all occupations. Physicians and surgeons must travel frequently between office and hospital to care for their patients. Those who are on call deal with many patients' concerns over the phone and may make emergency visits to hospitals or nursing homes.

Training, Other Qualifications, and Advancement

Formal education and training requirements for physicians are among the most demanding of any occupation—4 years of undergraduate school, 4 years of medical school, and 3 to 8 years of internship and residency, depending on the specialty selected. A few medical schools offer combined undergraduate and medical school programs that last 6 rather than the customary 8 years.

Premedical students must complete undergraduate work in physics, biology, mathematics, English, and inorganic and organic chemistry. Students also take courses in the humanities and the social sciences. Some students volunteer at local hospitals or clinics to gain practical experience in the health professions.

The minimum educational requirement for entry into a medical school is 3 years of college; most applicants, however, have at least a bachelor's degree, and many have advanced degrees. There are 146 medical schools in the United States—126 teach allopathic medicine and award a Doctor of Medicine (M.D.) degree; 20 teach osteopathic medicine and award the Doctor of Osteopathic Medicine (D.O.) degree. Acceptance to medical school is highly competitive. Applicants must submit transcripts, scores from the Medical College Admission Test, and letters of recommendation. Schools also consider an applicant's character, personality, leadership qualities, and participation in extracurricular activities. Most schools require an interview with members of the admissions committee.

Students spend most of the first 2 years of medical school in laboratories and classrooms, taking courses such as anatomy, biochemistry, physiology, pharmacology, psychology, microbiology, pathology, medical ethics, and laws governing medicine. They also learn to take medical histories, examine patients, and diagnose illnesses. During their last 2 years, students work with patients under the supervision of experienced physicians in hospitals and clinics, learning acute, chronic, preventive, and rehabilitative care. Through rotations in internal medicine, family practice, obstetrics and gynecology, pediatrics, psychiatry, and surgery, they gain experience in the diagnosis and treatment of illness.

Following medical school, almost all M.D.s enter a residency graduate medical education in a specialty that takes the form of paid on-the-job training, usually in a hospital. Most D.O.s serve a 12-month rotating internship after graduation and before entering a residency, which may last 2 to 6 years.

All states, the District of Columbia, and U.S. territories license physicians. To be licensed, physicians must graduate from an accredited medical school, pass a licensing examination, and complete 1 to 7 years of graduate medical education. Although physicians licensed in one state usually can get a license to practice in another without further examination, some states limit reciprocity. Graduates of foreign medical schools generally can qualify for licensure after passing an examination and completing a U.S. residency.

M.D.s and D.O.s seeking board certification in a specialty may spend up to 7 years in residency training, depending on the specialty. A final examination immediately after residency or after 1 or 2 years of practice also is necessary for certification by a member board of the American Board of Medical Specialists (ABMS) or the American Osteopathic Association (AOA). The ABMS represents 24 specialty boards, ranging from allergy and immunology to urology. The AOA has approved 18 specialty boards, ranging from anesthesiology to surgery. For certification in a subspecialty, physicians usually need another 1 to 2 years of residency.

A physician's training is costly. According to the Association of American Medical Colleges, in 2004 more than 80 percent of medical school graduates were in debt for educational expenses.

People who wish to become physicians must have a desire to serve patients, be self-motivated, and be able to survive the pressures and long hours of medical education and practice. Physicians also must have a good bedside manner, emotional stability, and the ability to make decisions in emergencies. Prospective physicians must be willing to study throughout their career in order to keep up with medical advances.

Employment
Physicians and surgeons held about 567,000 jobs in 2004; approximately 1 out of 7 was self-employed and not incorporated. About 60 percent of salaried physicians and surgeons were in office of physicians, and 16 percent were employed by private hospitals. Others practiced in federal, state, and local governments, including hospitals, colleges, universities, and professional schools; private colleges, universities, and professional schools; and outpatient care centers.

According to the American Medical Association (AMA), in 2003 about 2 out 5 physicians in patient care were in primary care, but not in a subspecialty of primary care.

A growing number of physicians are partners or salaried employees of group practices. Organized as clinics or as associations of physicians, medical groups can afford expensive medical equipment and realize other business advantages.

According to the AMA, the New England and Middle Atlantic states have the highest ratio of physicians to population; the South Central and Mountain states have the lowest. D.O.s are more likely than M.D.s to practice in small cities and towns and in rural areas. M.D.s tend to locate in urban areas, close to hospital and education centers.

Job Outlook

Employment of physicians and surgeons is projected to grow faster than average for all occupations through the year 2014 due to continued expansion of health care industries. The growing and aging population will drive overall growth in the demand for physician services, as consumers continue to demand high levels of care using the latest technologies, diagnostic tests, and therapies. In addition to employment growth, job openings will result from the need to replace physicians and surgeons who retire over the 2004-14 period.

Demand for physicians' services is highly sensitive to changes in consumer preferences, health care reimbursement policies, and legislation. For example, if changes to health coverage result in consumers facing higher out-of-pocket costs, they may demand fewer physician services. Demand for physician services may also be tempered by patients relying more on other health care providers—such as physician assistants, nurse practitioners, optometrists, and nurse anesthetists—for some health care services. In addition, new technologies will increase physician productivity. Telemedicine will allow physicians to treat patients or consult with other providers remotely. Increasing use of electronic medical records, test and prescription orders, billing, and scheduling will also improve physician productivity.

Opportunities for individuals interested in becoming physicians and surgeons are expected to be very good. Reports of shortages in some specialties or geographic areas should attract new entrants, encouraging schools to expand programs and hospitals to expand available residency slots. However, because physician training is so lengthy, employment change happens gradually. In the short term, to meet increased demand, experienced physicians may work longer hours, delay retirement, or take measures to increase productivity, such as using more support staff to provide services. Opportunities should be particularly good in rural and low-income areas, because some physicians find these areas unattractive due to less control over work hours, isolation from medical colleagues, or other reasons.

Unlike their predecessors, newly trained physicians face radically different choices of where and how to practice. New physicians are much less likely to enter solo practice and more likely to take salaried jobs in group medical practices, clinics, and health networks.

Earnings

Earnings of physicians and surgeons are among the highest of any occupation. According to the Medical Group Management Association's Physician Compensation and Production Survey, median total compensation for physicians in 2004 varied by specialty. Total compensation for physicians reflects the amount reported as direct compensation for tax purposes, plus all voluntary salary reductions. Salary, bonus and/or incentive payments, research stipends, honoraria, and distribution of profits were included in total compensation.

Self-employed physicians—those who own or are part owners of their medical practice—generally have higher median incomes than salaried physicians. Earnings vary according to number of years in practice, geographic region, hours worked, and skill, personality, and professional reputation. Self-employed physicians and surgeons must provide for their own health insurance and retirement.

Median total compensation for physicians with over one year of practice in the following specialties: Anesthesiology, $321,686; Surgery: General, $282,504; Obstetrics/gynecology, $247,348; Psychiatry, $180,000; Internal medicine, $166,420; Pediatrics, $161,331; and Family practice, $156,010.

Related Occupations

Physicians work to prevent, diagnose, and treat diseases, disorders, and injuries. Other health care practitioners who need similar skills and who exercise critical judgment include chiropractors, dentists, optometrists, physician assistants, podiatrists, registered nurses, and veterinarians.

PHYSICIANS RESOURCES

Don't forget! Refer to the general resources listed in Chapter Three.

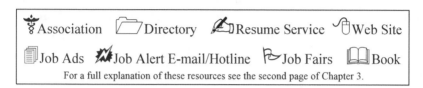

For a full explanation of these resources see the second page of Chapter 3.

⚕️ ▤ 🗁 📧 ✏️ 🖱️ **American Academy of Family Physicians (AAFP)** - 11400 Tomahawk Creek Parkway, Leawood, KS 66211; 800/274-2237. (**http://www.aafp.org**, fp@aafp.org) Information on residencies for medical school students considering this career and job ads posted by state. AAFP placement service is free for members.

⚕️ 🗁 ▤ 🖱️ **American College of Physicians (ACP)** - Independence Mall West, Philadelphia, PA 19106; 800/523-1546, x2600.Association of doctors of internal medicine. (**www.acponline.org**) Students/residents tab has information on the specialty, finding a residency, and financial aid. Jobs/careers tab lists opportunities by state.

⚕️ ▤ 🗁 🖱️ **American Medical Association (AMA)** - 515 N. State St., Chicago, IL 60610; 800/621-8335. (**http://www.ama-assn.org**) The AMA web site has extensive information on the process involved in becoming a physician, including planning and financing. Sponsors FREIDA the Fellowship and Residency Electronic Interactive Database containing over 7,800 graduate medical education programs accredited by the Accreditation Council for Graduate Medical Education, as well as over 200 combined specialty programs.

⚕️ 🖱️ **American Osteopathic Association** - 142 East Ontario St., Chicago, IL 60611; 800/621-1773. (**http://www.DO-Online.org**, msc@osteopathic. org) Web site has information on the mentoring program for students and residents, directory of colleges, directory of intern and residency programs, certification information, and job listings. Members can upload a résumé and be notified of openings.

📖 **Becoming a Physician: A Practical and Creative Guide to Planning a Career in Medicine** - by Jennifer Danek & Marita Danek, John Wiley & Sons, 1997, ISBN: 0471121665. Information on the MCAT.

Advice on selecting the right medical school. Current medical trends and the most attractive specialties.

☤ 📖 **Canadian Medical Association** - 888 855-2555. (**http://www.cma.ca**, cmamsc@cma.ca). Student membership gives access to the MD Financial Group, a one-stop source for all the financial needs of CMA members and their families, unlimited 24/7 access to the full text of 1000 peer-reviewed medical journals, the Canadian database of drug information, and more.

📖 **Get Into Medical School : A Strategic Approach** - by Maria Lofftus and Thomas C. Taylor, Kaplan Pub. 2003, ISBN: 0743240960 "As a pre-med student, you'll be working for at least two years without guarantee of a spot in medical school. It means publicly stating that you want something that in 2002 only 52 percent of those applying got - a position in medical school."

☤ 📖📇🖱 **National Medical Association (NMA)** - 1012 10th St. NW, Washington DC 20001; 202/347-1895, (**http://www.nmanet.org**, Publicaffairs@NMAnet.org) The NMA focuses primarily on health issues related to African Americans and medically under-served populations. Career opportunities tab of web site has placement service. Programs include breast-feeding, HIV/AIDS, asthma, traffic safety and tobacco control.

📇🖱 **New England Journal of Medicine** - 10 Shattuck Street, Boston, MA 02115; 617/734-9800. (**http://www.nejm.org/**, comments@ nejm.org) Web site has job ads published in the paper journal. You can also create a profile, and be alerted when jobs or opportunities that fit your criteria open up.

📇🖱 **The Physician Recruiter** - PO Box 698, Portland, OR 97207, 503/221-1260. (**http://www.therecruiter.com**, info@therecruiter.com) Permanent practice opportunities and locum tenens positions within primary care, emergency medicine, cardiology and surgical specialties.

☤ 🖱 **Specialties for Physicians** - Further information on the numerous specialties for physicians can be found through medical associations listed below. These links can be found on **http://healthcarejobs.org**. This site lists and provides direct links to many resources that will help including a list of 24 of the key medical associations.

Aerospace Medical Association (http://www.asma.org)

American Academy of Dermatology (http://www.aad.org)

American Academy of Neurology (http://www.aan.com)

American Academy of Pediatrics (http://www.aap.org)

American Academy of Allergy Asthma & Immunology
(http://www.aaaai.org)

American Association of Immunologists (http://www.aai.org)

American College of Occupational and Environmental Medicine
(http://www.acoem.org)

American Academy of Ophthalmology (http://www.aao.org)

American College of Sports Medicine (http://www.acsm.org)

American Gastroenterological Association (http://www.gastro.org)

American Medical Women's Association (http://www.amwa-doc.org)

American Podiatric Medical Association (http://www.apma.org)

American Psychiatric Association (http://www.psych.org)

American Psychological Association (http://www.apa.org)

American Society of Anesthesiologists (http://www.asahq.org)

American Society for Clinical Pathology (http://www.ascp.org)

American Society of Handicapped Physicians (Contact Will Lambert, Director, 3424 S. Culepper, Springfield, MO 65804; 417/881-1570.)

Radiological Society of North America (http://www.rsna.org)

Society of Nuclear Medicine (SNM) (http://www.snm.org)

Society of Critical Care Medicine (http://www.sccm.org)

VETERINARIANS

Significant Points
- Veterinarians should have an affinity for animals and the ability to get along with their owners.
- Graduation from an accredited college of veterinary medicine and a state license are required.
- Competition for admission to veterinary school is keen; however, graduates should have very good job opportunities.
- About 1 out of 5 veterinarians was self-employed; self-employed veterinarians usually have to work hard and long to build a sufficient client base.

Nature of the Work
Veterinarians play a major role in the healthcare of pets, livestock, and zoo, sporting, and laboratory animals. Some veterinarians use their skills to protect humans against diseases carried by animals and conduct clinical research on human and animal health problems. Others work in basic research, broadening the scope of fundamental theoretical knowledge, and in applied research, developing new ways to use knowledge.

Most veterinarians perform clinical work in private practices. More than 50 percent of these veterinarians predominately, or exclusively treat small animals. Small-animal practitioners usually care for companion animals, such as dogs and cats, but also treat birds, reptiles, rabbits, and other animals that can be kept as pets. About one-fourth of all veterinarians work in mixed animal practices, where they see pigs, goats, sheep, and some nondomestic animals in addition to companion animals. Veterinarians in clinical practice diagnose animal health problems; vaccinate against diseases, such as distemper and rabies; medicate animals suffering from infections or illnesses; treat and dress wounds; set fractures; perform surgery; and advise owners about animal feeding, behavior, and breeding.

A small number of private-practice veterinarians work exclusively with large animals, mostly horses or cows; some also care for various kinds of food animals. These veterinarians usually drive to farms or ranches to provide veterinary services for herds or individual animals. Much of this work involves preventive care to maintain the health of the animals. These veterinarians test for and vaccinate against diseases and consult with farm or ranch owners and managers regarding animal production, feeding, and housing issues. They also treat and dress wounds, set fractures, and perform surgery, including cesarean sections on birthing animals. Veterinarians euthanize animals when necessary. Other veterinarians care for zoo, aquarium, or laboratory animals.

Veterinarians who treat animals use medical equipment such as stethoscopes, surgical instruments, and diagnostic equipment, including radiographic and ultrasound equipment. Veterinarians working in research use a full range of sophisticated laboratory equipment.

Veterinarians can contribute to human as well as animal health. A number of veterinarians work with physicians and scientists as they research ways to prevent and treat various human health problems. For example, veterinarians contributed greatly in conquering malaria and yellow fever, solved the mystery of botulism, produced an anticoagulant used to treat some people with heart disease, and defined and developed surgical techniques for humans, such as hip and knee joint replacements and limb and organ transplants. Today, some determine the effects of drug therapies, antibiotics, or new surgical techniques by testing them on animals.

Some veterinarians are involved in food safety at various levels. Veterinarians who are livestock inspectors check animals for transmissible diseases, advise owners on the treatment of their animals and may quarantine animals. Veterinarians who are meat, poultry, or egg product inspectors examine slaughtering and processing plants, check live animals and carcasses for disease, and enforce government regulations regarding food purity and sanitation.

Working Conditions
Veterinarians often work long hours. Those in group practices may take turns being on call for evening, night, or weekend work; solo

practitioners may work extended and weekend hours, responding to emergencies or squeezing in unexpected appointments. The work setting often can be noisy.

Veterinarians in large-animal practice spend time driving between their office and farms or ranches. They work outdoors in all kinds of weather and may have to treat animals or perform surgery under unsanitary conditions. When working with animals that are frightened or in pain, veterinarians risk being bitten, kicked, or scratched.

Veterinarians working in nonclinical areas, such as public health and research, have working conditions similar to those of other professionals in those lines of work. In these cases, veterinarians enjoy clean, well-lit offices or laboratories and spend much of their time dealing with people rather than animals.

Training, Other Qualifications, and Advancement

Prospective veterinarians must graduate with a Doctor of Veterinary Medicine (D.V.M. or V.M.D.) degree from a 4-year program at an accredited college of veterinary medicine and must obtain a license to practice. There are 28 colleges in 26 states that meet accreditation standards set by the Council on Education of the American Veterinary Medical Association (AVMA). The prerequisites for admission vary. Many of these colleges do not require a bachelor's degree for entrance, but all require a significant number of credit hours—ranging from 45 to 90 semester hours—at the undergraduate level. However, most of the students admitted have completed an undergraduate program. Applicants without a bachelor's degree face a difficult task gaining admittance.

Pre-veterinary courses emphasize the sciences. Veterinary medical colleges typically require classes in organic and inorganic chemistry, physics, biochemistry, general biology, animal biology, animal nutrition, genetics, vertebrate embryology, cellular biology, microbiology, zoology, and systemic physiology. Some programs require calculus; some require only statistics, college algebra and trigonometry, or precalculus. Most veterinary medical colleges also require core courses, including some in English or literature, the social sciences, and the humanities. Increasingly, courses in practice management and career development are becoming a standard part of the curriculum, to provide a foundation of general business knowledge for new graduates.

In addition to satisfying preveterinary course requirements, applicants must submit test scores from the Graduate Record Examination (GRE), the Veterinary College Admission Test (VCAT), or the Medical College Admission Test (MCAT), depending on the preference of the college to which they are applying. Currently, 22 schools require the GRE, 4 require the VCAT, and 2 accept the MCAT.

In admittance decisions, some veterinary medical colleges place heavy consideration on a candidate's veterinary and animal experience. Formal experience, such as work with veterinarians or scientists in clinics, agribusiness, research, or some area of health science, is particularly advantageous. Less formal experience, such as working with animals on a farm or ranch or animal shelter, also is helpful. Students must demonstrate ambition and an eagerness to work with animals.

There is keen competition for admission to veterinary school. The number of accredited veterinary colleges has remained largely the same since 1983, whereas the number of applicants has risen significantly. Only about 1 in 3 applicants was accepted in 2004. AVMA-recognized veterinary specialties—such as pathology, internal medicine, dentistry, nutrition, ophthalmology, surgery, radiology, preventive medicine, and laboratory animal medicine—are usually in the form of a 2-year internship. Interns receive a small salary but usually find that their internship experience leads to a higher beginning salary, relative to those of other starting veterinarians. Veterinarians who seek board certification in a specialty also must complete a 3- to 4-year residency program that provides intensive training in specialties such as internal medicine, oncology, radiology, surgery, dermatology, anesthesiology, neurology, cardiology, ophthalmology, and exotic small-animal medicine.

All states and the District of Columbia require that veterinarians be licensed before they can practice. The only exemptions are for veterinarians working for some Federal agencies and some state governments. Licensing is controlled by the states and is not strictly uniform, although all states require the successful completion of the D.V.M. degree—or equivalent education—and a passing grade on a national board examination. The Educational Commission for Foreign Veterinary Graduates (ECFVG) grants certification to individuals trained outside the United States who demonstrate that they meet specified requirements for the English language and for clinical proficiency. ECFVG certification fulfills the educational requirement for licensure in all states. Applicants for licensure satisfy the examination requirement by passing the North American Veterinary Licensing Exam (NAVLE),an 8-hour computer based examination consisting of 360 multiple-choice questions covering all aspects of veterinary medicine. Administered by the National Board of Veterinary Medical Examiners (NBVME),the NAVLE includes visual materials designed to test diagnostic skills and constituting 10 percent of the total examination.

The majority of states also require candidates to pass a state juris-prudence examination covering state laws and regulations. Some states do additional testing on clinical competency as well. There are few recip-rocal agreements between states, making it difficult for a veterinarian to practice in a different state without first taking that state's examination.

Nearly all states have continuing education requirements for licensed veterinarians. Requirements differ by state and may involve attending a class or otherwise demonstrating knowledge of recent medical and veterinary advances.

Most veterinarians begin as employees in established practices. Despite the substantial financial investment in equipment, office space, and staff, many veterinarians with experience set up their own practice or purchase an established one.

Newly trained veterinarians can become U.S. Government meat and poultry inspectors, disease-control workers, animal welfare and safety workers, epidemiologists, research assistants, or commissioned officers in the U.S. Public Health Service or various branches of the U.S. Armed Forces. A state license may be required.

Prospective veterinarians must have good manual dexterity. They should have an affinity for animals and the ability to get along with their owners, especially pet owners, who tend to form a strong bond with their pet. Veterinarians who intend to go into private practice should possess excellent communication and business skills, because they will need to manage their practice and employees successfully and promote, market, and sell their services.

Employment
Veterinarians held about 61,000 jobs in 2004. About 1 out of 5 veter-inarians was self-employed in a solo or group practice. Most others were salaried employees of another veterinary practice. The federal govern-

ment employed about 1,200 civilian veterinarians, chiefly in the U.S. Departments of Agriculture, Health and Human Services, and, increasingly, Homeland Security. Other employers of veterinarians are state and local governments, colleges of veterinary medicine, medical schools, research laboratories, animal food companies, and pharmaceutical companies. A few veterinarians work for zoos, but most veterinarians caring for zoo animals are private practitioners who contract with the zoos to provide services, usually on a part-time basis. In addition, many veterinarians hold veterinary faculty positions in colleges and universities.

Job Outlook

Employment of veterinarians is expected to increase as fast as average for all occupations over the 2004–14 projection period. Despite this average growth, very good job opportunities are expected because the 28 schools of veterinary medicine, even at full capacity, result in a limited number of graduates each year. However, as mentioned earlier, there is keen competition for admission to veterinary school. As pets are increasingly viewed as a member of the family, pet owners will be more willing to spend on advanced veterinary medical care, creating further demand for veterinarians.

Most veterinarians practice in animal hospitals or clinics and care primarily for companion animals. Recent trends indicate particularly strong interest in cats as pets. Faster growth of the cat population is expected to increase the demand for feline medicine and veterinary services, while demand for veterinary care for dogs should continue to grow at a more modest pace.

Pet owners are becoming more aware of the availability of advanced care and are more willing to pay for intensive veterinary care than in the past because many pet owners are more affluent and because they consider their pet part of the family. More pet owners even purchase pet insurance, increasing the likelihood that a considerable amount of money will be spent on veterinary care for their pets. More pet owners also will take advantage of nontraditional veterinary services, such as preventive dental care.

New graduates continue to be attracted to companion-animal medicine because they prefer to deal with pets and to live and work near heavily populated areas. This situation will not necessarily limit the ability of veterinarians to find employment or to set up and maintain a practice in a particular area. Rather, beginning veterinarians may take positions requiring evening or weekend work to accommodate the extended hours of operation that many practices are offering. Some veterinarians take salaried positions in retail stores offering veterinary services. Self-employed veterinarians usually have to work hard and long to build a sufficient client base.

The number of jobs for large-animal veterinarians is likely to grow more slowly than that for veterinarians in private practice who care for companion animals. Nevertheless, job prospects may be better for veterinarians who specialize in farm animals than for companion-animal practitioners because of low earnings in the former specialty and because many veterinarians do not want to work in rural or isolated areas.

Continued support for public health and food safety, national disease control programs, and biomedical research on human health problems will contribute to the demand for veterinarians, although positions in these areas of interest are few in number. Homeland security also may provide opportunities for veterinarians involved in efforts to minimize animal diseases and prevent them from entering the country. Veterinarians with training in food safety, animal health and welfare, and public health and epidemiology should have the best opportunities for a career in the federal government.

Earnings

Median annual earnings of veterinarians were $66,590 in May 2004. The middle 50 percent earned between $51,420 and $88,060. The lowest 10 percent earned less than $39,020, and the highest 10 percent earned more than $118,430.

According to a survey by the American Veterinary Medical Association, average starting salaries of veterinary medical college graduates in 2004 varied by type of practice as follows: Small animals, predominantly $50,878, Small animals, exclusively, $50,703; Large animals, exclusively, $50,403; Private clinical practice, $49,635; Large animals, predominantly, $48,529; Mixed animals, $47,704; Equine (horses), $38,628 .

The average annual salary for veterinarians in the federal government in non-supervisory, supervisory, and managerial positions was $78,769 in 2005.

Related Occupations

Veterinarians prevent, diagnose, and treat diseases, disorders, and injuries in animals. Those who do similar work for humans include chiropractors, dentists, optometrists, physicians and surgeons, and podiatrists. Veterinarians have extensive training in physical and life sciences, and some do scientific and medical research, similar to the work of biological scientists and medical scientists.

Animal care and service workers and veterinary technologists and technicians work extensively with animals. Like veterinarians, they must have patience and feel comfortable with animals. However, the level of training required for these occupations is substantially less than that needed by veterinarians.

VETERINARIANS RESOURCES

Don't forget! Refer to the general resources listed in Chapter Three.

Association   Directory   Resume Service   Web Site

Job Ads   Job Alert E-mail/Hotline   Job Fairs   Book

For a full explanation of these resources see the second page of Chapter 3.

American College of Veterinary Surgeons - 11 N Washington St, Suite, 720, Rockville, MD 20850; 301/610-2000. *ACVS Directory of Diplomates*, online job ads, and information on becoming a veterinary surgeon. (**www.acvs.org**, acvs@acvs.org)

American Veterinary Medical Association (AVMA) - 1931 N. Meacham Rd., Suite 100, Schaumburg, IL 60173; 847/925-8070. (**http://www.avma.org**, avmainfo@avma.org). Web has directory of veterinary programs in the US. Student AVMA includes web based open mentoring. Anyone can view jobs posted on internet. Members can post résumé and be notified when jobs come up that meet their specifications.

Association of American Veterinary Medical Colleges - 1101 Vermont Avenue NW, Suite 301, Washington, DC 20005; 202/371-9195. (**www.aavmc.org**, vmcas@aavmc.org) Has directory of member programs. Operates the Veterinary Medical College Application Service (VMCAS), a one stop venue for applying to veterinary medical school.

📖 **Careers for Animal Lovers & Other Zoological Types** - by Louise Miller, McGraw-Hill, 2000, ISBN: 0658004638 Discusses dozens of ways to pursue a passion and make a living--including many little-known but delightful careers that will surprise readers.

📖 **Careers in Animal Care and Veterinary Science** - by Deborah A. Marinelli, Rosen Publishing Group, 2000, ISBN: 0823931854 A good resource for those who'd like to make a living working with animals.

 **California Veterinarian Medical Association (CVMA)** - 1400 River Park Drive, Suite 100, Sacramento, CA 95815; 916/649-0599. (**http:www.cvma.net**, staff@cvma.net) Web site lists graduating members of UC Davis vet program so prospective employees can contact them. Career classifieds section lists jobs and other career options. Search by practice type, employment type and city or region. Anyone can post a résumé ad, however members get special rates.

📖 **Opportunities in Animal and Pet Care Careers** - by Mary Price Lee and Richard Lee, McGraw-Hill, 2001, ISBN: 0658010433. Offers job seekers information about a variety of careers for animal lovers, including training and education requirements, salary statistics, and professional and Internet resources.

"If you think education is expensive, try ignorance!"
— Peter Drucker

Chapter

10

HOME HEALTH CARE & MEDICAL INFORMATION MANAGEMENT

Lily Chan, RN

Lily Chan, a registered nurse with Children's Home Care in Los Angeles, was born in Hong Kong May 23, 1953. She completed a three year nursing program and worked four years as a staff nurse there prior to moving to England. She took additional courses in pediatric and cardiothoracic nursing before coming to the United States.

When asked why she chose nursing, Lily said "I felt the need to take care of someone as a basic personality trait." In addition, she enjoyed studying biology and anatomy, and felt nursing could provide her with a good income. She also thought that "the education and experience in nursing would help me take care of my own health." Lily feels that the most satisfying aspect of a nursing career is "providing a quality environment for the patient. Even the more menial tasks become satisfying if you look at it that way."

A recruiting agency arranged for Lily to come to the United States in 1983 and take the NCLEX licensing exam for RNs. They also found employment for her at Methodist Hospital in Lubbock, Texas, as an interim permittee while waiting for her RN license. In April of 1984, she began working at Childrens Hospital Los Angeles. In 1995, Children's Home Care was formed as an affiliate of CHLA.

Lily pointed out the advantages to working in home health care. "In home health, you have time to deal with just one patient and family at a time. In the hospital you can get pulled in five directions at once when it gets busy." You also have a more flexible time schedule.

Lily was asked why she specifically likes pediatric home health care. "With pediatrics, you are interacting with the whole family." Once she was taking care of a child and complimented the mother on how good the chicken she was cooking smelled. When she finished with the patient, the table was set with dinner for her.

Lily advised that anyone considering home health as a career must evaluate their capabilities. "For home care you have to have a very broad knowledge base and be creative and flexible. You have to improvise a lot." She also warned, "the fear of many who transfer to home health care is that in a hospital, if there is any problem, you can just yell and get assistance, while with home care that security is lost. On the other hand, home care patients may not be as ill as those in the hospital and there is emergency help available, such as calling 911."

When asked for advice in finding employment, Lily responded, "It is hard for a new graduate to get into, as they need a few years in acute care in a hospital to develop the assessment skills." *NurseWeek* and the local newspaper are good sources for job ads. Check with hospitals, too. Some have their own home health care department.

I asked how to evaluate a home health care agency as a potential employer. "Look for leadership quality. The whole mission and philosophy of the agency has to support staff providing quality care. This affects how good you feel about yourself. The agency has to balance the quality with cost."

If you really enjoy working with people and have confidence in your skills, you will probably derive great satisfaction from caring for your patients in their homes.

This chapter features an overview of the home health field (one of fastest growing areas of medical care), and career descriptions with resources for

Homemaker-Home Health Aides   Computer Careers
Medical Information Technicians   Billing and Coding Specialists

Also presented are resources for the many professionals involved in caring for patients in the home. These include, but are not limited to:

Physicians   Dieticians
Nurses   Pharmacists
Physical Therapists   Social Workers
Occupational Therapists   Speech-language Pathologists

HOME HEALTH CARE OVERVIEW

The development of in-home medical technologies, substantial cost savings, and patients' preference for care in the home have helped make home health into one of the fastest growing segments of the health care industry. The National Center for Health Statistics reported 1,355,290 home health care patients in the United States in the year 2000.[1] The National Association for Home Care & Hospice estimates are higher: 7.76 million patients receiving home care from 20,000 agencies.[2]

The home health care services industry will be the fastest growing employer in the United States between 2004 and 2014. Expected to increase at a 5.4-percent annual rate to 1.3 million jobs by 2014, this industry's growth reflects an aging population, many of whom will have functional disabilities and will desire to maintain an independent, home-based life style.[3] Nurses and other health care specialists, including personal and home care aides, and home health aides, will be in great demand. One limit on home care growth is that Medicaid prefers to pay for nursing home care, which is often more expensive. Vermont is the first state to experiment with home care for Medicaid patients.[4]

A rapidly evolving facet of modern health care is telemedicine, the use of high-tech video equipment to facilitate communication among physicians, patients, families, nurses and other allied-health professionals. In home health, terms used are remote care technology, tele-health, and telehomecare. Having telemedicine equipment in the pa-tient's home, or in a van that can be driven to the home, means that fewer health care professionals are needed to monitor patients. Remote care is a supplement to home visits, not a substitute. Home health care workers can check in with patients as often as needed, even viewing the progress in wound healing by video camera.[5]

> **Personal and home care aides, and home health aides, will be in great demand.**

Not all patients needing home care are elderly. Disabled people of any age may need some degree of home care. Patients recuperating from acute illness or injury may need temporary home care. Children and adults with chronic illnesses may need medical treatment that can be provided at home by a home health professional, or may need training in specific medical therapies.

Home Health Care Defined

Home health care means providing health services and equipment to patients in their home. Depending upon the needs of the individual patient, services may be delivered 24 hours per day. Sometimes the purpose of home care is restoration of health and/or function, while other times it is to maintain comfort, as in hospice care. Home health care may provide for both the medical and the personal needs of patients and their family members. Professionals involved include phy-sicians, nurses, physical therapists, occupational therapists, dieticians, pharmacists, social workers, speech-language pathologists, and personal/ home care aides.

Many, but not all, patients are referred to home health care agencies after a period of hospitalization. Patients should have a thorough eval-uation, including not just medical needs, but also assessment of the mental state of the patient. In addition to evaluating the patient's ability to comply with treatment such as dietary recommendations and/or drug schedules, the family and social environment needs to be considered. Various health care professionals may be involved in the evaluation.

Numerous factors may influence the decision to provide care for the patient in the home rather than in a hospital, nursing home or other facility. Among these are studies that have shown patients tend to recuperate sooner from an accident or illness in familiar surroundings with caring family members. Another consideration is the availability of competent assistance from family or friends. The physical layout of the home must also be evaluated for adaptability to the patient's needs. For example, a patient in a wheelchair will need appropriate access to shower and toilet facilities.

Service is usually provided by a home health agency, hospice or homemaker/home care aide agency. Staffing and private-duty agencies can provide nurses, homemakers, home health aides or companions, but are not always required to be licensed. Pharmaceutical and infusion therapy companies employ pharmacists and nurses to assist patients requiring intravenous infusions. Medical equipment suppliers and manufacturers may provide installation of medical equipment and instruct patients on use. Some provide respiratory therapy services. Registries connect home health nurses and aides with individual patients, who employ them directly. Many home health care professionals are independent of agencies and are employed directly by the patient or are self-employed, often having several clients at once.

How Home Health Agencies Work

The National Council on the Aging defines a home health agency as "a company that provides many professional health care services, in the home, under the direction of a physician. These comprehensive services include skilled nursing, personal care assistance, physical, occupational and speech therapy, and medical social work. Medical equipment, supplies and infusion therapies may also be available. Home care agencies have an administrator or a director who is responsible for the business and managerial operations. This person is often a doctor, nurse, or social worker who has education or experience in administration."[6]

Certified agencies must meet licensing requirements. In addition, some are accredited by the Joint Commission on Accreditation of Healthcare Organizations, (**http://www.jcaho.org**) or Accreditation Commission for Health Care, Inc. (**http://www.achc.org**), Community Health

Accreditation Program (**http://www.chapinc.org**), and the National Committee for Quality Assurance (**http://www.ncqa.org**). Those participating in Medicare must also meet federal requirements.

Do You Have What it Takes?

A recent article by Lazelle Benefield, PhD, RN, in the *American Journal of Nursing* explored the personal qualifications required for nurses to be happy in their choice of home health nursing.[7] The considerations cited apply to many other professions.

One issue in caring for patients in their home is the freedom of making independent decisions versus the responsibility of making clinical decisions on one's own. Some people relish the independence, while others may feel comfortable with more structure and more interaction with peers and supervisors. Dr. Benefield emphasizes being proactive. Ask for advice from others in the field, subscribe to home health journals and focus your continuing education units.

A problem in home health is sorting out the variety of restrictions placed on patient services by all the different HMOs, PPOs and insurance companies. The home health nurse is responsible for documenting patient progress and justifying continuing care based on patient capabilities or safety.

In an accompanying article, Janet Dyer is very specific about the personality traits needed for success in the home health care field.[8] She writes, "Nurses who flourish in home health tend to be self-starters, independent and creative thinkers...they also need to be well-versed in the latest technology...home health tends to reward flexibility and well-rounded skills..."

REFERENCES

[1] National Center for Health Statistics, *Health, United States, 2004, With Chartbook on Trends in the Health of Americans.* Hyattsville, Maryland: 2004, p 287.

[2] National Association for Home Care & Hospice. *Basic Statistics about Home Care,* Updated 2004.

[3] Jay M. Berman, *Industry output and employment projections to 2014*, Monthly Labor Review, November 2005.

[4] Sara Miller LLana, *A push for stay-at-home healthcare*, The Christian Science Monitor, January 2, 2006.

[5] Home Health Care via Telemedicine, *Telemedicine Today Magazine*, Fall 1995

[6] "Family Care Resource - Home Health Care," The National Council on the Aging, Online, Available: http://www.ncoa.org, Dec. 22, 1997.

[7] Lazelle E. Benefield, PhD, RN, "Are You Really for Home Health Nursing?" *American Journal of Nursing*, Jan., 1998, pp 17-18.

[8] Janet Dyer, "Home Health Care: Where the Jobs Are", *American Journal of Nursing*, Jan., 1998, p. 18.

PERSONAL & HOME CARE AIDES

While many of the health professions featured in *Health Care Job Explosion* are utilized in home health care, Personal and Home Care Aides are specific to the field. Home health aides—who provide health-related services, rather than mainly housekeeping and routine personal care—are discussed in the statement on nursing, psychiatric, and home health aides, in Chapter 7.

Significant Points

- Job opportunities are expected to be excellent because of rapid growth in home health care and high replacement needs.
- Skill requirements are low, as is the pay.
- About 33 percent of personal and home care aides work part time; most aides work with a number of different clients, each job lasting a few hours, days, or weeks.

Nature of the Work

Personal and home care aides help elderly, disabled, ill, and mentally disabled persons live in their own homes or in residential care facilities instead of in health facilities. Most personal and home care aides work with elderly or physically or mentally disabled clients who need more extensive personal and home care than family or friends can provide. Some aides work with families in which a parent is incapacitated and small children need care. Others help discharged hospital patients who have relatively short-term needs.

Personal and home care aides—also called homemakers, caregivers, companions, and personal attendants—provide housekeeping and routine personal care services. They clean clients' houses, do laundry, and change bed linens. Aides may plan meals (including special diets), shop for food, and cook. Aides also may help clients get out of bed, bathe, dress, and groom. Some accompany clients to doctors' appointments or on other errands.

Personal and home care aides provide instruction and psychological support to their patients. They may advise families and patients on nutrition, cleanliness, and household tasks. Aides also may assist in toilet training a severely mentally handicapped child, or they may just listen to clients talk about their problems.

In home health care agencies, a registered nurse, physical therapist, or social worker assigns specific duties and supervises personal and home care aides. Aides keep records of services performed and of clients' condition and progress. They report changes in the client's condition to the supervisor or case manager. In carrying out their work, aides cooperate with health care professionals, including registered nurses, therapists, and other medical staff.

Working Conditions

The personal and home care aide's daily routine may vary. Aides may go to the same home every day for months or even years. However, most aides work with a number of different clients, each job lasting a few hours, days, or weeks. Aides often visit four or five clients on the same day.

Surroundings differ from case to case. Some homes are neat and pleasant, whereas others are untidy and depressing. Some clients are pleasant and cooperative; others are angry, abusive, depressed, or otherwise difficult.

Personal and home care aides generally work on their own, with periodic visits by their supervisor. They receive detailed instructions explaining when to visit clients and what services to perform for them. About one-third of aides work part time, and some work weekends or evenings to suit the needs of their clients.

Aides are individually responsible for getting to the client's home. They may spend a good portion of the working day traveling from one client to another. Because mechanical lifting devices that are available in institutional settings are seldom available in patients' homes, aides must be careful to avoid overexertion or injury when they assist clients.

Training, Other Qualifications, and Advancement

In some states, the only requirement for employment is on-the-job training, which generally is provided by most employers. Other states may require formal training, which is available from community colleges, vocational schools, elder care programs, and home health care agencies. The National Association for Home Care and Hospice (NAHC) offers national certification for personal and home care aides. Certification is a voluntary demonstration that the individual has met industry standards. Certification requires the completion of a standard 75-hour course and written exam developed by NAHC. Home care aides seeking certification are evaluated on 17 different skills by a registered nurse.

Personal and home care aides should have a desire to help people and not mind hard work. They should be responsible, compassionate, emotionally stable, and cheerful. In addition, aides should be tactful, honest, and discreet because they work in private homes. Aides also must be in good health. A physical examination, including state man-dated tests such as those for tuberculosis, may be required. A criminal background check also may be required for employment. Additionally, personal and home care aides are responsible for their own trans-portation to reach patients' homes.

Advancement for personal and home care aides is limited. In some agencies, workers start out performing homemaker duties, such as cleaning. With experience and training, they may take on personal care duties. Some aides choose to receive additional training to become nursing and home health aides, licensed practical nurses, or registered nurses. Some experienced personal and home care aides may start their own home care agency.

Employment

Personal and home care aides held about 701,000 jobs in 2004. The majority of jobs were in home health care services; individual and family services; residential care facilities; and private households. Self employed aides have no agency affiliation or supervision and accept clients, set fees, and arrange work schedules on their own.

Job Outlook

Excellent job opportunities are expected for this occupation, because rapid employment growth and high replacement needs are projected to produce a large number of job openings.

Employment of personal and home care aides is projected to grow much faster than average for all occupations through the year 2014. The number of elderly people, an age group characterized by mounting health problems and requiring some assistance with daily activities, is projected to rise substantially. In addition to the elderly, other patients, such as the mentally disabled, will increasingly rely on home care. This trend reflects several developments, including efforts to contain costs by moving patients out of hospitals and nursing care facilities as quickly as possible; the realization that treatment can be more effective in familiar rather than clinical surroundings; and the development and improvement of medical technologies for in-home treatment.

In addition to job openings created by the increase in demand for these workers, replacement needs are expected to lead to many openings. The relatively low skill requirements, low pay, and high emotional demands of the work result in high replacement needs. For these same reasons, many people are reluctant to seek jobs in the occupation. Therefore, persons who are interested in and suited for this work—particularly those with experience or training as personal care, home health, or nursing aides—should have excellent job prospects.

Earnings

Median hourly earnings of personal and home care aides were $8.12 in May 2004. The middle 50 percent earned between $6.83 and $9.70 an hour. The lowest 10 percent earned less than $5.93, and the highest 10 percent earned more than $10.87 an hour. Median hourly earnings in the industries employing the largest numbers of personal and home care aides in May 2004 were as follows: Residential mental retardation, mental health and substance abuse facilities, $9.09; Vocational rehabilitation services, $8.76; Community care facilities for the elderly, $8.49; Individual and family services, $8.48;Home health care services, $6.99.

Most employers give slight pay increases with experience and added responsibility. Aides usually are paid only for the time they work in the home, not for travel time between jobs. Employers often hire on-call hourly workers and provide no benefits.

Related Occupations

Personal and home care aides combine the duties of caregivers and social service workers. Workers in related occupations that involve personal contact to help others include childcare workers; nursing, psychiatric, and home health aides; occupational therapist assistants and aides; physical therapist assistants and aides; and social and human service assistants.

HOME HEALTH RESOURCES

Don't forget! Refer to the general resources listed in Chapter Three and in the chapter on your specific profession. One of the many resources you should check in chapter 3 is the **National Association of Health Career Schools.**

☤Association   ▭Directory   ✐Resume Service   Web Site

▤Job Ads   Job Alert E-mail/Hotline   Job Fairs   Book

For a full explanation of these resources see the second page of Chapter 3.

American Association for HomeCare - 625 Slaters Ave., Suite 200, Alexandria, Virginia 22314; 703/836-6263. (**http://aahomecare.org/**, info@aahomecare.org) This is a national trade association that represents all the elements of the home care industry. The web site has directories of home health care providers, consultants and state associations in the US and Canada.

CaregiversGuide - http://www.caregiversguide.com Search by state for long term care facilities, home care agencies, adult day care and alternative facilities.

the care guide - (**http://www.thecareguide.com**) Provided by Care Planning Partners Inc., this web site allows searches for home health care services and senior care facilities in Canada.

Google.com (www.google.com) has directories of hospices, extended care facilities and home health agencies. Click on the word "more" then on "Directory" and then on "Health" to access resources. Over 360 home health and hospice providers are listed.

Home Health Provider.com This site has well-designed job searches and lets you research industry sectors and post your résumé. (**http://www.homehealthprovider.com/**) It provides news, employer profiles, a school finder, career videos, magazines, salary surveys, and job seeker resources, such as résumé advice.

National Association for Home Care and Hospice (NAHC) - 228 Seventh Street SE, Washington, DC 20003, 202/547-7424. (**http://www.nahc.org/**) Members are agencies providing home care and hospice services. The Community area of the web site provides an

Agency Locator with information on more than 22,000 providers and a Job Exchange searchable by region. Contact information is available for home care and hospice state associations.

⚕ 🗀⁀🖰 **National Association of Area Agencies on Aging (NAAAA)** - 1730 Rhode Island Avenue, Washington, DC 20036; 202/872-0888. (**http://www.n4a.org/**) The NAAAA represents a majority of the more than 660 area agencies on aging (contact via Links section). The **Elder- care Locator** (**http://www.eldercare.gov**) provides free information on more than 4800 service providers, such as adult day care, personal care, senior housing and home health care. Search the web site for a local agency on aging by city, county or zip code. The Eldercare Locator, 800/677-1116, is available weekdays, 9:00 am to 8:00 pm (ET).

⚕ 🗀⁀🖰 **National Association of Psychiatric Health Systems** (701 13th Street, NW, Suite 950, Washington, DC 20005; 202/393-6700, (**http://www.naphs.org**). Institutions offering mental health and sub- stance abuse treatment. Membership Directory costs $35, but many members have links on the web site under Consumer Help.

🗀⁀🖰 **National Hospice & Palliative Care Organization (NHPCO)** - 1700 Diagonal Road, Suite 625, Alexandria, Virginia 22314; 703/837-1500. (**http://www.nhpco.org/**) Search the hospice care database by program name, state or zip code.

🗀⁀🖰 **Nursing Home INFO** (**http://www.nursinghomeinfo.com/**) Use the Facility Search feature to find nursing homes by facility name, state, city, county or type of service.

📖 **Opportunities in Gerontology and Aging Services Careers** by Ellen Williams, 2002, $12.95. Information on careers and training. Pub- lished by McGraw-Hill. ISBN: 0071390456.

🗀⁀🖰 Senior Mag - Has a directory of home care providers by state. (**http://www.seniormag.com/services/home_health_care/index.htm**)

🗀⁀🖰 **State departments of health or insurance** may be helpful in obtaining a Medicare Survey Report to locate home health care providers in your area. Use any search engine with the keywords "health depart- ment" and the name of your state or use the state government listings in your telephone book to contact them.

COMPUTERS IN YOUR HEALTH CARE CAREER

Most people working in the health care field will need to use computers. Some will be using programs written specifically for certain tasks, such as tracking patient specimens and reporting laboratory results, while others will use standard office suites, graphics or statistical programs. Medical researchers may even have to write their own database programs. A solid understanding of computers will at least lower your stress level and will probably make you a more valuable employee. The office computer guru can often save co-workers time and increase productivity.

Most community colleges and night schools offer basic courses in computer skills. Tutorials are available on CD, but do not offer the convenience of having an instructor to answer your questions. There are also courses available on the Internet, offered by computer publishers such as ZDNet (**http://www.zdnet.com**). Make sure your browser will view the virtual classrooms correctly before you sign up.

COMPUTER INDUSTRY CAREERS

The BLS Occupational Employment Projections for 2004-2014 state that computer and mathematical science occupations are projected to add 967,000 jobs and grow 30.7% — faster than other professional occupational subgroups. The demand for computer-related occupations should increase as organizations continue to adopt and integrate increasingly sophisticated and complex technologies. Growth will not be as rapid as during the previous decade, however, as the software industry begins to mature and as routine work is increasingly outsourced overseas. Employment in this "information supersector" is expected to increase by 54.6% for network systems and data communications analysts, by 46% for computer software engineers, by 38.4% for network and computer systems administrators, by 38.2% for database administrators, by 31.4% for computer systems analysts, 23% for computer support specialists, but by only 2% for computer programmers.

A major component of health care is the managing of information, including patients' medical records, which can contain massive amounts of data. The push to digitize medical records will require a number of computer professionals for implementation. First instituted by Beth Israel Deaconess Hospital of Harvard Medical School, some facilities are providing patients with online access to their medical records. (Neil Osterweil, *CNN MedPage Today*, Dec. 27, 2005)

Computer and Information Systems Managers

Computer and information systems managers plan, coordinate, and direct research and facilitate the computer-related activities of firms. They direct the work of systems analysts, computer programmers, support specialists, and other computer-related workers. These managers plan and coordinate activities such as installation and upgrading of hardware and software, programming and systems design, development of computer networks, and implementation of Internet and intranet sites.

A bachelor's degree usually is required for management positions, although employers often prefer a graduate degree, especially an MBA with technology as a core component. Computer and information systems managers must possess strong interpersonal, communication, and leadership skills. Median annual earnings in May 2004 were $92,570.

Computer Programmers

Computer programmers write, test, and maintain the detailed instructions, called programs, that computers must follow to perform their functions. Programmers also conceive, design, and test logical structures for solving problems by computer. Programmers write programs according to the specifications determined primarily by computer software engineers and systems analysts. Programmers in software development companies may work directly with experts from various fields to create software.

The level of education and experience employers seek has been rising due to the growing number of qualified applicants and the specialization involved with most programming tasks. Bachelor's degrees are commonly required. The job calls for patience, persistence, and the ability to work on exacting analytical tasks, especially under pressure. Median annual earnings were $62,890 in May 2004.

Computer Scientists and Database Administrators

Job tasks and occupational titles used to describe these workers evolve rapidly. Computer scientists work as theorists, researchers, or inventors. Database administrators determine ways to organize and store data. They identify user requirements, set up computer databases, and test and coordinate database systems. Network systems and data communications analysts are needed to design, test, and evaluate systems such as local area networks (LANs), wide area networks (WANs), the Internet, intranets, and other data communications systems.

A bachelor's degree is a prerequisite for many jobs; however, some jobs may require only a 2-year degree. Relevant work experience is also very important. For more technically complex jobs, persons with graduate degrees are preferred. Technological advances come so rapidly in the computer field that continuous study is necessary. In May of 2004 median annual earnings of computer and information scientists in research were $85,190, of database administrators: $60,650, and network systems and data communication analysts: $60,600.

Computer Software Engineers

Systems software engineers work for companies that configure, implement, and install complete computer systems. Computer software engineers often work as part of a team that designs new hardware, software, and systems.

Most employers prefer to hire persons who have at least a bachelor's degree and broad knowledge of, and experience with, a variety of computer systems and technologies. A bachelor's degree in computer science or computer information systems is typical. Most training authorities feel that program certification alone is not sufficient. These engineers must have strong problem-solving, analytical and communication skills. Median annual earnings in May 2004 were about $74,980.

Computer Support Specialists and Systems Administrators

Computer support specialists provide technical assistance, support, and advice to customers and other users. Network administrators and computer systems administrators design, install, and support an organization's local-area network (LAN), wide-area network (WAN), network segment, Internet, or intranet system. Systems administrators are the information technology employees responsible for the efficient use of networks by organizations. Computer security specialists may plan, coordinate, and implement the organization's information security.

Due to the wide range of skills required, there are many paths of entry to a job. Many employers prefer to hire persons with some formal college education. A bachelor's degree in computer science or information systems is a prerequisite for some jobs; however, other jobs may require only a computer-related associate's degree. Median annual earnings of computer support specialists were $40,430 in May 2004, while network and computer systems administrators earned $58,190 in May 2004. Starting salaries in 2005 ranged from $26,250 to $53,750 for help desk and technical support staff.

Computer Systems Analysts

Computer systems analysts solve computer problems, plan and develop new computer systems, or devise ways to apply existing systems' resources to additional operations. Because of the importance of maintaining up-to-date information, systems analysts work on making the computer systems within an organization, or among organizations, compatible so that information can be shared. Many systems analysts are involved with networking.

Rapidly changing technology requires an increasing level of skill and education on the part of employees. Companies look for professionals with a broad background and range of skills, including technical knowledge and interpersonal skills. Many employers seek applicants who have at least a bachelor's degree in computer science, information science, or management information systems (MIS). Median annual earnings of systems analysts were $66,460 in May 2004.

COMPUTER CAREER RESOURCES

Those interested in pursuing a career in computers and health care may want browse the Digital Library at (**http://www.acm.org/**) and check out other publications by the Association for Computing Machinery. The ACM Career Resource Center has a section for students to network with professionals. Other organizations and/or web sites include:

American Medical Informatics Association (**http://www.amia.org/**)

National Association of Health/Data Organizations
    (**http://www.nahdo.org**)

Healthcare Information and Management Systems Society
    (**http://www.himss.org**)

Institute of Electrical and Electronics Engineers Computer Society
    (**http://www.computer.org/**

Medical Records Institute (**http://www.medrecinst.com**).

Computer professionals who want to find work in health care will probably prefer to do their own surfing. A great place to start is the **Google.com** directory "Information Technology" under Business. Sites specific for computer jobs include:

> **http://geekfinder.com**
> **http://www.dice.com**
> **http://www.nationjob.com/computers**
> **http://www.computerjobsbank.com**
> **http://www.guru.com**
> **http://information-technology.thingamajob.com**
> **http://www.computerjobs.com**

Computer magazines often rate career web sites, so check your local library or bookstore. **Chapter 3 has many good general job sites that can help you locate employment listings.** Use the directories there or in the appendix to locate companies in your area. Contact their employment or human resources offices for specific job openings. The associations listed in this book may employ network administrators or other specialists. The appendix lists many directories of companies you could investigate as job sources.

MEDICAL RECORDS AND HEALTH INFORMATION TECHNICIANS

Medical Records and Health Information Technicians
- Employment is expected to grow much faster than average.
- Job prospects should be very good; technicians with a strong background in medical coding will be in particularly high demand.
- Entrants usually have an associate degree; courses include anatomy, physiology, medical terminology, statistics, and computer science.
- This is one of the few health occupations in which there is little or no direct contact with patients.

Nature of the Work
Every time a patient receives health care, a record is maintained of the observations, medical or surgical interventions, and treatment outcomes. This record includes information that the patient provides concerning his or her symptoms and medical history, the results of

examinations, reports of x-rays and laboratory tests, diagnoses, and treatment plans. Medical records and health information technicians organize and evaluate these records for completeness and accuracy.

Technicians assemble patients' health information. They make sure that patients' initial medical charts are complete, that all forms are completed and properly identified and signed, and that all necessary information is in the computer. They regularly communicate with physicians and other health care professionals to clarify diagnoses or to obtain additional information.

Some medical records and health information technicians specialize in coding patients' medical information for insurance purposes. Technicians who specialize in coding are called health information coders, medical record coders, coder/abstractors, or coding specialists. These technicians assign a code to each diagnosis and procedure. They consult classification manuals and also rely on their knowledge of disease processes. Technicians then use computer software to assign the patient to one of several hundred "diagnosis-related groups," or DRGs. The DRG determines the amount for which the hospital will be reimbursed if the patient is covered by Medicare or other insurance programs using the DRG system. In addition to the DRG system, coders use other coding systems, such as those geared toward ambulatory settings or long-term care.

Some technicians also use computer programs to tabulate and analyze data to improve patient care, control costs, provide documentation for use in legal actions, respond to surveys, or use in research studies. For example, cancer (or tumor) registrars maintain facility, regional, and national databases of cancer patients. Registrars review patient records and pathology reports, assign codes for the diagnosis and treatment of different cancers and selected benign tumors. Registrars conduct annual follow-ups on all patients in the registry to track their treatment, survival, and recovery. Physicians and public health organizations then use this information to calculate survivor rates and success rates of various types of treatment, locate geographic areas with high incidences of certain cancers, and identify potential participants for clinical drug trials. Cancer registry data also is used by public health officials to target areas for the allocation of resources to provide intervention and screening.

Medical records and health information technicians' duties vary with the size of the facility where they work. In large to medium-sized facilities, technicians might specialize in one aspect of health information or might supervise health information clerks and transcriptionists while a medical records and health information administrator manages the department. In small facilities, a credentialed medical records and health information technician sometimes manages the department.

Working Conditions

Medical records and health information technicians usually work a 40-hour week. Some overtime may be required. In hospitals—where health information departments often are open 24 hours a day, 7 days a week—technicians may work day, evening, and night shifts.

Medical records and health information technicians work in pleasant and comfortable offices. This is one of the few health occupations in which there is little or no direct contact with patients. Because accuracy is essential in their jobs, technicians must pay close attention to detail. Technicians who work at computer monitors for prolonged periods must guard against eyestrain and muscle pain.

Training, Other Qualifications, and Advancement

Medical records and health information technicians entering the field usually have an associate degree from a community or junior college. In addition to general education, coursework includes medical terminology, anatomy and physiology, legal aspects of health information, coding and abstraction of data, statistics, database management, quality improvement methods, and computer science. Applicants can improve their chances of admission into a program by taking biology, chemistry, health, and computer science courses in high school.

Hospitals sometimes advance promising health information clerks to jobs as medical records and health information technicians, although this practice may be less common in the future. Advancement usually requires 2 to 4 years of job experience and completion of a hospital's in-house training program.

Most employers prefer to hire Registered Health Information Technicians (RHIT), who must pass a written examination offered by the American Health Information Management Association (AHIMA). To take the examination, a person must graduate from a 2-year associate degree program accredited by the Commission on Accreditation for Health Informatics and Information Management Education (CAHIIM).

Technicians trained in non-CAHIIM-accredited programs or trained on the job are not eligible to take the examination. In 2005, CAHIIM accredited 184 programs for health information technicians.

Experienced medical records and health information technicians usually advance in one of two ways—by specializing or managing. Many senior technicians specialize in coding, particularly Medicare coding, or in cancer registry. Most coding and registry skills are learned on the job. Some schools offer certificates in coding as part of the associate degree program for health information technicians, although there are no formal degree programs in coding. For cancer registry, there were 11 formal 2-year certificate programs in 2005 approved by the National Cancer Registrars Association (NCRA). Some schools and employers offer intensive 1- to 2-week training programs in either coding or cancer registry. Once coders and registrars gain some on-the-job experience, many choose to become certified. Certifications in coding are available either from AHIMA or from the American Academy of Professional Coders. Certification in cancer registry is available from the NCRA.

In large medical records and health information departments, experienced technicians may advance to section supervisor, overseeing the work of the coding, correspondence, or discharge sections, for example. Senior technicians with RHIT credentials may become director or assistant director of a medical records and health information department in a small facility. However, in larger institutions, the director usually is an administrator with a bachelor's degree in medical records and health information administration.

Employment

Medical records and health information technicians held about 159,000 jobs in 2004. About 2 out of 5 jobs were in hospitals. The rest were mostly in offices of physicians, nursing care facilities, outpatient care centers, and home health care services. Insurance firms that deal in health matters employ a small number of health information technicians to tabulate and analyze health information. Public health departments also hire technicians to supervise data collection from health care institutions and to assist in research.

Job Outlook

Job prospects should be very good. Employment of medical records and health information technicians is expected to grow much faster than average for all occupations through 2014 because of rapid growth in the number of medical tests, treatments, and procedures that will be increasingly scrutinized by health insurance companies, regulators, courts, and consumers. Also, technicians will be needed to enter patient information into computer databases to comply with federal legislation mandating the use of electronic patient records.

Although employment growth in hospitals will not keep pace with growth in other health care industries, many new jobs will, nevertheless, be created. The majority of new jobs is expected in offices of physicians as a result of increasing demand for detailed records, especially in large group practices. Rapid growth also is expected in home health care services, outpatient care centers, and nursing and residential care facilities. Additional job openings will result from the need to replace technicians who retire or leave the occupation permanently.

Technicians with a strong background in medical coding will be in particularly high demand. Changing government regulations and the growth of managed care have increased the amount of paperwork involved in filing insurance claims. Additionally, health care facilities are having difficulty attracting qualified workers, primarily because of the lack of both formal training programs and sufficient resources to provide on-the-job training for coders. Job opportunities may be especially good for coders employed through temporary help agencies or by professional services firms.

Some cancer registrars may have difficulty finding open positions in their geographic area because of a limited number of registrars employed by health care facilities and low job turnover. However, when a position does become vacant, qualified cancer registrars have excellent prospects because of the limited number of trained registrars available for employment.

Earnings

Median annual earnings of medical records and health information technicians were $25,590 in 2004. The middle 50 percent earned between $20,650 and $32,990. The lowest 10 percent earned less than $17,720, and the highest 10 percent earned more than $41,760. Median annual earnings in the industries employing the largest numbers of medical records and health information technicians in 2004 were as follows:

General medical and surgical hospitals, $26,640; Nursing care facilities, $26,330; Outpatient care centers, $23,870; Offices of physicians, $22,130.

Related Occupations

Medical records and health information technicians need a strong clinical background to analyze the contents of medical records. Other workers who need knowledge of medical terminology, anatomy, and physiology but have little or no direct contact with patients include medical secretaries and medical transcriptionists. Medical transcriptionists listen to dictated recordings made by physicians and other health care professionals and transcribe them into medical reports, correspondence, and other administrative material. Career information for medical transcriptionists can be found at Bureau of Labor Statistics, U.S. Department of Labor, Occupational Outlook Handbook, 2006-07 Edition, at **http://www.bls.gov/oco/ocos271.htm.**

Resources for health information technicians are combined with medical billing, claims examining and patient accounting below.

MEDICAL BILLING, CLAIMS EXAMINING and PATIENT ACCOUNTING
Contributed by Suzan Hvizdash

Suzan Hvizdash presents a comprehensive review of the medical billing field including nature of work, working conditions, job outlook and employment, training, other qualifications, advancement, and earnings. Ms. Hvizdash started in the medical billing business working as a Claims Analyst at Nationwide Insurance, the Medicare carrier for West Virginia and Ohio. She moved to the Pittsburgh area where she became a billing coordinator for two doctors, and was asked to sit on the Physician Relations Board at Mercy Hospital. Hvizdash was the Medicare Supervisor in Patient Services at Stadtlanders Pharmacy (now Pharmacare Specialty Pharmacy) and then the Medicare Specialist at HMI Pharmacy (now part of Pharmacare Specialty Pharmacy). Ms. Hvizdash also taught Medial Billing/Health Claims Examining at North Hills School of Health Occupations (now Career Training Academy). She was also the Senior Reimbursement Supervisor for Gentiva Health Services (a National Home Infusion company that has since been divided into several new companies) Currently, Suzan is the Physician

Education Specialist for the Department of Surgery at the University of Pittsburgh Medical Center. She educates and audits over 200 staff and faculty members on the intricacies of patient documentation. She also holds the position of Senior Audit for the Coding and Reimbursement Network. She has had the opportunities to speak on several teleconferences, at conventions and corporate meetings which included a regional sales meeting for Novartis Drug Company (formerly Sandoz), The Michigan Nurses Conference, local and national meetings of the American Academy of Professional Coders, and the University of Pittsburgh School Of Health Information Management. She also sits on the Advisory Board for General Surgery Coding Alert.

OCCUPATIONAL TITLES

Billing Specialist	Coding Specialist
Patient Account Representative	Medical Collector
Claims Analyst	Claims Processor
Electronic Claims Processor	Claims Reviewer
Reimbursement Specialist	Billing Coordinator
Claims Assistant Professional	Revenue Cycle Coordinator
Collection Specialist	

Nature of the Work

A successful biller/examiner/coder will know medical terminology, anatomy, proper forms completion, ICD-9 and CPT coding. They may possibly need to have further coding knowledge such as HCPCS or DRGs. This person will also need to be proficient on the computer having a typing speed of at least 35-45 words per minute. As we approach Electronic Medical Records, this is vital. Billers and Coders work with patients, other offices' staff, medical personnel and other office personnel. Examiners may also work with all of these people in addition to Medical Directors, auditors, etc. Coders should be able to establish a good relationship with the physicians for which he/she codes. Communication at this level is extremely important to proper coding and understanding. Customer Service is very important, as the people contacted are either colleagues or part of the practice, or they are patients who could be at stressful points in their lives.

Working Conditions

Medical billers usually work in an office setting. Sometimes billers don't work near where the patients are being seen. There are billing offices and services in large corporate buildings, in small suburban offices, and in the doctor's office itself. Work hours are usually daylight, Monday through Friday, 40-hour work weeks. Overtime is often available, and sometimes mandatory. Positions at insurance companies are more likely to have a few overnight or late hour shifts available.

A lot of billers and coders have been able to work from home. They can either work for themselves getting independent physicians as clients or they can work for larger firms that provide them with their workload via electronic means.

Job Outlook and Employment

Medical Billing and its related occupations continue to be the fastest growing opportunities in health care. Insurance companies and the government are spending more time and money researching and controlling claims' fraud, abusive practices, and medical necessity issues. Because of this, insurance companies, doctors, hospitals, pharmacies, and other providers are hiring more.

Most companies and practices are looking for experience and or schooling, again because of the legal ramifications of incorrect billing practices. There are also some requiring false claims insurance to be taken on each of their coders/billers.

Medical billers are also able to work independently out of their homes. They can set up electronic billing through their home computers. Also available is the ability to be an insurance specialist or consultant. This would be a position of self-employment to help patients understand their insurance bills and what they should be paying. This could require additional licensure.

Positions are available in doctors' offices, hospitals, pharmacies, nursing homes, and rehabilitation centers, insurance companies, accounting offices, legal offices, and consulting firms.

Training, Other Qualifications and Advancement

At present, there is no set standard for educational requirements in these fields. However, more employers are looking for some formal training at an accredited vocational or career training school. These schools range in training time from nine months to two years. Anything shorter is not advised.

Certification in these fields is not always required, but is highly recommended. There are several organizations sponsoring certification examinations in the resource section. There are several types of certifications available for different specializations. Some certifications are fairly new, so it is advised to research your field to find the best one suited to your needs.

It's also important to know that the advancement opportunities are unlimited including office managers, supervisors, managers, and directors of billing or examining departments, directors of coding, reimbursement, revenue cycles, etc.

Earnings

These fields have a wage range between $8-$10 an hour to start and up to $40-$60 an hour for years of experience and responsibility.

MEDICAL BILLING, CLAIMS EXAMINING, PATIENT ACCOUNTING, MEDICAL TRANSCRIPTIONISTS, HEALTH INFORMATION TECHNICIANS and MEDICAL OFFICE MANAGER RESOURCES

The organizations for these careers are listed below. It is recommended that you join at least one, but research them beforehand, to find the appropriate one for your career goals. Keep in mind that these organizations may have a local chapter as well, so check your local telephone directory, or the association's web site for local groups.

Don't forget! Refer to the general resources listed in Chapter Three (such as **HEALTHeCAREERS.com**).

 Association   Directory   Resume Service   Web Site

 Job Ads   Job Alert E-mail/Hotline   Job Fairs   Book

For a full explanation of these resources see the second page of Chapter 3.

▤▷‿ᵕᵗ **ADVANCE Newsmagazines** - (http://advanceweb.com/) *ADVANCE for Health Information Professionals,* and *ADVANCE for Health Information Executives.* Call 800/355-1088 for additional information. Free to qualified professionals, these publications have extensive classified ads and meeting lists online. Contact the Job Fair Staff at 800-546-4987 or **http://health-care-job-fairs.advanceweb.com/** or JobFair@merion.com.

⚕‿ᵗ **Alliance of Claims Assistance Professionals (ACAP)** - 873 Brentwood Drive, West Chicago, IL 60185-3743. (**http://www.claims.org/**, askacap@charter.net).

⚕▤▨✐‿ᵗ **American Academy of Professional Coders (AAPC)** - 2480 South 3850 West, Suite B, Salt Lake City, Utah 84120; 800/626-CODE. (**http://www.aapc.com/**, info@aapc.com) Certification and extensive information for Coders, Office Managers, Claims Examiners, Hospital Outpatient Coders, Experienced Reimbursement Specialists and Coding Educators. The web site job ad section lets you post your résumé and receive job alerts by e-mail.

⚕▤‿ᵗ **American Association of Healthcare Administrative Management (AAHAM)** - 11240 Waples Mill Road, Suite 200, Fairfax, VA 22030; 703/281-4043. (**http://www.aaham.org/**)Includes a Technical Certification Study Guide, links to local chapters, information about the CPAT/CCAT certification exams, job openings, a list of local chapters and networking.

⚕▤▱▨✐‿ᵗ **American Association for Medical Transcription (AAMT)** - 100 Sycamore Avenue, Suite M, Modesto, CA 95354; 800/982-2182. Their Web site at **http://www.aamt.org** has career information, employment opportunities, networking, local associations and approved education programs. You can post your résumé online and receive e-mail job alerts.

⚕‿ᵗ **American College of Medical Practice Executives (ACMPE)** - 877/275.6462, ext. 889. (**http://www.mgma.com/acmpe/**) Affiliated with the MGMA (see below, same address) this group for office manager and practice administrators has branches for different specialties such as Endocrinology, Cardiovascular, etc. Jobs ads in monthly publication *MGMA Connections,* or on MBMA web site. Core Learning Series on MGMA web site has education information.

⚕▤▱‿ᵗ **American Health Information Management Association (AHIMA)** - 233 N. Michigan Ave., Suite 2150, Chicago, IL 60611-5800;

312/233-1100. **(http://www.ahima.org,** info@ahima.org) AHIMA provides brochures for those considering entering the health information management (HIM) profession. Web site has information on careers (including a career counselor), a job bank, financial aid, certification, schools, independent study and state associations.

✡ ⌒⊖ **American Medical Billing Association** (AMBA) - 4297 Forrest Drive, Sulphur, OK 73086; 580/622-2624. Their web site presents information about online courses, networking opportunities, and information on preparing for the examination to become a Certified Medical Reimbursement Specialist. Visit **(http://www.ambanet.net/AMBA.htm)**.

✡ ▤⌕◿🖰⌒⊖ **Healthcare Information and Management Systems Society (HIMSS)** - 230 East Ohio, Suite 500, Chicago, IL 60611-3269; 312/664-4467. **(http://www.himss.org,** himss@himss.org). Includes a membership directory, résumé posting, job alerts, and you can research potential employers and Career Development Resources with résumé and interviewing advice and more. Members only.

✡ ⌒⊖ **Health Professions Institute (HPI) -** PO Box 801, Modesto, CA 95355-0801; 209/551-2112. **(http://www.hpisum.com/,** hpi@hpisum.com) Publishes many books, periodicals and conducts seminars for the medical transcription community. HPI has a free Student Network and information on medical transcription courses. *Perspectives* magazine (an e-zine) is free to medical transcription professionals.

⌒⊖ **Medical Coding and Billing** - Information about coding and billing careers on **http://www.medicalcodingandbilling.com** includes certification, education, and also medical office management career information. Lists of professional associations.

✡ ▤⌒⊖ **Medical Group Management Association** (MGMA) - 104 Inverness Terrace East, Englewood, CO 80012, 303/799-1111or 877/275-6462. **(www.mgma.com)** This organization is designed for the supervisors of medical group practices. The Web site has job ads, networking, internship information and a Core Learning Series for education. Jobs ads are in monthly publication *MGMA Connections*.

✡ ⌒⊖ **Medical Records Institute** - 425 Boylston Street, 4th Floor, Boston, Massachusetts 02116; 617/964-3923. This organization's web site **(http://www.medrecinst.com,** cust_service@medrecinst.com) promotes electronic health records, mobile health, and related applications.

Medical Transcription Career Handbook, by Keith A. Drake, Paperback, $21.80. Published by Prentice Hall, 1999. ISBN: 0130115401

Medical Transcription Education Center, Inc. (M-TEC) Their Web site at http://www.mtecinc.com offers courses in medical transcription and an online tests to see if the career is right for you. Advice on financial aid and a placement service.

Medical Transcription Industry Alliance (MTIA) - 233 N. Michigan Avenue, Suite 2150, Chicago, Illinois 60601; 800/543-MTIA. (http://mtia.com). MTIA is an association for medical transcription services. The web site directory of member services.

MT Daily for Medical Transcriptionists - PO Box 982276 Park City, UT 84098; 435-655-8949. (http://www.mtdaily.com/)*MT Daily* provides medical transcription networking information and information on training. free weekly e-mail newsletter.

MT Jobs - http://www.mtjobs.com/ Sponsored by *MT Daily*, this site provides free job searches, résumé posting. email job alerts and employer profiles.

MT Monthly (http://www.mtmonthly.com) - 106 Norway Lane, Oak Ridge, TN 37830; 800/951-5559, 865-387-5555 *MT Monthly* is a national newsletter for medical transcriptionists. for $15 you can purchase the book *Working as a Medical Transcriptionist at Home*. The web site has links to placement services, products and web sites.

National Cancer Registrars Association - 1340 Braddock Pl., #203, Alexandria, VA 22314; 703/299-6640. (http://www.ncra-usa.org/, info@ncra-usa.org) Career information and job bank.

National Healthcareer Association (NHA) - 134 Evergreen Place, 9th Floor, East Orange, NJ 07018; 800/499-9092 or 973/678-9100. The National Healthcareer Association (NHA) offers education, training and certification for many health care jobs, including Certified Medical Transcriptionist (CMT) and Certified Billing and Coding Specialist (CBCS). (http://www.nha2000.com/)

Professional Association of Health Care Office Managers (PAHCOM) - 461 East Ten Mile Road, Pensacola, Florida 32534-9714; 800/451-9311. (http://www.pahcom.com/) Web site has information on education, local chapters, and on the Certified Medical Manager exam. The Benefits page of the web site posts job openings.

Appendix

HEALTH CARE CORPORATIONS!

Thousands of companies manufacture products or provide services for the medical profession. The major manufacturers have large research and development budgets and many operate health care facilities. The demand for medical equipment and supplies is expected to experience healthy growth: 4.7% annually until 2014. (Bureau of Labor Statistics, *Monthly Labor Review*, Nov., 2005)

Additional positions include sales representatives, computer experts and consultants. Research facilities must be staffed by medical professionals: technicians, physicians, bio-statisticians and PhD scientists. Many fields in health care publish magazines focusing on sales such as *The Magazine of Dental Sales* and *Home Care*. The web site of *HomeCare* (**http://www.homecaremag.com**) offers an industry links section with national and state associations for medical equipment services.

Corporate contacts offer abundant employment opportunities for health care workers in sales, manufacturing and research. Large corporations like Merck, Medtronic, AmerisourceBergen, and Baxter International realize billions in sales yearly. Baxter International's 2005 sales increased by 3.6 percent and total sales reached $9,849,000,000. They employ approximately 48,000 people in 100 countries, market thousands of health care products, and operate outpatient health care centers.

Directories of health care service providers, medical supply companies, and manufacturers are available at many public or college libraries and are listed below. These directories provide names and contact information for thousands of companies in the health care field. The American Chemical Company publishes a directory of scientific corporations listed by product or service. Many medical companies are highly diversified and are not restricted to a single product or service. Check out the "Yellow Pages" entry near the end of this appendix.

Refer to the *Thomas Register* at your local library to start your search for companies that manufacture specific products or visit them on line at **http://www.thomasnet.com**. The *Thomas Register* provides a cross reference between product and company. To locate manufacturers of x-ray equipment you would look up x-ray equipment in the index and it will direct you to the appropriate manufacturers. The company name, address and phone number is provided along with other valuable data. (Their web site is listed below.)

Publicly traded companies will generally be listed in either the *Value Line Investment Survey* (1700 listings), Standard and Poor's (over 4300 listings), or the *Moody's Manual* (12,000 public companies). These references are generally available at larger libraries and provide com-pany information including product lines, gross sales, number of employees, etc. Stock brokers' Internet sites may have company profiles. If you or your parents own stock, your broker may provide profiles free.

Another way to find information on a company is to go to the web site of the Secretary of State of the state where it is incorporated. Secretary of State offices may be found by typing Secretary of State and the name of the state into a search engine such as Google. There may be a minimal charge in some states, in others the service is free.

Don't forget! Refer to the general resources listed in Chapter Three, especially the ones with directory icons, or any other chapter discussing a profession that interests you. The search engines/directories can be especially helpful in finding corporate web sites.

Achoo Healthcare Online (http://achoo.8media.org) Achoo is a search engine with an extensive category structure. One of the directory options is "Business of Health," with companies, products and services.

Allbusiness.com (http://www.allbusiness.com) Use the directories tab to search for companies by category or name. There are many categories containing the term "medical."

American Chemical Society Publications (http://pubs.acs.org). Use the web site to search for products, companies or services. The ACS Directory of Graduate Research (DGR) at **http://dgr.rints.com/** has information on chemical research and researchers at universities in the U.S. and Canada. The Chemjobs page is a complete job search tool.

BizWeb (http://www.bizweb.com) There are more than 600 companies listed in the Medical category alone.

Dentistinfo.com (http://www.dentistinfo.com) Web site has Find a Dentist section and a Job Search section for sales reps.

EMSresponder (http://www.emsresponder.com) Directories of organizations and companies. Introducing free job service in March 2006.

HealthcareRecruitment.com (http://www.healthcarerecruitment.com) Search the jobs database. Sign up, post your résumé, and have them send information relating to your job interests.

Hoover's Online (http://www.hoovers.com) This site, associated with Dun and Bradstreet, provides profiles and contact information for thousands of companies.

Hospital Web (http://adams.mgh.harvard.edu/hospitalwebusa.html) Created by the Department of Neurology at Massachusetts General Hospital, this site's goal is to list all of the hospitals on the Internet.

Magellan Health Services (http://www.magellanhealth.com) Nationwide company providing behavioral health services to employers. Site has career section for jobs with the company.

MedCatalog.com (http://www.medcatalog.com) The Medical links tab has extensive links to articles and medical information sites. This is a long page, so be sure to scroll down to see all that is there.

Medical and Pharmaceutical Sales: How to Land the Job of Your Dreams! by Nikki K. Kerzic, Executive Connection Pub., 2002, ISBN: 0967331544. This book will give you information to land a job in sales, including information on résumé writing, recruiting strategies, networking, interviewing tips, and up-to-date industry and company research.

MedSearch Health Care Careers (http://www.medsearch.com) Part of MyMonster.com. Search extensive list of companies, hospitals, medical facilities by keyword or by discipline or click on major employers listed.

ODONT.COM (http://odont.com) This site has numerous links to dental and medical information, products, and job opportunities.

Pharmaceutical Online (http://www.pharmaceuticalonline.com) Employment Opportunities area of web site allows you to view ads in their searchable database of companies, or post your résumé.

PharmInfoNet (http://pharminfo.8media.org) Has a list of links to pharmaceutical companies and educational programs.

PharmWeb (http://www.pharmweb.net) From the PharmWeb Yellow Pages to the Virtual Library, to many other resources to the pharmacy industry, this site has lots of information and links.

Proofs: The Magazine of Dental Sales (Omeda Communications, Inc. 610 Academy Drive Northbrook, IL 60062; 847/564-8900. Features sales and manufacturers' representative positions under "Want Ads".

The Riley Guide (http://www.rileyguide.com) Employment opportunities and job resources on the internet from A to Z.

Sciencejobs.com (http://www.sciencejobs.com) Job search service operated by *New Scientist Magazine*. Search by state or region, and occupational interest.

Science Careers (http://aaas.sciencecareers.org) Associated with the American Association for the Advancement of Science, this web site is another major search engine for job seekers

Search engines and web directories - Two of the best are **Yahoo!** (http://www.yahoo.com) and **Google** (http://www.google.com). Yahoo! has a Finance section with profiles of companies. Google has a directory called Medical Equipment Manufacturers.

superpages.com (http://yellowpages.superpages.com) Health and medicine section has directories of many specialties.

Yellow Pages Most large libraries have Yellow Pages for major cities all over the country. Business-to-Business Yellow Pages often have the best information. Look up "Medical Equipment & Supplies" among other categories. There are several "yellow page" services on the Internet.

Appendix

B

SCHOLARSHIPS / TUITION HELP

Wouldn't it be great to get an education and have someone else pay for it? In some health care fields, competent workers are in such short supply that employers are willing to pay part or all of a student's tuition and sometimes companies also offer monthly payments of $1000 or more for living expenses.

For those who are willing to commit to working in rural or inner city health care, several programs offer tuition, tuition with living expenses or loan repayment. The Rural Recruitment and Retention Network, and the National Rural Health Association (see both in chapter 3) and the Rural Information Center (800-633-7701) can be contacted for specific information and guidance. Visit **www.nal.usda.gov/ric/** to find out more about these programs. One of the most informative web sites is RuralNet **http://ruralnet.marshall.edu/** provided by the Marshall University School of Medicine. Review their Rural Health Resources section for excellent annotated links. There are at least 82 state-sponsored programs for scholarships or loan forgiveness or loan repayment for physicians, nurse practitioners, nurse midwives, physician assistants and others who commit to serve in high-need areas. Contact your state department of health, the Rural Assistance Center **www.raconline.org** or the National Health Service Corps **www.bphc.hrsa.gov/**. The NHSC also has information on loan-repayment programs for health care workers in inner-city areas.

Assistance is available to minority students through programs offered by institutions such as the Indian Health Service. Visit their web site at **www.ihs.gov**. Contact the financial aid office of your college or of the nearest medical school.

The United States Armed Services offers abundant educational opportunities. If you enlist for several years they will train you for many health care or computer-related careers. Their Tuition Assistance Program currently pays up to $4,500 per year for full-time active duty members. Eligible *College Fund Program* enlistees receive up to $65,000 toward college tuition, when combined with the Montgomery G.I. Bill, and upon honorable discharge. Registered nurses who enlist, in addition to loan repayment or sign-up bonuses, may work towards a degree as a nurse practitioner or physician assistant. Students who have their pre-med degree can arrange to have their medical or dental school paid for. Call your local recruiter to get details on education programs or visit the U.S. Army's web site at **www.todaysmilitary.com/**.

There are many programs available for those who take the time to seek them out. Contact local hospitals that are short staffed and other medical providers to ask about tuition assistance programs. Directories with hospital contact information are described in Chapter 3. Many employers offer tuition assistance to current employees who show initiative and maintain good grades. It is amazing just how many programs are available especially when demand for workers is high and competition is fierce between recruiters and medical facilities in general.

There are also magnet schools that specialize in health care training in cities like Los Angeles and Baltimore. The Chicago Public Schools has a program to encourage minorities to go into medicine and the AMA has a "Doctors Back to School" program, sending physicians to speak in schools to get young people interested in medical careers.

Locate programs that you find attractive through the use of the resources listed in this chapter and in all of the other resource sections located throughout this book. Don't forget to contact occupational associations to find out what information they may have concerning scholarships and tuition assistance programs. The more contacts you make the more programs you will uncover in your research.

Index